GW01393149

Leonard of Mayfair

Leonard of Mayfair

Leonard Lewis
with Andrew Crofts

Hutchinson
London

First published in the United Kingdom in 2000 by Hutchinson

The Random House Group Limited
20 Vauxhall Bridge Road, London SW1V 2SA

Random House Australia (Pty) Limited
20 Alfred Street, Milsons Point, Sydney,
New South Wales 2061, Australia

Random House New Zealand Limited
18 Poland Road, Glenfield
Auckland 10, New Zealand

Random House (Pty) Limited
Endulini, 5a Jubilee Road, Parktown 2193, South Africa

The Random House Group Limited Reg. No. 954009
www.randomhouse.co.uk

A CIP catalogue record for this book is available
from the British Library

Papers used by Random House
are natural, recyclable products made from wood grown in
sustainable forests. The manufacturing processes conform to the
environmental regulations of the country of origin

ISBN 0 09 180070 6

Typeset in Bembo by SX Composing DTP, Rayleigh, Essex
Printed and bound in Great Britain by
Biddles Ltd, Guildford and King's Lynn

For my dearest sister, Rene, who brought me up and looked after me when times were bad, and for my son, Dominic, whose loving support I cherish.

CONTENTS

LIST OF ILLUSTRATIONS

1st Section

1 In the days when I had long hair. (Clive Arrowsmith)
2 My sister, Rene.
   This photograph of me, aged five, was used by Cow & Gate for one of their ads.
3 No.6, Upper Grosvenor Street. My salon.
4 This cartoon caption was suggested by the millionaire businessman, Charles Clore.
   Twiggy. (Barry Lategan)
   Grace Codington. (Richard Young)
5 Me and Liza Minnelli. (Richard Young, Rex Features)
   I also used to cut the hair of Duran Duran's Nick Rhodes, and his wife, Julie. I was also one of the best men at their wedding. (Clive Arrowsmith)
6 With my son, Dominic, in the salon. (Barry Lategan)
   A special drawing from my old friend, Tony Curtis.
7 Andy Warhol presented me with a sketch while he was in London. Francis Bacon did one on the other side. (Peter Beard)
8 With my first wife, Ricci, and our son Dominic. (Clive Arrowsmith)

2nd Section

1 On Top of the World (Mont Blanc in the background).
2 Top left: Twiggy. (Barry Lategan)
   Top right: Ingrid Boulting. (Barry Lategan)
   Bottom left: Sarah Miles and son, Ben. (Barry Lategan)
   Bottom right: Maudie James. (Barry Lategan)
3 Top left: Louise Nordell. (Barry Lategan)
   Top right: Jean Shrimpton. (Barry Lategan)
   Bottom left: Twiggy. (Barry Lategan)

Bottom right: A *Vogue* shoot in the Pre-Raphaelite mode. (Barry Lategan)

4 On one of Dodi Fayed's yachts. Dodi took the picture.
  Below: With Petra Arzberger and Greta Morrison in India.

5 Top left: Marella Oppenheim with Peter Morton and one of his girlfriends in the Bahamas.
  Top right: *Mutiny on the Bounty*. On location with Anthony Hopkins (centre), Mel Gibson (left) and Daniel Day Lewis (right).
  Centre: My one-second 'starring' role as a hairdresser in Stanley Kubrick's *Barry Lyndon*.
  Bottom left: With Anna Roberts in Kenya.
  Bottom right: Loadsamoney, which you needed at the Colombe d'Or in St Paul de Vence.

6 After my operation for a brain tumour. Photograph, flowers and baseball hat courtesy of Dodi Fayed.

7 With Michael Rasser, Nicky Clarke and John Frieda at the Hairdressers' Benevolent Ball given in my honour. (Richard Young, Rex Features)
  With Vidal Sassoon. (Richard Young, Rex Features)

8 The old Mayfair salon.

FOREWORD

There are many reasons why Leonard will be known as one of the most important hair artists of our time. Allow me to illuminate . . . having joined me early in my own career, he seemed to understand immediately my sense of direction, but was fated to go his. A brilliant individualist, he created a '*Leonard Look*', which brought even more esteem to London as the dynamic force in hair.

When John Frieda called to explain Leonard's health problem, so many of London's top-named stylists whom he had trained and inspired were anguished by his condition. Their feelings were proven by their generosity and love to a man who had given them so much. He had instilled amongst his pupils a fidelity of commitment to our art form, and a loyalty that can only be earned.

His hair-house in Mayfair had great style which personified the man. This, together with his intuitive understanding as a leading fashion creator, and with his extraordinary work in films, gave to our craft a credence: through his technique, and his hands, you knew the man. He is a friend and a colleague who stretched me all the way. In fact, he uplifted our craft by bringing the best out of all who had the joy of working with him.

Vidal Sassoon

ACKNOWLEDGEMENTS

I should like to thank a number of close friends for their help with this book, especially Richard Compton Miller and Neville Shulman, who have stood by me in good times and bad. I am also grateful to Barry Lategan and Clive Arrowsmith for letting me use their photographs and for their constant kindness to me. Other friends who have been wonderfully loyal to me include the master tailor, Edward Sexton, Mimmo, Peter Kromberg, Johnny Gold, Peter Blake, Kathy Phillips, Barbara Daly, Meredith Etherington-Smith, Willy Bauer, Robert Lacey, Bryan and Greta Morrison, Mara and Lorenzo Berni, Dick Burnett, and Michael Stephenson. Nor must I forget the great support that I have received from hairdressing colleagues like Stephen Way, John Frieda and his PA Claire Jackson, Karen Dunsford, Daniel Galvin, Nicky Clarke, Michael Rasser and particularly Geoffrey Bonn of the Hairdressers' Benevolent. I am also eternally grateful to Vidal Sassoon for all he taught me and for writing his generous Foreword. I also must give special thanks to my long-suffering co-writer Andrew Crofts, my editor Paul Sidey, and my agent Andrew Lownie, who have helped to turn my chequered life story into this book. Finally, I owe a huge debt of gratitude to Professor John Duncan, who helped stabilize my epilepsy.

CHAPTER ONE

As Jack Nicholson often said to me, 'Len, there are some mornings, to me most mornings, when it's just not worth getting out of bed. Especially if someone is raising that little eyebrow.' Whatever he meant, this was probably one of those mornings.

I had been working late at the salon on the new styles for a Zandra Rhodes spring collection which was to be shown in a few days' time. It was always easier to work in the evenings when the phones had quietened down and most of the clients had left. When we had eventually finished, a group of us went on to San Lorenzo for dinner and then drank and danced at Annabel's and Tramp until the small hours of the morning.

When I'd left home in Belgravia that morning Ricci was still fast asleep. Our son, Dominic, had been up with his nanny having breakfast when I came downstairs, and I had joined him for something to eat before setting off to work. I can't have had more than four hours' sleep but I was buzzing with anticipation for the day ahead.

By the time I walked into the salon, after a second breakfast with some of the senior stylists in the Italian restaurant down the road, the limousines were already dropping clients in Upper Grosvenor Street and they were making their way up the steps to the elegant, brass-studded door of Number Six, the House of Leonard.

Dennis, the Australian minicab driver whom I had somehow recruited to the company during a ride home one night, was parking his Volvo up the street, ready to pick me up as soon as I needed him. He kept asking to drive one of my cars now he was on the payroll, but I knew how fast he drove as he whipped me back and forth around London every day. I thought it would be better if he kept to his own car.

One or two of the arriving clients were regulars, like the elderly lady from round the corner who came in almost every day, just to be washed and dried. She saw me arriving and called out.

'You look wonderful,' I exclaimed, brushing my lips to her heavily beringed old fingers and noticing Catherine Deneuve, the French film star, alighting from a car which had just drawn up. Catherine was at that time being acclaimed as one of the most beautiful women in the world, a description I would not argue with. She still looks wonderful today. To the public she was famous as a film star, as the face of Chanel, that ultimate symbol of Parisian chic, as David Bailey's ex-wife and as a blonde. In fact, she was a brunette and absolutely obsessive about her colouring, never wanting to show even the slightest hint of dark roots. She came to us for retouching whenever she was in London.

As she swept in she almost collided with Joan Collins, an unashamed brunette who preferred to wear glamorous wigs to cover her slightly sparse hair. Joan was caped in a full-length mink coat which seemed hardly necessary for the walk from her chauffeured car to the front door. After some cheek kissing I ushered the two stars into the VIP room to be plied with fresh coffee and croissants while the stylists rushed around preparing themselves for a busy day.

There was a sense of movement everywhere, reflected in the many elegant floor-to-ceiling mirrors which decorated the walls. Girls in impossibly high heels and minute skirts bustled around with piles of soft, clean towels in preparation for the day. There was a hushed atmosphere of luxury and the heavy scent of expensive beauty products hung in the air.

I relieved Joan of the amazing coat, passed it to a receptionist to take care of and she made her stately progress up to the second floor to have a manicure before being seen by Clifford Stafford, one of the senior stylists.

It was important never to allow anything to upset the calm atmosphere of the salon. There might have been any number of panics going on behind the scenes, but the customers could never be allowed to see them. It was like putting on an all-day fashion show, presenting an immaculate face to the world. Even the juniors wore designer clothes, often spending their whole week's money on a pair of Gucci shoes to wear to work. I dare say their chic appearance helped to boost the lavish tips they received. I always insisted that the VIPs must feel they were being dealt with discreetly and with the deference necessary to their status – nobody was ever allowed to ask for autographs from clients. Like first–class butlers we had to ensure that none of the dramas going on below stairs disturbed their peace of mind.

At that stage everything seemed to be going well. The Mayfair mansion started to hum around us pleasantly and I set about my own business, moving amongst clients, starting a cutting session by making suggestions at one mirror and then handing over to a junior stylist and moving to another mirror to make some judicious cuts.

The morning was passing smoothly as I concentrated on a dozen things at once, partly absorbed in my work, partly planning whom I would meet for lunch and dinner and who might like to make up a party and go to a club that night. Every so often I would be summoned away by a receptionist to take a telephone call from a friend and I would persuade whoever it was to join me for a meal or a drink later. Sometimes I would have to go to greet somebody new as they arrived downstairs.

'The Aga Khan's wife is on the phone. She wants a word,' I was told a few hours later.

'I'll take it in the office,' I replied. Sally Croker-Poole had been a good client for a number of years, from the days when she had been a debutante and then one of the many successful models on the London Sixties scene. Now she was the wife of the Aga Khan, a man that millions of Ismaili Muslims believe to be a living God . . .

Every few weeks, it seemed, Karim sent in a new girl to have her hair done in preparation for a date with him. They were usually going to go straight from the salon to the Gavroche, an expensive restaurant just down the road, to meet him for lunch or dinner. They were always very glamorous and would be twittering with excitement, never realising they were just the latest product in an assembly line.

I was always embarrassed by this because Sally had been a very faithful customer and friend to me over the years and through dozens of different hairstyles.

'Leonard,' she said as I got to the phone. It sounded as if she was calling long-distance. 'I have a small problem. That diamond hair clip you sold me the other day . . .'

'The Cartier?' I asked. I had been worried about the fact that Cartier had asked me to carry a showcase of their new diamond-studded clips in the salon. They were very beautiful and just the sort of thing that my clients liked, but at around £2,000 each I thought they would be too tempting to robbers and I was considering asking Cartier to take them away.

'Yes,' she said. 'I've mislaid it. I need you to replace it.'

'Well, you'll have to buy another one, Sally,' I said. 'I can't afford just to replace it at that price.'

'Oh, Leonard,' her voice was wheedling, the beautiful charmer that I had known for so long.

'I'm sorry, Sally,' I said, noticing that one of the receptionists was standing in the door of the office signalling wildly for my attention. 'I've got to go, I'll talk to you later.'

'Mr Leonard,' the girl cried as I put down the phone, 'come quickly, there's a problem.' She clattered away on her high heels, without telling me what was happening.

I swept downstairs to find an air of barely suppressed panic enveloping the usual calm of the reception hall.

'It's Miss Collins,' one of the receptionists whispered to me.

'What about her?' I demanded. I had been with Joan just a few minutes before and she had been perfectly happy.

'She's on her way down,' the girl squeaked, 'and we got her coat out of the cupboard to be ready . . .'

'Yes?' I was getting annoyed. What could possibly be so terrible to justify all this hysteria?

'One of the juniors hung it in a cupboard which had fresh paint on it,' she said. 'The decorator hadn't put a sign up. She had no idea!'

She held up the priceless coat. The tips of the fur all down one sleeve carried a vivid white stripe where it had brushed against the wet paint.

'What are we going to do?' the receptionist wailed. A small crowd of employees was forming around us. 'She's on her way down.'

'Stall her,' I barked.

Several of them scurried off to the main staircase to intercept the descending star, who was not renowned for her patience with fools. I stared at the coat for a moment, wondering what I could possibly do to remove the paint in the time it would take Joan to descend the last few steps. I knew that my good friend and accountant, Neville Shulman, would not be best pleased if I told him we were going to have to buy her a new coat. It seemed like hours, but it can only have been a matter of seconds before I knew what had to be done.

I whipped my comb and scissors out of my top pocket. At the speed of light I ran the comb down the sleeve and trimmed off the painted ends of the fur, like mowing hideously expensive grass. I had to work fast but at the same time I had to be careful not to cut too much. When I reached the top of the stripe I realised that the other sleeve now looked different. Swinging the coat round I repeated the exercise on the other side. I could hear Joan becoming irritated by the people fussing over her on the staircase, asking if she would like a drink or coffee before she went. Her voice was clearly audible above their chatter, the ringing tones that would later make her so effective as the terrifying vamp, Alexis, in *Dynasty*.

'I'm in a hurry,' she announced as she tried to shoo them out of her way. 'I have a lunch appointment. Will you please fetch my coat and let me through?'

As she entered the reception area she saw that 'Mr Leonard' himself was waiting to usher her from the premises, holding out her coat. Her face softened into a beautiful smile at this obvious tribute to her importance to us as a client. I draped the mink flamboyantly over her shoulders, whisked my fingers through her hair exclaiming at the perfection of the cut, and kissed her on both cheeks. She stalked from the salon, purring happily. If you are reading this now, Joan, please forgive me.

Breathing a sigh of relief I returned to the first floor to see how my other clients were faring.

'I can't wake my client up,' Clifford complained as I came on to the floor.

'What do you mean?' I demanded.

'She's fallen asleep under the dryer.' He indicated the elderly lady I had seen coming in earlier that morning.

I went over to her and pressed her hand gently. There was no movement. In fact there was no pulse.

'This client is not asleep, Clifford,' I hissed out of the corner of my mouth. 'She's bleeding dead.'

'Oh God,' Clifford looked horrified. 'What happens to my commission?'

I ignored the question and started issuing muted instructions to all and sundry. The husband, an infamously ferocious QC, needed to be informed and an ambulance called. Until they arrived I could see no need to move her or alert the other customers. Like Clifford they all assumed she was asleep. Let them continue in their peaceful ignorance and we would continue with our business around her. We would maintain the facade for as long as possible, casually moving other clients to different parts of the building so that they didn't have to witness the undignified sight of a client leaving the premises feet-first. Nothing should be allowed to disturb the tranquillity of their morning at the world-famous Leonard House of Hair and Beauty.

An hour or two later the corpse had been discreetly spirited away and I was able to go for a well-earned lunch with my friends, and an even better earned drink at the Trattoria Terrazza in Soho. Dennis was still waiting outside the front door with the Volvo by the time I swept out.

'Ah, Mr Leonard!' Franco, the manager greeted me warmly as I made my way into the restaurant. 'You look wonderful! All your friends are already here.'

He steered me to my usual table where several friends had been waiting for me for some time. Other acquaintances waved from neighbouring tables as I sat down, a drink in my hand, feeling on top of the world.

'I've had the strangest morning,' I announced.

CHAPTER TWO

TWENTY-FIVE YEARS later, I observed the young policeman's eyes, as he looked around my sister Rene's front room. His colleague let out a guffaw, quickly stifling it and trying to recompose his face into an expression which would be appropriate for an officer investigating a reported crime. I was still shaky and upset and my nerves must have communicated themselves to Rene. The gloom of the room was oppressive and the policemen seemed too big in their uniforms to be invading such a small living space. They were being as polite as they could be but I could tell that they found my slowness exasperating.

The one I had been telling my story to was obviously trying to think of a kind way of suggesting to me that I was a deluded old fool, wasting their time with my rambling fantasies. My manner must have seemed very distracted as I groped for the right way to express myself, and I wished I could muster some authority.

I always used to have authority. I used to be able to turn heads wherever I went. When I entered a fashionable boutique, club or restaurant, people would automatically treat me with respect, call me 'Mr Leonard' and run around at my beck and call. For years and years I heard almost nothing but praise from everyone I came into contact with. If I ever seemed inarticulate they would smile and tell one another I was 'vague' and 'eccentric' and 'such an artist'. Nothing about me that cold, dark December day would have made those two young policemen say anything like that.

Not much has happened in the way of redecoration in Rene's front room since we all moved there as a family nearly fifty years ago. The little council house was full of people then. Mum and Dad were still alive, and, as well as me, there was Rene and her husband, Sam, and a constant stream of visiting friends and relatives. My two elder brothers, Arthur and Fred, had left home by then but it wasn't long before Rene gave birth to her son, Colin. There were always people in every room. The house is much quieter and more gloomy now.

There are two comfortable but well-worn television chairs either side of the electric fire and not much else. They look like the sort of chairs you see in old people's homes. They probably looked like that even when they were new. Everything is overwhelmingly brown. Rene likes it that way and I've given up trying to suggest that we should smarten the place up a bit. I don't know how I would set about arranging it these days. I used to think nothing of flying fashionable interior designers and decorators in to Mayfair and Belgravia from New York or San Francisco for meetings whenever I felt like it – now I can't even organise a local painter and decorator to slap on a coat of emulsion.

The younger man's eyes alighted on the peeling paint of the wood-work and the piles of old newspapers on the table by the wall. The two policemen were sitting on hard chairs, pushed back against the walls of the narrow room. They had taken their caps off and one was balanced incongruously on top of the newspapers.

In the awkward silence that had fallen between us we could all hear Rene chatting to herself in the kitchen as she made them tea or coffee. She had almost certainly forgotten exactly what they had asked for but it didn't matter, they would drink whatever she brought them. She was always more comfortable if she was doing things for people rather than having to answer their questions. I could imagine that she was annoyed with me for bringing yet more drama into her deliberately quiet and uneventful life.

The young constable lifted his notebook and took a deep breath. 'Are you sure it was a genuine Rolex, Sir?' he enquired. 'Some of these copies can be very good. Could fool anyone.'

I knew immediately what he was thinking. He was looking at me and wondering how on earth a shuffling old man, living with his elderly sister in a run-down terraced house in south London, could possibly have acquired a Rolex watch.

'Yes, it was a genuine Rolex,' I said. 'It was a gold one. I've had it some time.'

'Would you be able to find the receipt, do you think, Sir?' he asked, obviously willing to devote only a little more time to humour-ing me and my fantasies.

'Oh yes,' I said. 'I think I have it somewhere. It might take me a little while to find it.'

'If you could, Sir, that would be very helpful.'

I pulled myself to my feet. Since the operation I had to take everything slowly, consider each movement before I made it. It was all too easy to stumble and make a fool of myself and I hated that. I was aware that I was moving like an old man, like a drunk trying to appear sober, but there was no alternative. I was trapped in a body that I couldn't trust any more. It had let me down too many times.

Rene came in from the kitchen with the cups for the policemen rattling in their saucers. It was hard to tell what she had made for them, but they politely jumped up and took the murky brown drinks from her, fearful that she might drop them in her nervous state.

'I'm just going to look for the watch receipt for the officers,' I explained as I made my way slowly out of the room. Their patronising attitude was making me angry, but I was determined not to show it. I was trying to think where I would find the relevant receipt.

Paperwork was never my strong point. Even when the business was booming I had never been able to get interested in the financial side. It used to drive my accountant, Neville Shulman, who tried so hard to help me, mad. No doubt things would have turned out very differently if I had been able to focus my mind a little more on the money side of things.

I could hear the policemen talking to Rene as I pulled myself upstairs. It took a lot of concentration to place each foot on the next step without losing my balance. I was carrying too much weight because of my medication and I was frightened that I might have one of my fits and fall. I was finding it hard to get used to being over-weight. I had always been as thin as a rake, and able to wear whatever clothes I liked. I seemed to have lost interest in how I looked in recent years.

Eventually I reached the bedroom where what was left of my life was packed up into cardboard boxes. I started to hunt for the receipt.

It wasn't an easy task. Even once I found the right pile of papers there were an awful lot to sort through. I had bought quite a few watches over the years, many of them Rolexes, some of them Cartier, some of them Boucheron. I had never worried too much about the receipts. Well, you don't, do you?

Downstairs the policemen were trying to find out more about me from Rene. I knew they wouldn't have much luck. She could tell them about my childhood and how she had had to bring me up, and she could tell them that I had been a hairdresser up in the West End, that I used to appear in the newspapers and magazines, but she didn't know much more about my life after I left home. She had never wanted to know. It wasn't a world that interested her. Rene was always someone who preferred a simple life; she had never felt comfortable with the trappings of wealth and fame. Nothing she would tell them would dispel the impression that I was imagining the whole thing. My hands were shaking as I rummaged through the papers, trying to concentrate on what I was searching for.

I could never have imagined anything as horrible as what had happened to me that day. Never, in all the years that my family had lived in Roehampton, just south of the river in London, had we been the victims of violence or crime. It just wasn't something that happened in the area.

I suppose I had become a sitting target, but I never realised it. I had been making my way back to Rene's house from the bus stop. I had been to the West End, stocking up on presents for Christmas. For anyone else it would not have been a long walk, maybe ten or fifteen minutes. For me it took a great deal longer.

I don't know how long the young man had been watching my shuffling progress as I made my way home with the carrier bags full of Christmas puddings, chocolate logs, mince pies and cream cakes for Rene. Cream cakes are her great love in life. God knows how she manages to stay so sparrow thin – she should be the size of an elephant with all the sugar she consumes. The sweeter and stickier they are, the happier she is. Cream cakes are all she ever asks me to bring her when I go anywhere. No Cartier watches or Hermès scarves for Rene, just a nice cream bun to have with her tea.

When the young man sprang out it took me a moment or two to work out what he wanted.

'Can you tell me the time, mate?' he asked.

I lifted my arm with difficulty because of the weight of the carrier bags. I don't know if he had already seen the watch and was lying in wait specifically to grab it, or whether it was just his lucky day. But once he spotted it, he was in a hurry to get it off my wrist. Rene's cream cakes were hurled to the ground and I watched in horror as he stamped on them threateningly. I could just imagine how disappointed she was going to be when I came home empty handed.

He ripped the watch off my wrist and was gone. It must all have been over in a few moments. No one else seemed to have noticed, or, if they had, they didn't want to get involved. I stood for a moment, not sure what to do first. Should I scrape up the mess of food lying on the pavement, or sit down and rest, or head straight back home? After a few moments of dithering I plodded on home with what was left of Rene's cakes.

The police probably thought I was racist because when they asked me for a description, all I could think to say was that he was young and black. I started to explain that I could never be described as racist, that one of my best friends was a black hairdresser called Earl Lewis. I started to tell them a story about how we had both gone to New York separately to work in the salon I had opened there and the hotel gave him my room because we had the same surname. They thought he was my brother. It was a memory that always made me chuckle but I could see they weren't in the mood for my faltering reminiscences. They couldn't imagine me in a swanky New York hotel anyway. I tried with every fibre of my being to charm them, to win their sympathy, but I just couldn't hit the right note.

What I hated most about the incident was the feeling of helplessness. Because I couldn't run or fight I could do nothing to stop the man from stealing what he wanted from me. I couldn't escape from him, or punch him, or run after him as he made his getaway.

After what must have seemed like hours to the young policemen downstairs, I actually found the receipt and went carefully back down again. Their expressions changed slightly when I gave it to them. They scrutinised me as if trying to picture me ever shopping in smart places like Cartier or Tiffany's in Bond Street. When you are young it is often hard to imagine that the old people you hardly notice going about their business around you were once young too. It slowly dawned on them that perhaps I had a past which was more interesting than they had at first imagined.

'We'll look into it,' they said as they prepared to leave, 'and we'll get back to you.'

I knew what they meant. They were going to check up to see if my story was true. Had I really been a West End hairdresser with the sort of money needed to buy Rolex watches? It wouldn't take them long to find out the truth. There were plenty of people who would vouch for me. My fall from grace had been extraordinarily fast. There were still a lot of people in society and in Hollywood who didn't even realise that I had disappeared from Mayfair. I dare say there were others who had already written me off as dead.

Whatever I might have looked like to the young policemen, I was still on the right side of sixty. Most of my friends and contemporaries were still at the peaks of their careers. Hairdressers, film stars, artists, restaurateurs, they were all still doing the things they loved to do, still treated with respect, their services still in great demand.

I never did get the Rolex back and the insurance on it had long since lapsed. It is not important. Material possessions have never obsessed me. They are not what I miss most about my old life. At least the thief hadn't hurt me, that was the most important thing.

I recently went back to 6 Upper Grosvenor Street, where the House of Leonard once stood in all its glory. It is a handsome building on the outside, a six-storey Georgian town house standing right behind the American Embassy, but inside there is now a ghostly air of sadness. The property company which uses it as office space has done nothing to the decor. The grey drapes at the high windows of my old reception room are still there, but now they hang, tired and lank. The odd desk has been moved in to provide practical working surfaces, but they are too small for the room. It resembles how I imagine many stately homes looked when they were requisitioned by the government in the war. The glamour and magic is long gone and the air is stale and musty.

Just ten years before it was in the final days of its greatest glory. Some of the richest, most beautiful and most famous faces in the world walked up that elegant staircase. Waiting limousines and carelessly parked sports cars lined the road outside. Fires burned in the hearths and the scent of gigantic flower arrangements mingled with the perfumes and lotions that I had specially created. It was simply the most famous salon in London and had been for twenty years. It would have been impossible to imagine that, almost overnight, the whole thing could disappear like the *Titanic*.

CHAPTER THREE

MY MOTHER DID everything she could to get rid of me before I was born. She made no secret of the fact that the last thing she wanted was another child. Rene, my sister, was nearly twenty by the time Mum fell pregnant with me, and both my brothers, Arthur and Fred, were adults, out earning their livings, ducking and diving around Shepherd's Bush. I dare say she had grown careless about contraception, believing that she was too old to have to worry any more. The thought of starting all over again with a screaming baby must have been dreadful. With my brothers and sister grown up and going to work she must have thought that, financially, things would ease up on her and my father and then along comes another responsibility.

Some people are naturals at bringing up children but for most of us it is something we can only do when we are young. Life at the bottom of the pile was hard enough for my mother as it was, without another mouth to feed. I can just picture the terrible dread she must have felt when she realised that she was about to go through the whole ordeal of childbirth and motherhood again, just when she was preparing herself to be a grandmother.

This was many years before abortions were made legal and a back-street abortionist would have cost a fortune. There was no one she could turn to for help, so she tried everything she could think of to rid herself of me. She sat in hot baths, drank gin and took a variety of poisons so horrible that she ruined her own health in the process.

I was obviously a stubborn foetus, because I held on for the full term, refusing to give in to my mother's efforts to shake me loose, and arrived as a healthy and, apparently, beautiful baby. Friends say that I'm still stubborn and that by rights I should have been dead years ago with all the things that I have put my body through, but I just keep on going. I must have had a powerful urge to live, even at that embryonic stage. Perhaps I knew what excitements were in store.

Once I had arrived and there was nothing else she could do about it, Mum was perfectly nice to me, although I later overheard her telling several people that she had never wanted me in the first place which was very hurtful. But her health was so bad by then that she didn't do much more than sit around the house, blind and tired, leaving everything to Rene. She was more of a grandmother figure to me than a mother.

I think I must have been an attractive child. I certainly remember that old ladies around the tower block where we lived behind the dog track in White City used to coo over me when they passed me on the walkways, and would plant kisses on the top of my head at every opportunity. They would all exclaim what a rogue I was and how they couldn't think what would become of me, but they always smiled when they saw me. I used to ring their door bells and run away before they opened them, all the innocent tricks that kids indulged in in those days.

I remember once my picture turned up on a tin of Cow and Gate baby food. I have no idea how it got there, I just remember going into a shop and seeing my own angelic face smiling out at me from the label. I must have allowed a photographer to snap me at some time and in those days there weren't such things as child modelling agencies. In the picture my hair was all curled up on top of my head and Rene always tells me that she used to do that for me. I think, if the truth were told, she would rather have liked to be a hairdresser herself, but she went into the clothes-alteration and mending business, letting out seams, putting up hems and darning holes. Her customers were all local women, keen to make their clothes last as long as possible, unable to afford anything new.

Once I was born and our mother's eyesight began to fail dramatically, the task of bringing me up fell totally on poor old Rene. She was always the most easy-going of women, content to spend her life running around after her father and brothers, tutting and muttering to herself. She seemed to have no ambitions for her own life, happy to spend her days with Mum, cooking and caring for a bunch of men who undoubtedly took her for granted. What she would have liked most in the world would have been to have a daughter or a sister who could have taken over Mum's place in her life once Mum died. But it wasn't to be. When Rene married Sam he came to live with the rest of us and they had a son, Colin. Rene's role in life as·a carer of selfish men was destined never to change. Sam was a nice man, an upholsterer by trade who had been courting her for a long time before she finally gave in.

As a tiny child during the war I was evacuated for a while, when there were fears that German bombs would be falling so hard and fast that all the children of the city would be wiped out. I dare say it was a relief to the adults in the family to see me go; one less plate at the tea table, one less thing to worry about during such hard times. I was sent to different places all over the country on my own and rather enjoyed the experience. I went to Cheshire, Kent and Nottingham, and every time I was sent back to White City the bombs would start again, sometimes hitting blocks of flats around ours, and I would be dispatched once more. I was happy to get out of the city. The bomb shelters were damp, crowded and unpleasant places to spend our nights.

I remember staying on farms and being startled by the beauty of the countryside after the relentless grey of the smoky city. The air was clean and the food was fresh, and I was puzzled by the contrast with life on London housing estates where ration books ruled everyone's lives and my father and brothers spent their whole time chasing ever more elusive and expensive black market goods. There was one farm that had a cow which I grew particularly fond of. One day I couldn't find it and I asked one of the farm hands where it was.

'Over there,' he gestured towards a shed I had never been into before. When I got there I found that only the head of my friend remained. The rest of her had gone to market. I was horrified.

They used to take our photographs before they sent us off and I think that must have been where the picture on the baby food can originated. Apart from these small adventures, I saw nothing outside of my family's narrow and simple world until I was a teenager.

Nothing much about the local schools in White City caught my imagination. I don't suppose there were many inspirational teachers working in the Shepherd's Bush area during the war or just after; certainly none has stuck in my memory. The real world seemed much more exciting than anything that might happen in the classroom. Not far from our estate there was a heavily fenced-in dump where they stored unwanted armaments from the war. I was forever wriggling through the wire and wandering amongst the various intriguing pieces of equipment; proudly bringing home guns and hand grenades with which to frighten Rene, and which I would then sell to school friends.

The school authorities would sometimes come round to find out why I wasn't attending classes, but poor Rene had no idea what to say to them. All she knew was that I left the house in the morning after breakfast and then didn't come home until the evening. Working-class families like ours didn't attach too much importance to the idea of formal education. Sometimes I went to school; usually I found more interesting things to do. Although I did have friends, I was very much a loner from the start, wanting to find out about the grown-up world for myself.

In those days there was a limited number of career options open to a boy like me from an area like ours. It seemed likely I would either become a boxer, work in the docks or on the market stalls, or become a villain. It was the same for boys growing up in all the outlying areas of London. It was the Eastenders who became best known for their working-class roots and their connections with the world of crime, but it was the same for those of us who lived in the west, the south and the north of the city. As we grew older we all came together in the melting pot of the West End, where gangsters ruled the illegal drinking and gambling clubs and where we could move amongst the rich and the ambitious and search for ways to escape from our backgrounds.

I couldn't help feeling that there must be something better to do with my life than the traditional options, although I didn't know what it was.

'You wait till I'm famous,' I would tell Rene if she gave me any sort of scolding.

'That'll be the day,' she'd say, chuckling at the very thought of such a thing happening to her troublesome little brother. People like us didn't become famous unless we ended up with our faces on 'Wanted' posters outside police stations or in the newspapers on our way to prison.

Dad wouldn't have been worried either way. He was an easy-going, quiet man who liked to place a bet now and again and who made his living down at Goddard, Davidson Smith, the auction house on the river in Putney, where they sold second-hand cars. It was a world of dodgy deals and fast talking, attractive both to the wide boys who had learnt their trade on the market stalls and the hard men of London's thriving underworld who needed getaway vehicles and status symbols to show off their growing wealth. There were virtually no laws regulating the state of cars in those days. It was a new industry which was growing at a tremendous rate, with plenty of opportunities for wads of cash to change hands without the authorities knowing anything about it. Everyone wanted a car but no one knew anything about them, the perfect trade for the street salesmen to practise their skills.

On the days when I hung around there with Dad I got to meet all the gangsters like Billy Hill and Jack Spot who were the biggest underworld figures at the time. They were hard men whose names were whispered respectfully around the streets of London, men with dark, glamorous legends of ruthlessness and violence attached to them. They were always good to me, and sometimes they would offer me little jobs to do for them. They used to have me running messages or passing over mysterious packages. I was happy to run errands but I was never tempted to emulate these men. Something told me that there were better ways of making your mark on the world, although I had no idea what they might be. I knew that I could never be a 'hard man'; I wanted to be everyone's friend. I would never have been able to hit or threaten anyone. I couldn't possibly have managed to create the air of menace needed to gain respect as a 'face' on the London gangster scene.

I always found that I got on well with women. As I grew out of my cherubic phase I had something of a Latin look which they seemed to like and I always felt comfortable in their company. A flower-seller called Gypsy Tim, who used to have a barrow on the corner of Mount Street in Mayfair, always said that he would do anything for me because Dad was a 'king of the gypsies'. It was something Dad never mentioned, but I can believe it was true. Our family came from Wales originally and, looking back at photographs, I can certainly see that I had the look of a gypsy about me.

Gypsy Tim didn't just sell flowers. He used to come round to my flat to sweep the chimneys and was always telling me that if I ever wanted someone 'sorted out', he was the man to come to. I knew that he meant I would not be seeing that person again. Luckily I never had cause to call on that aspect of his services.

It wasn't just the physical side of women that I enjoyed. I found their talk about clothes and fashion intriguing and I liked to watch them making themselves beautiful for their boyfriends and husbands. Rene never seemed to want to get involved in anything like that. Young men used to come calling at the door of our flat for her before she was married and she used to hide in her bedroom, giving me threepenny pieces to answer the door and tell them she wasn't there.

When I was twelve the woman next door invited me in on the pretext of some chore she needed doing.

'I need this table shifting into the other room,' she told me, pointing to a table which she could easily have lifted on her own.

I was happy to oblige, thinking I might get a tip at the end.

'Come over here and sit next to me,' she said, once the table was moved, patting the seat on the sofa next to her.

I noticed that she had drawn the curtains and the lights were dim. I sat beside her and she stroked my leg, slipping her blouse off her shoulder with her other hand. I had no idea what she expected me to do but it didn't matter because she was happy to guide me all the way. She unbuttoned my shirt and slipped her hands inside. She showed me how to undo the complicated catches which held women's underwear together in those days. I was a willing pupil and before long we were stretched out on her bed in the next room and I had lost my virginity before I had even truly realised I possessed it.

I loved every minute of it. It wasn't just the actual act of sex, it was the whole sensual involvement with a woman's body. The way she looked, the way she felt, the way she smelled. When I was touching her I knew that I was in the right place, a sort of spiritual arrival. It wasn't love or anything like that, it was something more basic. I wanted as much of this as I could get. While I enjoyed the company of men at the auction house or down the market or the pub, joining in the endless story-telling with gusto, happy to hear everyone's yarns, I was equally eager to spend time in the sweetly scented company of the opposite sex.

At the same time I was wary of becoming too involved with any girls of my own age. I watched young men like my brothers falling straight into marriages, having children and immediately becoming old married couples. I knew I didn't want that, not yet, not while I was still trapped in Shepherd's Bush. I wanted to escape first to a place where life was altogether more heady and exciting, where there was money to be made and where the women were breathtakingly beautiful. What young boy doesn't harbour such dreams?

In the cinema I felt I could spy a world that I would be happy to join. I went to every film I could, always hungry for more of the images which flickered across the screen, giving me insights into places that seemed a million miles away from Shepherd's Bush. To begin with a group of us would go to Saturday morning shows at the cinemas around Shepherd's Bush Green – one of us buying a ticket and letting the others in through the back door. As we became more adventurous we would walk along to Notting Hill and let ourselves into the Gate Cinema, or up to the ABC in Fulham Road.

It was like glimpsing a magic kingdom. We would sit with our mouths open watching stars like Tony Curtis and Errol Flynn and dreaming of living lives just like theirs. It always seemed quite plausible to me that I could do everything that they did, although I still had no idea how I would manage it. I was a cheeky kid from the estates with nothing to lose, I felt sure something would turn up if I just kept my wits about me and my eyes wide open.

I dreamed of meeting stars like Curtis and Flynn, but never imagined it might actually be possible. I thought what great mates they would make, how we could sit around their swimming pools and yachts swapping stories in the sun, drinking champagne and watching the beautiful girls go by. And it all came true for me.

I was keen to get into the adult world as soon as possible. I wanted to feel the weight of money in my pockets. I wanted to be able to go out dancing on a Saturday night and pick up girls. I wanted to be able to wear clothes that felt good against my skin and showed off my elegant young physique. I wanted to test my skills in real life.

To do any of these things I had to find a way to earn money. The first paid work I took was feeding the greyhounds at the nearby White City Stadium which was on the site that is now the BBC Television Centre. Word soon got around that young Len had access to the dogs' food, and several of the men whom I knew through Dad and my brother, Fred, started approaching me with little packets of powder and tablets which they wanted put into the various bowls.

'What for?' I asked innocently.

'To make them go faster,' I was told.

I did as I was asked for a while and then it dawned on me that I was actually taking the risks of fixing the races and not getting anything for it. They all said they would 'look after me' if I did as they asked, but most of them didn't. I was too young to argue with them at that stage, being no more than ten or eleven, but I didn't feel comfortable about it and decided to look around for something else to do.

In Shepherd's Bush market I started working for a man on a fruit and vegetable barrow. I would rise before dawn and drive with him to Covent Garden to buy the produce. I loved getting up early, when the world was quiet and empty of people, letting myself out of the flat while the rest of the family was still sleeping. There would be hardly any other vehicles on the road until we got to the market.

However early we arrived, Covent Garden would already be alive with lorries and stalls by the time we got there, trolleys rattling, voices shouting out prices and people who had been working all night haggling with one another about the prices of their produce. The narrow streets which are now so clogged by tourists, street performers and shoppers would then be filled with trucks and lorries loading and unloading. Stacks of crates would be balanced precariously as business was done around them. The gutters would be filled with discarded cabbage leaves and damaged fruit, the pavements wet and slippery as traders tried to keep their own patches clean with buckets of soapy water.

I would stand and stare in amazement at the banks of flowers waiting for the florists to whisk them away to the grand houses of Mayfair and Belgravia, Kensington and Chelsea, to decorate the lives of people who could afford to spend more on a bunch of flowers than my whole family needed to live on for a week. I couldn't believe how beautiful the colours and scents were and how high the boxes were stacked.

My boss and I would be back in Shepherd's Bush with a barrow-load of produce before the first shoppers were out of their homes, setting up our wares, ready for a day's trading once the men had all gone to work and the women came out to buy food for the day.

I can't have been more than twelve when I started on the barrows as a Saturday job. As soon as I could get out of school, before they were able to teach me more than the basics of reading and writing, I began working in the market every day and by fourteen I had graduated to having my own barrow.

Even after we moved as a family out of White City and down to the house in Roehampton where Rene still lives, I went on working in the market. I loved the hustle and bustle of being in business, handling the money, calling out my wares – 'Nice cabbages, two for sixpence. Apples a shilling a pound' – chatting to the customers - 'My word, you're looking well, Mrs Brown' – and going home with my pockets bulging at the end of the day. I found it easy to give them the chat, to sparkle and make them feel good. I was young, handsome, charming and life was very promising indeed.

My barrow was outside a mirror shop which did a good trade. Mirrors were becoming very fashionable. Ordinary people were starting to use them to decorate their houses, just as the rich had been doing for centuries, discovering how they could bring light and space into small, cramped rooms. There was a young Italian lad called Michael Birri working in the shop and we got to know one another, sharing cups of tea on the pavement to warm us up on chilly mornings, chatting about girls and comparing dreams about the future. I don't think there is any pleasure in life greater than just sitting around with someone, swapping stories.

Our paths crossed in Mayfair many years later and Michael ended up married to the fabulously wealthy Princess Meriam of Johore and living in tax exile in Florida. He was the manager of the Mayfair club, Harry's Bar, where all the richest and most fashionable people used to eat, and still do. It is owned by Mark Birley who also owns Annabel's, which has been the premiere London night club for the jet set for decades now. When Princess Meriam took a shine to Michael she used to eat at the club every day, sometimes twice a day, until he was unable to resist the temptation any longer.

When my salon was at its most successful I would eat in Harry's Bar often, knowing that I would be bound to meet a mixture of friends and clients, as well as getting some of the best cooking in London. When I realised that the new manager was my childhood friend from the mirror shop, we fell to reminiscing about the old pie and mash shop in the market, where we used to buy our lunch to eat while we worked.

I knew the shop was still going and, as a treat for Michael, I rang them the day after meeting him in Harry's Bar and asked them to send him over a portion of pie and mash in a cab. It arrived at the bar at lunchtime. Michael unwrapped it and put it on a plate just as Sir James Goldsmith, the billionaire, came in for lunch.

'What's that you're eating, Michael?' Sir James asked.

'It's the dish of the day,' Michael joked.

'Looks good,' Sir James said, sniffing the pie, 'I'll have some of that.'

'You'd better have this one,' Michael said, and handed it over. God knows what sort of a mark-up he put on that meal.

I bumped into Sir James on a bus a few months before he died, after I had moved back in with Rene. It was just before the general election in 1997 that brought the Labour Party back into power. He was running his Referendum Party from an office in Putney and he was getting the bus up to the West End, so we travelled together, reminiscing about the old days.

He was already dying of cancer then, although the world didn't yet know it. It seemed odd to me that one of the richest men in the world should be hopping on and off buses in south London.

'It's more convenient than driving,' he said when I expressed my surprise. 'I don't have to worry about parking or having a driver. I just go where I want when I want.'

I think he was probably surprised to meet me there too. By coincidence we found ourselves on the same number 74 bus back to Putney that evening and he sat down beside me once more, lighting up a huge cigar. I warned him that you aren't allowed to smoke on London buses, but he just smiled at me indulgently.

'Rules are for other people, Leonard,' he said and kept on puffing away as we chatted amiably about mutual acquaintances and about his family.

His daughter Jemima, whom I remembered as a little girl, had recently married the Pakistani cricketer Imran Khan, which Sir James seemed pleased about. Although he was a terrible tyrant and bully to many of the people he dealt with, he was a great romantic at heart.

As a young man he had eloped with Isabel Patino, the heiress to a Bolivian tin fortune. She was expecting his child and died tragically of a brain haemorrhage the night after the birth. After a number of affairs, and another marriage, Sir James had started an affair with Lady Annabel Birley. At the time she was married to Mark Birley and he had named his famous night club after her. She eventually became Sir

James' third wife and was the mother of Jemima. Despite all that, Sir James and Mark remained friends and would often dine together.

The bus conductor, whom I knew quite well from my travels up and down to town, spotted the clouds of smoke emanating from the cigar and came over.

'No smoking on this bus,' he said sharply.

'Have you any idea who I am?' Sir James boomed. 'I could buy this company tomorrow.'

He kept on smoking defiantly and the man shrank back. Once the tycoon had got off he came back to me.

'Who does your friend think he is, Sir James bleeding Goldsmith?' he enquired.

'He is Sir James Goldsmith,' I told him.

'Well,' he replied, 'I don't care who he says he is. Tell him he's not to smoke on my ****ing bus again.'

But this was all still a long way in the future. In the days when Michael Birri and I worked in Shepherd's Bush market my ambitions were just vaguely formed dreams which I had no idea how to fulfil and Sir James was only just leaving Eton to begin his adventures. I enjoyed working on the barrow, but I knew I wanted more from life than a few quid in my pocket and a sore throat from shouting my wares.

I had started to discover the world of fine art and it had opened my eyes to the possibilities of life. Nothing I had come across at home or at school had taught me anything much about the world. I don't remember there being a single picture on the walls at home, but Hammersmith Secondary Modern did manage to develop an interest in art and in carpentry in me. I came across some pictures of horses by Stubbs in a magazine and was struck by their beauty. I decided I wanted to find out more about the artist. And I discovered that I could take a bus or tube up to the centre of London and wander around art galleries for free. I started by going to the Victoria and Albert Museum, spending whole days gazing at everything on display. I was particularly intrigued by the furniture, and by drawings from the end of the nineteenth century.

I would go on from one gallery to another, staring at pictures and sculptures, simply drinking in everything that I saw. I had no idea what I was looking at. I didn't understand any of the history or philosophy behind the works, I just knew that the idea of creating such beautiful things made my skin prickle with excitement. It was like a longing which I couldn't satisfy, an inner itch which I could find no way to scratch, a hunger that would never be satisfied however much I ate. I had no reason to think that I could paint or sculpt or carve, or do anything like that. I just knew I wanted to do something creative. I wanted to express myself and produce something with my own hands, guided by my own eye.

I used to look at glossy art and photography books in shops, spending as long as I dared turning over the luscious pages, before some suspicious shop assistant would start to close in and I would have to scarper. I longed to be able to own such beautiful things for myself. I was never much into reading, but I loved to gaze at beautiful images, soaking them up, longing to make them part of my own life.

'Why don't you come down to the auction rooms and work with Arthur and me?' Dad suggested one evening when we were sitting around in the kitchen. 'You can earn a good living from cars. Every-one's going to have one soon.' My brother, Arthur, had been helping Dad with the cars at Putney Bridge and Fred had gone into engineer-ing. I was intent on leaving school as soon as possible and, since I had no other ideas, I took his advice and went to work at the auction rooms. It occurred to me that the best way to make a little money was to buy and sell a car myself.

Within a week or two I had put together all the money I had managed to make in the market and purchased my first car, an old black Packard. I bought it very cheaply and spent weeks polishing it up, making it shine like new. I then put it back into the auction. One of the gangsters who hung around the showroom bought it and I made a £100 profit. For a moment I thought that maybe my old dad had given me sound advice.

'You're good,' the proud new owner of the shiny Packard told me as he wandered around the car, caressing the gleaming chrome work on which I had lavished so much love and attention. 'You're wasted in a business like this.' I was quite happy to agree with him, but I still couldn't think of any alternative.

It felt fine to have the money in my pocket, but it did not satisfy the craving I was feeling inside to express myself creatively in some way. Not having had much education I had no idea how to channel my urges, I only knew that not using my talents was leaving me with a frustrating emptiness which I had no way of filling.

The night after I sold the Packard I went to see a film at the Curzon cinema in the West End. They always showed films that were a bit different, a bit more artistic than the local cinemas, often foreign movies with subtitles. They still do. This particular one was French. It was called *An Artist with Ladies*. I had no idea what I was about to see as I sank down into the plush seat. I was hungry for anything that would teach me something new about life. I also liked the luxury of the Curzon. Because of its location in the heart of Mayfair it was much more comfortable than most of its rivals, the seats feeling almost like armchairs. There was plenty of leg room and a sense of thickly carpeted hush everywhere, even in the foyer.

The film starred an actor called Fernandel who was playing a hairdresser. Like most men at that time I had assumed that all hairdressers were gay, or 'queer' as we termed it then. Fernandel's character definitely was not gay and his profession gave him access to a constant supply of willing women who were bewitched by the way in which he touched their hair and made them beautiful. They opened up their hearts to him in more ways than one.

The realisation came to me with blinding clarity. This was the world I wanted to join. The salons where the film was shot were sumptuous sets, decorated with the most luxurious furnishings, a million miles from the dreary flats and houses where I had spent my childhood. That was what I wanted: to be a hairdresser and be part of all this glamour. Not only would I be able to meet as many women as I could possibly want, I would also have a way of satisfying some of the artistic yearnings which had been troubling me, trying to find an outlet.

'A barber?' Dad said when I broke the news. 'You want to be a barber?'

'A ladies' hairdresser, Dad,' I corrected him. 'I want to be a ladies' hairdresser.'

'They're all sissies, aren't they? Poncing about.'

Hairdressing was very different in those days. To start with men and women wouldn't have considered for a single minute going to the same salon. Men went to barbers who were normally bald old men with pictures on the walls of the cricketer, Denis Compton, advertising Brylcreem. The more fashionable ones might have movie stills of

Tony Curtis and his quiff in the window to persuade young men that getting their hair cut would make them more desirable to women. Most of them used electric clippers, which they ran up the back of the customer's neck, allowing bristles to grow back in the coming weeks, leaving a short back and sides style just like they did in the army.

Women on the other hand went for permanent waves, which entailed a lot of rollers and sitting under dryers for hours. Rich women would go to their hairdresser several times a week; the rest would only go every few weeks or even months. Famous hairdressers were people with salons in Knightsbridge and Mayfair who could win competitions by building a woman's hair up into a stately galleon or something resembling Marie Antoinette.

None of our family knew anything about this trade or how a young man would start out in it, but some of Dad's more worldly friends, the men who frequented the illegal gambling and drinking clubs of the West End and knew a bit about how the 'better classes' lived, realised that I was on to something.

'Good trade for the boy to get into,' Jack Spot reassured Dad. 'He'll meet a fine class of person. Open a salon in a good area and you can make a very decent little living.'

The next time he came to the auction room, Jack brought me a copy of *Hairdressers' Journal*, a magazine I would never have dreamt even existed, and showed me some of the advertisements for trainees and apprentices. Suddenly I could see a way forward.

CHAPTER FOUR

ALTHOUGH THE WEST End of London is just a short bus ride from Shepherd's Bush and White City, it was – and still is – a different world. It was one I couldn't get enough of. It wasn't just the cinemas and art galleries which I came into the centre for. I was getting to know all the parts of London life which would later earn the city the nickname 'Swinging London'.

Although on the surface British life still seemed to be stuck in the dull post-war mould, beneath the surface a generation of young people was getting ready to break through in an explosion of talent and new ideas. Art, music, fashion, photography, publishing, design – everyone was there but still in their teens, looking for a way to make their voices heard. The many people who were soon to be household names, from Mary Quant to Terence Conran, the Beatles to David Bailey, were all teenagers with ideas on how they wanted to change their parents' world.

Of course at the time we didn't see it like that. We were more interested in getting a bit of money in our pockets and having a good time. On Friday and Saturday nights I would be putting on my best shirts and sharpest suits, which I would buy in flash shops in Shaftesbury Avenue and Oxford Street, and heading to the Tottenham Royal or the Wimbledon Palais or the Hammersmith Palais, to meet friends and listen to Ted Heath and the big swing bands.

On Sunday nights, from seven till eleven, all the young men would be at the Lyceum-in-the-Strand, just off Covent Garden, in search of fun and female company. There would be lads from south London and north London, from the East End and from my neck of the woods in west London, all mingling. There were some rivalries bubbling under the surface but they didn't often flare up. We might growl at one another but there weren't many fights. After we had danced and flirted for a few hours we would go to the nearby Black and White café and drink coffee and milkshakes into the small hours of Monday morning.

There was a feeling amongst the working-class youth of London at that time that we were as good as anyone else, we could do whatever we wanted. We were emerging from the drab post-war world of rationing and shortages and we were ready to have some fun.

Many of the lads who were hanging around London's dance halls went on to make it in fashion and showbusiness. The photographers David Bailey and Terence Donovan were there, and actors like Michael Caine and Terence Stamp, and the boys who went on to make it in the brave new world of advertising and public relations. There were also young men who would follow different careers, gangsters like the Kray twins and the Richardsons who were waiting for their chance to challenge the old gang leaders like Billy Hill and Jack Spot.

We were all mixed together, getting our suits and shirts made by little tailors in the back streets of Soho, all eager to make our mark on the world. A lot of the lads used to have their hair cut by a man called Sid Sieger, who had a little barber's shop in Archer Street, in Soho. The hookers who worked upstairs used to use him as a message-taking service while we were sitting in the chair and he was trying to achieve the Tony Curtis look on us.

'Tell my next customer I'll be back in ten minutes,' one of them would call out as she passed through the shop. 'I'm just going for a coffee with Lil.'

I loved the street life of the city. I loved the hot, noisy dance halls with their primitive, tinny acoustics, the cheap, informal coffee bars, the smoky pubs and the endless talking and laughing and planning and dreaming. I loved to hear the gossip from high society and from the underworld. Living at home cost me nothing and so any money I managed to make I could spend on enjoying myself, and I did.

But it was the streets of Mayfair which most impressed me, where the terraced houses were the size of mansions and the shops displayed paintings and pieces of furniture so expensive that the traders didn't even dare put prices on them. These largely residential streets were more discreet than the glare of Piccadilly Circus and the Strand, filled with expensive cars which wafted the locals around from restaurant to night club and back home again. I could smell the cigar smoke in the air. The forbidding facades of the grand hotels like the Connaught and the Dorchester, the Grosvenor House and Claridge's, hid interiors so lavish and luxurious that they took my breath away as I got my first glimpses through the heavily guarded doors. It was obvious that this was where the real money was. This was where the most elegant and most gracious living would be found. These were the people I wanted to meet and live amongst. Soon, I told myself, I would be walking through those doors and chatting to those stern-faced liveried doormen as if I had known them all my life.

As I studied the pages of the *Hairdressers' Journal* I came across an advertisement for a salon called French of London, just off Park Lane. They wanted to employ some apprentices. My heart throbbed with excitement. This could be the door which would let me into the magical world of the rich and famous. I rang them immediately from the phone box on the corner of the street, forcing the coins into the slots with trembling fingers, and made an appointment for an interview the next day.

I rose early, having hardly slept at all, and dressed in my smartest Italian suit. I was so clean and well groomed I must have squeaked as I walked to the bus stop. I was determined to make an impression. I was sure I looked good because everyone was always telling me that I did, but I was still nervous. Would they realise just how much they needed my services? Or would they spot me for the ambitious barrow boy and second-hand car salesman I actually was, and send me packing back to Shepherd's Bush?

As the bus rolled into Knightsbridge, I felt my heart beginning to speed up. It was still early morning and the grand shops were opening up. Taxis were starting to drop early shoppers around Harrods and Harvey Nichols. Hyde Park looked lush and green as the driver negotiated his way around the race track of Hyde Park Corner and turned into the bottom of Park Lane. I was shaking with excitement by the time I got to the door of the salon. On the outside I might have been able to make myself look like a confident young man about town, although I doubt it, but inside I was just like any other quaking fifteen-year-old setting out from home for the first time.

The rich smell of the salon swept over me as I walked in, intoxicating and strange, a mixture of perfume and chemicals. The scented air was warm and I felt a little faint, as if I might be suffocating. There were already clients being moved around from chair to chair, being brought coffee and being fussed over by immaculately turned-out staff, none of whom paid me any attention at all.

The receptionist did not trouble to make eye contact with me. Had there been a tradesman's entrance I'm sure she would have sent me round to it. When I told her I had an appointment she waved me to a chair and gave me a form to fill in. No one bothered to greet me or make me feel more at ease. I was left in no doubt where my place would be in the pecking order in this establishment.

I dare say they were used to eager young boys coming in off the streets for jobs. I didn't care how they treated me. I just stared around me. I expect my mouth was hanging open. This was nothing like the hairdressers round our way, where people like Mum and Rene went for their perms. Everything about the customers here reeked of style and money. They were all so chic and so confident in their fur coats and discreet day jewellery. There was such an air of excitement and bustle.

It was exactly how I pictured life behind the scenes at a theatre or on a film set. I could imagine these women were being prepared for great social events: balls in grand hotels, race meetings and formal dinners. Perhaps some of them were even famous actresses from West End shows or film stars staying at the Dorchester or Claridge's. My imagination was racing as I watched them, and they all looked right through me.

After a few minutes I remembered the form which I was gripping tightly in my lap. The thought of filling it in made me nervous. Reading and writing had not been my best subjects at school, but I was determined to have a go.

I stared hard at the questions and started to fill them in with all the honesty I could muster. Then I got stuck. They were asking what I thought of *Vogue* magazine and *Harpers Bazaar*. Plucking up my courage I stood up and went back to the woman who had given me the form.

'Excuse me,' I said, 'what are these magazines?'

She looked at me in silence for a moment, apparently stunned by my ignorance. Eventually she managed to find her tongue. 'If you don't even know that,' she said icily, 'you will never become a hairdresser.'

Crushed, I left the salon and fled back home to my copy of the *Hairdressers' Journal*. Having been inside French's I was now more sure than ever that this was what I wanted to do with my life. I realised that I hadn't prepared myself well enough for the interview. I needed to find another vacancy to apply for, and this time I would be ready.

I bought all the glossy fashion magazines I could find at the newsagents and studied their pages avidly. If I had been entranced by the Fernandel film and by the atmosphere of French's, the pictures in these bibles of style overwhelmed me. Now, of course, they look extraordinarily dated. The art of fashion photography was still in its infancy in the Fifties, the models still stiff and formal, usually wearing hats and gloves. But to me it was an enchanted world. The feel and smell of the expensive, glossy paper and the beauty of the photographs enthralled me. No wonder the woman at French's had been so dismissive. These magazines were like a dream. They transported me to a place where every woman was a perfect beauty and where every-thing in life was elegant and ordered. They gave me access to a world which I did not yet have any chance of entering for real. Not only did they give a glimpse into high society, they also painted an idealised picture of the people who populated it.

With renewed enthusiasm I went back to the *Hairdressers' Journal* and found another advertisement offering apprenticeships in a salon in Mount Street called Evansky's. It was run by Rose and Albert Evansky. I knew Mount Street. It was right at the heart of Mayfair, exactly where I wanted to be. This time I would be ready for whatever questions they threw at me. I had soaked myself in the glamour of the magazines and would not be thrown by anyone trying to put me down.

Rose Evansky was a lovely woman, and didn't make me feel in the least inferior. Even though she was obviously distracted by the clients who were all round the salon awaiting her attentions, she took the time to sit down and talk. I don't think she spotted any particular talent in me, she simply thought I was keen enough and looked the part. So she offered me an apprenticeship. I felt like I had won the pools.

In those days, and for many years to come, there was a price attached to entering the magic kingdom of hairdressing. Eager young apprentices had to pay their new employers a premium for the privilege of being trained by them. That was as well as being their virtual slaves. No one gave a thought as to how the poor apprentices were supposed to support themselves during this time. I didn't care. I was willing to pay whatever I could afford to be given a chance to become part of this world. The hundred pounds I had made on the sale of the Packard became my stake in my future career.

I broke the news to Dad, who took it philosophically. By that stage he had talked to a few more of the West End 'faces' about hairdressing as a career for his boy, and they had all been encouraging. I don't know if he had decided I must be queer and that he was going to let me get on with it – it certainly wasn't a subject we would have talked about openly.

There were plenty of other young men eager to fill my shoes at the car auction rooms. I was replaced by a young villain called Gordon Goodey. Gordon had already started on a life of crime and, over the next few years, would develop a reputation as a safe blower and armed robber. In 1963 he became part of a gang which planned to rob the Glasgow to Euston Royal Mail train. The job was carried out and they got away with two and a half million pounds (about thirty million at today's rates). It was the biggest robbery of its kind ever staged and the gang became famous as the Great Train Robbers. The majority of them, however, including Gordon, were captured within a few days of the job and were sentenced to a record thirty years in jail each.

Rose Evansky was a talented hairdresser by the standards of the day and highly thought of within the trade. Like most of them she really had only one hairstyle which she could do, but she had built up a loyal clientele who loved her work. She was particularly good at dressing hair, which was what grand Mayfair ladies wanted at that time. They would come in to have their hair prepared for a specific event like Royal Ascot, a debutante ball or a grand dinner party, and they would be back a day or two later for something else. They provided a steady flow of customers to the salon and made it a solid business.

Rose's husband, Albert, was a good hairdresser as well but his ambitions were directed more towards acting. I doubt if he was very successful at that, although I do remember him going off to do bit-parts in commercials every so often. I still see him occasionally on television, usually playing Einstein or some other mad professor. He was a flamboyant character who enjoyed playing the hairdresser for the amusement of the clientele and staff alike.

Like all the apprentices, Rose set me first to shampooing her clients, which was a job I enjoyed because it meant I could chat to them as I worked, but she was worried about my accent. I think she thought that my rough edges might damage the genteel atmosphere of her salon which catered almost exclusively for rich, upper-class ladies.

There was a mixture of other trainees, some with different accents but none who talked like barrow boys. Deciding she must do something about smoothing down the rough edges, Rose sent me to a local drama coach for elocution lessons.

It was just like a scene from *My Fair Lady*. Most of the other pupils were young girls hoping to get jobs as receptionists or secretaries and the teacher would spend her time making us parrot phrases like 'How now brown cow' after her, with nicely rounded vowels. I was a very keen pupil, willing to do anything to improve my chances of getting on in the world, but I found it hard not to giggle. Even a few years later the idea of such classes was laughable. Can you imagine people like John Lennon, David Hockney or David Bailey putting themselves through such a ridiculous ordeal?

I hadn't been there long before Rose rang during the school day.

'Leonard,' she said, 'the customers are missing you. You must come back. You've done enough time there.'

'I haven't finished the course,' I protested.

'Never mind. We need you back.'

I was very flattered, but worried as to how I was going to master the necessary improvements to my voice after such a short course. When the customers asked me where I had been I explained.

'Oh, don't worry about that,' they said. 'Everyone likes the way you work. Your accent will change in time just from being around different people.'

They were right. In the end people used to accuse me of sounding 'rather grand'. I don't think I did it on purpose, I just sort of soaked it up.

I was desperately keen to learn all there was to know about hairdressing. I would watch Rose and the other stylists like a hawk, trying to see what they were doing and working out ways to do it better. I was always happy to stay late and practise cutting and dressing hair on anyone who would allow me near them, with Rose watching my every move. I began to think that perhaps I was going to do all right in this game. I managed to persuade some of the ladies from the

33

elocution classes to come to the salon in the evenings to be my models, so that I could try out a few of the ideas which were starting to form in my imagination. The women were always very keen. I guess it was as exciting for them to be able to get free haircuts in a posh establishment like Evansky's as it was for me actually to be using my creativity at last.

I was always very polite to the clients, whether they were paying or not, perhaps to compensate for the roughness of my voice, and I found that whenever a stylist was away for some reason, the regular paying clients started asking for me to do their hair.

At that time it was largely a matter of setting hair rather than cutting it, but I had already worked out that hairdressing is a basic service industry and that a good hairdresser will do whatever the client wants while they are in the salon in order to make them feel good about themselves.

I had learned the skills of selling on the barrow, where customers would always respond better if I took the trouble to show them the fruit that I thought they should be buying. It was the same in the salon. I would make sure they had their coffee the way they liked it, their newspapers and magazines. They were always so nice to me. I never seemed to have any trouble with anyone and my confidence started to grow. Soon I was actually plucking up the courage to suggest ideas to them rather than simply letting them tell me what they wanted me to do. Sometimes, when the stylists returned from their holidays, the clients would continue asking for me. It seemed that I had the knack. I had found something that I was good at.

While most of the customers wanted to be given the same hairstyles they had always had, and didn't want anything new or experimental, I was finding other ways of improving my cutting technique. Models who were just starting out in the business and couldn't afford to go to top stylists, would seek out trainees like me who wanted to build reputations and establish client bases. The deal was simple. They would get free hairstyling and might even get their pictures taken, and I got the chance to work with girls who had beautiful hair and beautiful faces, girls who would photograph well and would be an advertisement for my skills.

Such close proximity to a variety of young models also gave me a chance to spend time with the sort of women I had only ever dreamed

34

about before. To start with I guess they were charmed because I was so young and inexperienced and I don't think any of them took me very seriously. Models in those days were mostly upper-class girls filling in time until they managed to hook a rich husband. None of them would have considered going out with a working-class hairdresser's apprentice. I didn't mind. I was in no hurry. I could see my path ahead and it all looked very promising. By then I was only sixteen years old. Today I would still be trapped at school, getting ready to take my A Levels, but I was already out and about and gaining worldly experience. I knew where I was going and there now seemed no reason I wouldn't be successful.

As the months passed, many of the young models whose hair I had cut started to get work and become successful, but they still kept coming back to me. Most importantly of all, they talked to other people.

'Who does your hair?' they would be asked by photographers, clothes designers or other models.

'I go to Leonard at Evansky's,' they would reply, wanting to make it sound as if only the best was good enough for them, and my name began to become familiar in the right circles.

Even while I was serving my apprenticeship I was building up the base of clients which would eventually propel me right to the top of the tree. Looking back now, it is almost as if I planned it all, which in a way I did. But it didn't feel like that at the time. Life was so busy, working, travelling to and from home and socialising with my mates in the evenings, that I never really had any time to think about my career path in the sort of structured way that young people do today. I just knew I was doing the right things and enjoying myself.

This training period took three years, and a lot of people could get to hear about a 'hot' young hairdresser in that time. Hairdressing is a small industry, at least it was then, and everyone knew who was doing what at the rival salons. If a customer was pleased with something you had done they would be happy to tell their friends all about it – everyone likes to think that they have found something new and exciting that they can recommend to others. My name continued to be passed around.

Whenever there was an opportunity to accompany a model to a photographic session I would grab it. I wanted to climb inside those glossy magazine pages that I had pored over so eagerly and be part of the creative process which led to the final pictures of the flawless beauties who gazed so haughtily out at the readers. I wanted to learn how to dress hair for the photographs as well as cut it. I loved the excitement of the lights, the tripods and the tantrums. The mounting tension as the photographers disappeared under their hoods, shouting orders at their assistants. It was exciting watching the girls coming in off the street looking quite ordinary and then transforming themselves with make-up. I became fascinated by what was possible, how they could create a world of fantasy for the readers with brushes and combs, filters and reflectors, making eyes wide and lips lustrous, heightening cheekbones and abolishing all blemishes from the skin. I could see that the hair should be playing a much bigger part in the beauty process than it had so far been allowed to do.

Fashion and beauty photographers were just beginning to become stars in their own rights. One of the biggest names at the time was John French. When I went along to assist at a shoot in his studio in Mayfair I met his young assistant, Terence Donovan, a working-class lad like myself who would soon become one of the biggest photographer stars of the Sixties and a long-term mate.

'It's a crying shame, isn't it,' he said to me as we stood watching his boss taking the final pictures of some model I had been working on a few minutes before.

'What is?' I asked.

'You do all that work and he just sticks a bleeding hat over the whole lot so you can't see a thing. I mean,' he went on, warming to his subject, 'who the hell wears a hat any more unless they're going for tea with the Queen? We should be taking pictures where the models actually look alive. Their hair should be blowing in the wind, not jammed into some twenty guinea titfer!'

I couldn't have agreed more, and it wasn't long before we were doing exactly that. Without realising it, we were all starting to meet one another: the models, the photographers, the actors, the fashion designers, the make-up artists and the hairdressers who would later be seen as the founders of the Swinging Sixties. We had no idea that was what we were doing at the time. We were just ambitious young people trying to establish ourselves in jobs which we loved doing. We were also keen to have fun.

The Fifties were drawing to an end and everything was about to change, although none of us could foresee just how great the changes were going to be. I was growing increasingly eager to do more with customers' hair. Rose Evansky was good at dressing hair, but, in common with nearly every hairdresser at the time, she had no particular technique for cutting. I soon felt that there should be more to it than the razor cutting which was still going on. I didn't like the unnatural, bouffant Doris Day styles which were fashionable and which seemed to me to make everyone look years older than they actually were. Well-cut, healthy hair could be so beautiful and yet the customers seemed to be doing everything they could to disguise its natural attractions.

One day a new lad came to the salon to work as a junior, sweeping up hair and shampooing. I knew immediately that he was from the same sort of background as myself. He was a cockney, very cheeky and a terrible hairdresser. He was calling himself Christian St Forget, but his real name was Nigel Davies. His friends and family called him Nagels.

'Why did you choose a name like St Forget?' I asked him once, as we worked together at the basins, up to our wrists in shampoo.

'Just in case anyone asked me my name and I forgot it,' he replied, straight-faced.

It didn't take long for Nagels and me to discover that we had a lot of contacts in common – most of them villains. The reason why he was at Evansky's was because he had been fired by the man who was then the hottest name in hairdressing, Vidal Sassoon. In fact, Nagels told me later, Sassoon had been so frustrated with him that he had hurled his scissors into the air with such force that they had stuck into the salon ceiling and hung there, precariously, above the upturned heads of astonished customers and stylists.

Vidal was another working-class bloke, although a little older than Nagels and me, who was making his way in the world, having started as a shampoo boy at the age of fourteen. He had a first-floor premises in Bond Street and it was becoming the most talked-about salon in London. There they were starting to do radical new things with hair, the sort of things that Terence Donovan and I had been talking about.

Women who no longer wanted to be set and permed every week were discovering that it was possible to have cuts which would allow them to be more natural. Not only would their hair look healthier and suit their faces better, it would also be far easier to look after. Instead of having to go to the salon every few days they could go every few weeks. They could wash and dry it themselves and it would look just as good, well, almost as good, as when they first walked out of the salon.

'How come you were working at Sassoon's in the first place?' I asked Nagels as we deposited our customers under the dryers and went off to start the next round of shampooing. I could see that he wasn't there because he was any sort of genius with the scissors.

'Ah,' his eyes lit up at the prospect of telling a good story. 'Do you know Big Jackie Myravitch?'

'Sure, I know him.' Jackie was a well-known villain. I had met him around the car showrooms with my dad.

'He's known Vidal since they were both kids,' Nagels explained. 'Anyway. I'd knocked off a lorry-load of wine – real crap – and I was looking for an outlet. I'd also knocked off a big pile of serious labels, Rothschild, Mouton Cadet, that sort of thing. Big Jack told me that his pal – a hairdresser called Sassoon – was getting married at a big posh do in a Park Lane hotel and asked if I could supply the wine. "As it happens," I said, "I can."

'I have a pal, Stephen Way, do you know him?'

I knew Stephen was another young stylist working at Sassoon's. Later he was to prove himself a true friend to me but I didn't know him personally at that stage, as I told Nagels.

'Well, Jackie is his brother-in-law. Anyway, Stephen's mum was a gypsy, fabulous, big, handsome, red-haired woman. She was in on the scam with me and the night before the wedding we got down the family bath tub, filled it with hot water and scrubbed the old labels off. We then stuck on the posh ones.

'The wine itself was like paint stripper, but I thought we might get away with it. Vidal sent a cab the next day and off I went with the crates. I watched in amazement as the guests just glanced at the labels, satisfied themselves that it was a good wine and then drank it without turning a hair.

'Towards the end of the reception Vidal – or Victor Baboon as I like to call him – called me over. "Nagels," he said, "can I have a word?" I stood close to the exit, ready to run. "Listen," he said, "would you like to be my personal assistant? You're such a lively lad and I'm really pleased with you." So that's how I got to be there, but he keeps firing me for things.'

I couldn't believe the luck of the man. Everyone else was having to pay for the privilege of being trained and he was being given it as a reward for ripping off the best hairdresser in London. This was a man I wanted to get to know better.

Over the following months we became close friends and used to hang around the West End together after work. Nagels' mum lived in the East End, which was a lot further from the centre of things than Roehampton, so, during the week, he used to come back with me. We would arrive home at all hours after hanging around the pubs and clubs in the West End and Chelsea. By that time, my mum had passed away and we had a couple of camp beds up in Dad's bedroom. He used to grumble at us to get to sleep when we kept chattering excitedly away about our experiences in the salon that day and our wild dreams for the future. Dad and Nagels always got on well because they had a lot of friends in common.

Any money either Nagels or I earned we used to spend on clothes, having suits and shirts made whenever we could. A man in Lexington Street used to make us suits for a fiver. Ronnie 'the Chink', who had a stall in Castle Street, off Petticoat Lane, used to make the shirts. Our hero was the film star Laurence Harvey, who was impossibly sophisticated, all smooth Italian suits, slicked-back hair, gold cufflinks and cigarette holders. We would have done anything to have looked that cool but we were still working to pretty tight budgets. We never had more than the price of a meal in our pockets but we looked the business as we strutted around the streets of Mayfair. I usually had a bit more than Nagels because I got better tips.

We used to have our shoes made for us as well. The fashion at the time was for winkle-pickers, shoes so long and narrow that they made us hobble like ancient Chinese women with bound feet. We had ours made by Stan the Shoemaker in Soho. Nagels always went that little bit further in the cause of fashion than I did and I remember many a time, as we walked about the streets, when he would have to stop somewhere like Sloane Square, ease his shoes off and immerse his throbbing feet in the cool water of a fountain.

These days the clothes we wore as young men have become

museum items. Nagels gets requests from the Victoria and Albert Museum for his old suits and shoes. He's kept a lot of them in perfect condition. His flat in Chelsea is a bit like a little shrine to the period with Nagels as some sort of eccentric old curator. They teach the Sixties in school history lessons now. The things Nagels and I did a few years after we first met have become historical events. If you'd have predicted that at the time we would have thought you were mad.

Strolling along Park Lane together one evening, when it was still just an elegant single carriageway, not the six-lane motorway it has since become, looking up at the grand buildings running along the side of Hyde Park, I pointed to the top of the Dorchester Hotel where the Oliver Messel suite was being created.

'One day, mate,' I said, 'that will be us up there, sipping champagne, up to our necks in beautiful girls.'

'Yeah,' Nagels laughed. 'And I can just see us ten years later; a couple of old tramps, walking along here, saying, "Do you remember when we lived up there?" '

I'm sure he was joking at the time, but his prediction was to come frighteningly close to reality.

CHAPTER FIVE

NAGELS WAS ALWAYS keen to get back to Vidal Sassoon's from Evansky's, knowing that it was the most exciting salon in London, probably in the world, at the time.

'Let me talk to Vidal,' he said, 'and see if I can persuade him into taking you on as well.'

I was grateful to him. While I was very happy at Evansky's I knew that Sassoon's place was where the really interesting work was being done and where the really interesting people were going. Only later did Nagels admit to me that he was using me as his ticket to get back in. Apparently my reputation as a cutter was already getting about and he thought that Vidal would be more likely to forgive him, whatever his latest sins had been, if he could bring a potential 'top stylist' into the fold from a rival salon.

As usual, Nagels' scheme worked and he came back to tell me that Vidal wanted to meet me. I went along for an interview. This was a million miles from my previous interview experiences. Then I had nothing to offer except my adolescent enthusiasm and the training fee. Now I had a fledgling reputation, plus a couple of years' experience and training. I could actually give a demonstration of my skills without worrying that I would make a fool of myself. More importantly, I could see that this salon was full of young stylists like me, working-class girls and boys who wanted to do something different and make a stir, none of whom would have considered taking elocution lessons. There was an air of creativity and excitement the moment you walked into the place. The customers were also younger and more fashionable than the grand ladies at Evansky's. I knew immediately that I would fit in.

Vidal himself was very impressive. Immaculately groomed and tanned, he looked more like a pop star than a hairdresser. He was very friendly, with none of the old-fashioned snobbery associated with grand hair salons, and obviously as enthusiastic about hair and beauty and all the new things that were happening in the fashion world as I was. He invited me to join him there and then. He later told me that he just had to see my hands while I was doing a test cut for him, to know that he wanted me on board.

'There was such marvellous control,' he enthused, 'such dexterity.' He was also happy to take on anyone who had been trained by Rose Evansky.

Vidal himself was one of the most glamorous figures in London at the time. Young, confident, handsome, fit and ambitious, part designer, part entrepreneur, part showman, he was preparing to take over the world.

I felt a surge of excitement at this new opportunity. It was like a footballer being promoted to the first division. Nagels was also back in the fold again. Although how he had managed to stay there as long as he had, I don't know. He had developed a particular hairstyle which was a sort of square flick-up. It was completely terrible and depended heavily on the use of rollers to cover up his cutting shortcomings, but he got away with it because he was able to chat his way out of trouble. All the women thought he was wonderful. He was like a character from some Dickens novel, always reinventing himself.

'You need a better name,' Vidal told him one day. 'St Forget is too ridiculous.'

'I fancy changing Christian, too,' Nagels said.

They batted a few names back and forth and came up with Justin de Villeneuve (Nagels thought he would be able to remember it because it translated into 'New Town', like Crawley, Croydon and Milton Keynes). And that was the one that stuck. It was the name that he would be using when he accidentally made a discovery that set the seal on the whole Swinging Sixties scene a few years later, but to me he has always remained Nagels.

Within six months everyone was talking about me as being Vidal's 'top stylist'. There was a tremendous sense of electricity and competition amongst the young cutters on the floor. It was a great feeling, to discover that I actually had a natural talent for a profession which I enjoyed. If I was asked to describe my talent with scissors I would find it difficult to put it into words. It was like an instinct. I was able to look at a customer's face and just see how their hair should fall. When I started cutting I wouldn't always be sure how I was going to achieve the final result, but my fingers would seem to know what to do. It was almost like working in a trance. Someone once compared me to a diamond-cutter, a craftsman who knew exactly how to cut round the flaws. I know that many people found me vague and distant when I was at work – some translated it as being 'a bit grand' – but it was just the way it happened. It was as if my fingers had some sort of magic skills that I could do little to influence. Whenever I made a cut it always seemed to be the right one. It was a gift I was, and still am, profoundly grateful for.

As I became more mature and self-confident I found that I was able to impress the girls, just as I had always wanted. I was now seventeen and successful, a very different animal to the little boy who had first caught the bus up to the West End and hadn't known what *Vogue* was. If you are a little shy and nervous about meeting people, as I was, despite all my cheek, being a hairdresser gives you the perfect excuse to strike up a conversation with a beautiful woman. What girl doesn't like to talk about her hair or appearance and how it might be improved?

Just as Fernandel had depicted in the film that had set me on this course, I found that being a hairdresser is the perfect profession for a young man in search of sex. The women have time to get to know you as you work on their hair, chatting about any number of things with no sense of urgency. They trust you. They open up their hearts and allow you to see them at their most vulnerable. They talk about their problems with dandruff and boyfriends, unwanted pregnancies and unwanted offers of marriage. For a young man willing to spend time listening, it was a perfect education into what makes women tick. They are grateful to you for making them look beautiful and you have every opportunity to flatter and pamper them. Cutting someone's hair is a very intimate, often sensual business. It is inevitable that sparks will be struck from time to time. How often a warm-blooded young hairdresser takes advantage of these opportunities depends upon their conscience.

There was another young stylist at the salon, an Italian called Raphael, who was developing something of reputation for himself as a womaniser. He had a wonderful habit of swearing at the clients in Italian. They never had any idea what he was saying, thinking him very dashing and romantic. In fact he was an appalling old Latin chauvinist, but a very glamorous figure. He spoke four languages and had once trained as a matador, which was what he looked like as he swept and swirled around the floor of the salon, all fire and temperament.

Raphael had left home in Italy at fourteen and run off to join the Foreign Legion. He then escaped and took up bull-fighting, before moving on to London and hairdressing. He had a little flat just behind St George's Hospital on Hyde Park Corner, where the Lanesborough Hotel now stands. He was reputed to have a mirrored ceiling in his bedroom and the women seemed to be lining up to spend the night there. Raphael was spinning like a top just trying to keep up with them all.

The salon's reputation was blossoming and Vidal was becoming the first hairdresser whose name was known to the general public since the legendary Raymond in Knightsbridge, who was always known by the media as Mr Teasy Weasy. The newspaper editors were hungry for success stories of young, creative people and Vidal was a genius at marketing and public relations. He was brilliant at getting the fashion and beauty editors from the newspapers and magazines in to have their hair done, and entertaining them royally.

'Vidal gets them in and spends a hundred pounds on entertaining them,' Stephen Way once told me, 'then you do their hair and make them look as good as they feel. Then Raphael takes them off to bed.' There was more than an element of truth in that.

Raphael was also very fond of 'purple hearts', which were the first amphetamines to be sold illegally on the streets and in the clubs. Compared to the sort of things that are available to the young people today, these were extremely mild stuff, but they seemed temptingly wicked to us at the time, which is what mattered, and the Establishment managed to get highly alarmed and irate about the threat that drugs posed to the future of the nation's youth.

Nagels, forever the eager entrepreneur, always seemed to be able to get bagfuls of the things and kept Raphael stocked up. It was something I was never comfortable with. I was discovering many of the pleasures of the high life, like sex, drink and good food, but drugs were never amongst my pleasures.

Although Raphael had a reputation for using women like tissues, Nagels and I, both being teenagers with all our hormones racing, were no saints either. I discovered that if I managed to persuade a young lady to join me in the lift to the salon, I could stop it between floors for long enough to complete a hasty seduction. Nagels, rather coarsely, nicknamed me 'Leg-Over Len'.

There was only one potential pitfall in my new life. National Service was looming. At that time, every able-bodied young man was expected to serve in the army for a couple of years. The idea of marching round and round parade grounds, going on early morning runs and wearing baggy, scratchy uniforms was not attractive at all. I was also fairly sure that a rather effete young Mayfair hairdresser was likely to be given a pretty hard time by his fellow squaddies until they got to know him.

I began to hatch a plan. Ladies' hairdressers, I reasoned to myself, were generally assumed to be queer. I was a slim young man with a pretty face and a rather distracted habit of waving my arms around. I was aware that many people assumed that I was no exception to this tradition until they got to know me better. It occurred to me that I could make this work in my favour. There was a tinter at the salon called Laurence, who was about as camp as it was possible to be. I asked him if he would dye my hair red for me the day before my interview with the army. He was more than happy to oblige.

When I turned up for the interview, dressed in my tightest and most fashionable clothes, the recruitment officer took one look at me and suggested that I forget all about enlisting. In those days hetero-sexual men did not go around dyeing their hair.

Once I was safely back in the salon I asked Laurence to return me to my natural colour and resumed my blooming career.

It wasn't long before Vidal had outgrown his salon and had moved to glamorous new premises just down the road in Old Bond Street, where there was actually a viewing gallery so that the public could come in and watch London's most fashionable hairdressers at work. Bond Street was a wonderland of outrageously expensive shops, possibly the most expensive in the world at the time. Old Bond Street was the grandest part of all, with names like Asprey's, Cartier and Agnew's art gallery setting the mood for the area.

It was a time when a number of things were happening on the fashion scene, although it was all still in its infancy compared with what was to come. Mary Quant had started designing miniskirts which showed shocking amounts of leg, and the concept of boutiques was being born. British Leyland had also brought out the Mini car which was to become another symbol of the times. The magazines and newspapers were full of articles about the 'youth revolution'. Until then, fashion and beauty had largely been the domain of the rich and aristocratic. Now young people were designing clothes and hairstyles for other young people. Ordinary boys like us began to have money in our pockets and we were determined to have some fun with it.

In a few years' time Carnaby Street would emerge as the Mecca of street fashion in the heart of Soho. Groups of young musicians were working around the northern clubs circuit trying to break through into the big-time, where Elvis Presley was reigning as the king.

In Bond Street Vidal had perfected a look which he called the 'five point cut'. He gave Mary Quant a lovely, simple, straight geometric cut which became like a trademark for both of them for many years. It was the look of the moment and it was different from anything else that had gone before. Hairdressing was beginning to be accepted as a visual art and those of us who were good at it were starting to be feted as 'artists'.

I became more and more interested in working with photographers because that was where I could really put my imagination to work. There was a limit to how experimental you could be if you were working with clients in a salon, but in the studio, often working with wigs, we could do whatever we liked as long as the editors liked it too. I now knew all there was to know about *Vogue, Harpers Bazaar, Queen* and *Tatler*. I had been in behind the glossy images and seen how they were created. I was part of the process and believed that I could add something to it. But I needed more freedom to experiment and be outrageous.

For years the London fashion industry had been ruled with a rod of iron by grandees like Norman Hartnell and Hardy Amies. They had been around for as long as anyone could remember and did not take easily to new ways of doing things. But the influence of young people coming up inside the magazines, as well as outside in the design world, was growing every year. Soon we would be the ones with the power to invent the images we wanted.

For ex-barrow boys like Nagels and me, Sassoon's new place was heaven. Once we started getting good tips we had plenty of cash in our pockets. We were mixing with beautiful women all day and all night. We felt like the City dealers of the Eighties must have felt during the Thatcher years – 'Masters of the Universe'.

One of my clients was Nicole, Duchess of Bedford. She and her husband once invited me down to Woburn Abbey for a ball for which Nicole wanted her hair dressed. It was the first really grand house that I had ever been to and when I was shown into the dining room for dinner and saw the walls lined with genuine Canalettos, I could hardly contain my excitement. The Duke was obviously surprised that a hair-dresser would know anything about painting – all those afternoons spent in art galleries had paid off. From then on I went to Woburn regularly to do both the Duke and Duchess and their children.

My mates and I still used to go to the dance halls together on Saturday nights. I was more aware of the roughness of some of the customers now. There was always a danger of a fight at some stage of the night. But I was keen to stay out of it, not wanting to damage my new clothes or go to work with a shiner. One evening at the Lyceum a man was thrown off the balcony above our heads and practically landed on me. Nagels saw him coming and managed to pull me out of the way, muttering, 'Mind the whistle, Len.' He crashed on to a couple of girls standing next to us, sending all of them sprawling across the floor. He then stood up, dusted himself off and went back upstairs to find the blokes who had pushed him. We helped the irate girls back on to their feet and out to the ladies to repair the damage.

Most of all, I loved the glamour of Mayfair. To me it was like living in a fairy tale. I was able to go to the openings of art galleries as a guest, seeing all the paintings which I admired in the art books I had started buying. I had a tremendous thirst for every bit of art and fashion that I could find. I just wanted to drink it all in, soak myself in it, stoking up my creative juices.

As well as the fashionable crowd, many of the celebrities of the day were coming to Sassoon. At the same time, old contacts from the criminal world started to come in, asking for me to do their wives' and mistresses' hair. The villains loved mixing with the society people and I think the nobs rather liked the idea of rubbing shoulders with notorious gangsters. I was always more than happy to oblige people like Jack Spot. After all, it had been him who had got me into the business in the first place. But I was always aware that they were sussing out their fellow clients for potential robberies. Billy Hill had a girlfriend called Gypsy, who often used to come in and get chatting to the other customers in the hope of finding out something about their lives and habits.

You could always tell the gangsters; they had the most expensive suits, flashy and bright, but cut wide to accommodate their weapons, whether knuckle-dusters, iron bars or even guns. One time a ferocious-looking heavy came in to see his girlfriend and as he bent over to kiss her his gun fell out and cracked the sink. He wasn't fazed and just tucked it away again as I pretended not to notice. It was better that way. I doubled her bill and he was happy to pay it.

I also socialised with a lot of underworld characters in the evening. We went to the Star pub in Belgravia, set in the midst of elegant houses that they would later be robbing.

As in every sphere, there was a new generation of crooks coming up as well. Young hoods like the Krays and the Richardsons were starting to make names for themselves around town and were mixing with the same people as Nagels and me.

I was known always to carry a comb and scissors in my pocket and never turned anyone down who requested a trim, whether we were in a restaurant, a club or a private house. Some hairdressers get fed up with being asked to cut hair when they are off duty. I never minded. I loved to cut, all the time. I knew that I was good at it and the more I did it the better I became. It gave me a reason to be. It was my identity. I wasn't interested, as most hairdressers at the time seemed to be, in exhibition work, trying to outdo other hairdressers with ever more ludicrous and extravagant designs. I was interested in cutting hair for people so that it would work in their everyday lives as well as when they were dressed up to go out.

Designers like Mary Quant, Ossie Clarke and Barbara Hulanicki, who went on to found Biba, were doing the same, creating clothes which could be worn to the office and on a picnic as well as to a posh evening out. Lifestyles were changing and people's hair needed to adapt. I would also cut hair for men friends if they asked me, although none of them would have been seen dead being cut in a women's salon at that time.

It is good to feel that you are becoming a master of your chosen trade. It is my belief that you can teach anyone the basic techniques of hair cutting. Whether or not they turn out to be any good will depend on whether they have any artistic ability. That is something that is born in you, you cannot learn it. Almost any architect in the world could design you a house. Only a few of them would be able to design you a house so beautiful it makes your heart lift just to look at it. So it is with hairdressing.

Nagels never seemed to be out of trouble for long. One evening I was busy with a client when I heard loud music coming up from the basement below. Someone was drumming and a voice was singing 'Be-Bop-A-Lu-La!' More voices joined in and the clients began to look around to see where it was coming from. I followed everyone else downstairs, just in time to hear Vidal yelling, 'Nagels, you're fired.'

Nagels put down the biscuit tin he had been drumming on and pulled on his coat. 'See you, Len,' he said cheerfully and disappeared into the night.

Vidal and I continued to get on well. We shared a vision which meant that we had an endless amount to talk about. He became something of a mentor to me in those early years. He even took me on holiday to St Tropez in the South of France. It was the first time I had been out of the country. I did not even have a passport. In those days the package holiday had not yet been invented and only the wealthy and adventurous went abroad for their holidays.

I had seen pictures and films but I had never actually been anywhere so glamorous, with the blue of the sea and the scent of the flowers, the pretty little villages and the elegant resorts. St Tropez itself was still little more than a fishing village at the time and had only just been colonised by people like Brigitte Bardot. Bardot was then something of a scandalous figure, seen by the older generation as symbolic of the immoral younger generation. She had bought a villa in the village and suddenly it was one of the most famous resorts in the world. Topless girls were beginning to appear on the beaches, playboys arrived in their yachts and the world began to hear about the jet set life down on the Côte d'Azur.

Vidal and I went to Cannes one day. We went on to the terrace at the Carlton Hotel, where all the rich men and the beautiful hookers used to hang out. We were watching the girls go by when I heard a familiar voice.

'Hello, Leonard! Have you got time to do my hair?'

I turned and found myself face to face with Billy Hill's Gypsy. 'What are you doing here?' I asked.

'We're down here on business,' she replied in a tone which suggested I shouldn't ask any more questions.

In 1956 Grace Kelly, the American film star, arrived in Monaco further up the coast, to marry Prince Rainier and become Princess Grace, adding another chapter to the mythology of the area. Later when she was in London Grace started coming to my salon to have her hair cut – she was the first big star that I was able to work on. She had a beauty which took my breath away. She was like a precursor of Princess Diana, bringing a fresh glamour and beauty to a previously rather dowdy royal family. It was extraordinary that both of them should meet the same tragic fate, both killed in car crashes in France, both of them pursued beyond the grave by rumours of illicit affairs, cover-ups and indiscretions.

At least Diana stuck to the right age group. Grace's male partners seemed to get younger and younger. Perhaps she was trying to recapture that incredible time when it seemed every man in the world fancied Grace Kelly. But as I well know, you just can't turn the clock back.

Grace was amazed by how many of her films I'd seen.

She used to reminisce about her Hollywood days and particularly her male co-stars. She'd often talk about Clark Gable, Cary Grant, David Niven and Frank Sinatra, sounding quite dreamy as she remembered them all. She was still in touch with Frank, and told me that she could quite understand why women found him so attractive.

Once I had my own salon I was always very embarrassed when people offered me tips, always suggesting they give the money to the juniors. Princess Grace knew this but one day she told me that she was so grateful for what I had done for her she was going to give me something she knew I would really like.

'The thing I would most like is you,' I said.

She wagged a finger at me and laughed. 'You are a cheeky young man.'

Later that day a case of Dom Pérignon champagne was delivered with her compliments. She knew I liked champagne because she and I had drunk Kir Royals together (champagne mixed with blackcurrant

In the days when I had long hair

My sister, Rene

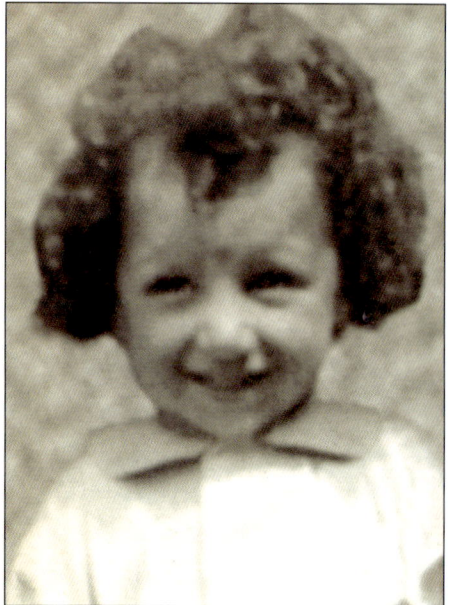

This photograph of me,
aged five, was used by
Cow & Gate for one of their ads

No.6, Upper Grosvenor Street. My salon

This cartoon caption was suggested
by the millionaire businessman,
Charles Clore

Twiggy

Grace Codington

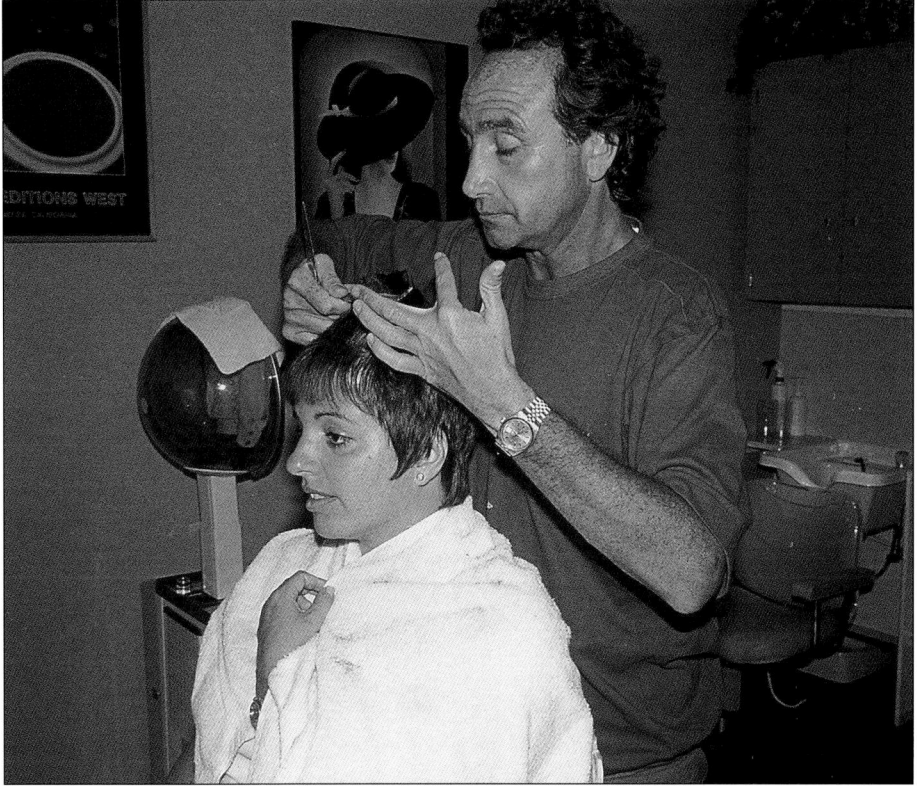

Me and Liza Minnelli

I also used to cut the
hair of Duran Duran's
Nick Rhodes, and his
wife, Julie. I was one
of the best men at
their wedding

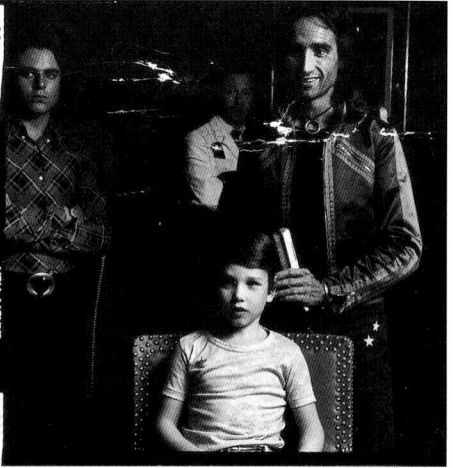

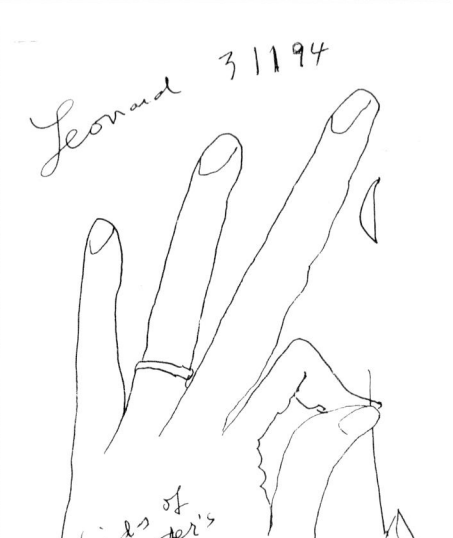

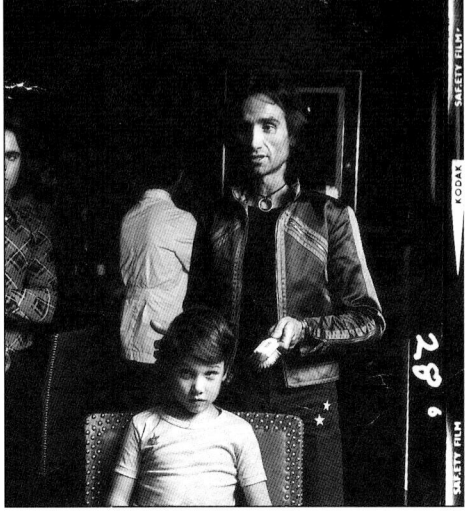

Leonard 31194

friends of
each other's
youth

Tony Curtis

A special drawing from my
old friend, Tony Curtis

With my son, Dominic,
in the salon

Andy Warhol presented me with a sketch while he was in London.
Francis Bacon did one on the other side

With my first wife, Ricci, and our son Dominic

liqueur) when she flew me down to the palace at Monte Carlo to dress her hair for a special annual ball. That was the sort of tip I was happy to accept.

Finding myself at the palace in Monte Carlo was extraordinary. While I was there I did Prince Rainier's hair as well, and the children's. Both Princess Stephanie and Princess Caroline came to the salon in London with their mother when they were in London. Both of them grew to be great beauties, their lives dogged by scandal and gossip. Princess Grace was always very strict with them as children, insisting that they behave properly, but she allowed herself to be far more informal as they grew older. She tried to be their friend as much as their mother, and I think she was a little envious of the freedoms they insisted upon, while she, officially at least, was bound by the protocol of the palace.

The South of France remained an exciting place even after St Tropez had become a hugely expensive tourist trap with vast showy yachts and bars crammed with beautiful poseurs. Later I would go back to Cannes for its annual film festival with Tony Curtis, who spent most of his time in pursuit of large-breasted starlets. It wasn't a town I ever particularly liked.

I took to the St Tropez life immediately. I loved water sports – later I discovered skiing as well – and Vidal was an expert in all that sort of thing. I was like a kid who had been let loose in a candy shop. I wanted to go everywhere and try everything. Whenever we were together we were talking about hair and creativity and fashion. We were both so full of ideas, our minds racing all the time with plans and ideas.

Vidal was completely immersed in the world of beauty, and believed you should change anything you didn't like about yourself, not just your hairstyle. He had a model girlfriend called Maggie London and he had persuaded her to have her nose changed. He was soon into having facelifts himself, seeing no reason why he should give in to ageing at any stage. I didn't feel ready to go quite that far myself, although I had to admit that he did look good, seeming to get younger every year. He still looks amazing for his age.

Over the years I saw some terrible sights caused by bad plastic surgery. There was an American woman who used to stay in the Connaught Hotel when she came to London. She asked me to come to the hotel because she didn't want to be seen in the salon. When I arrived I could see why. Her face had been so pulled and stretched over the years that it looked as if the skin had given up all its elasticity, dropping from the bones like melted wax.

While the idea of head-to-toe beauty treatments did seem to be the way the business was going, my over-riding interest was with hair. Although Vidal's geometric cuts were an enormous step forward, I still felt that the results could be rather like a helmet. His cut was so successful that the clients came knowing what they wanted, and the style became something of a formula rather than something personal created to suit the individual.

I believed that hair should have as much freedom as possible. It should not be curled and permed into unnatural positions, forced to stay there with sprays. Every face and head shape needed a different approach, and I was worried that Vidal's style was becoming so widely copied that it was being given to people who would have been better off with something different, something more personal to them. It was a bit like forcing everyone to wear the same dress, even if it was by Chanel!

Everyone who cut for Vidal had to do things his way. That was the secret of his success. But there were many clients who now wanted more freedom with their hair. They wanted to be able to put it up and dress it when they felt like it. They wanted something more romantic and flowing than the geometric cut. I also wanted to experiment and I began to feel held back by Vidal's strict regime. We started to have disagreements over the things that I wanted to do for clients, particularly the models who were no longer keen to look exactly the same as all their competitors.

'You're limiting hairdressing,' I would tell him. 'I don't want to keep producing uniform haircuts for everyone.'

'As long as you work here you've got to,' he replied.

Vidal always said he believed that people like us, had we been educated, would have been architects. He was fascinated by the work of architects like Le Corbusier and the Bauhaus Movement. He was constantly studying and improving his understanding of the fine arts, although he was finding less and less time to actually do any cutting himself.

It is always a danger, when a hairdresser becomes successful, that the tasks of running a business and dealing with all the public relations will leave no time for practising the skills that got them there in the first place. I was always determined to concentrate on the cutting rather than the business, which may be why Vidal is where he is today and I am where I am.

I started to develop a technique of dividing the oval shape of the head into sections. I would cut the hair, either sharply or softly, in ways which made it fall naturally into shapes which would flatter and complement the shape of the head and face beneath. Once the basic cut had been achieved the client could then dress it up for special occasions but the hair would still look good, even if they did nothing but brush it through in the morning.

The idea was based on the dome of ancient geometry which was used to build the Pyramids and the Inca temples. It came from the realisation that the head is an oval, not a round shape, as many people believed. I worked out that if you took eight points – from the chin to the crown, the temple to the neck – from ear to ear and from nose to neck, you had an oval shape which could be divided into sections. If you treated the head as a round then you ended up with a pudding basin cut. The dome cut was a method which was to become the basis for all the top hairdressers now working in London, many of whom started out with me over the following years.

It is a fact of life in the world of hairdressing that good stylists will leave and set up their own salons. Every hairdresser has to be prepared to lose their best people, because the best people want the chance to spread their wings and work for themselves.

It wasn't long before I was convinced that I had learned all I could from Vidal and should be running my own show. I was very sad to leave Sassoon's because Vidal had been such a good friend and they had been such exciting times. But I could see that I would never be allowed to become a partner, and I would always just be one of his stylists. I had to move on. I wanted to do wonderful romantic things with hair which Vidal would never encourage as long as he was convinced that everyone who came to the salon had to have the same cut.

Raphael felt the same and, since we got on well together, the two of us decided to open a modest salon together in Mayfair's Duke Street, called Leonard and Raphael. We were well enough established for plenty of clients to follow us without our having to do anything to poach them. It was not a great risk. We could finance it simply by going to our banks and asking for overdrafts. The salon was a modest-sized room – it has been turned into a dry cleaners since then – and Raphael and I were able to decorate it ourselves over a weekend.

But going into business with Raphael did not prove to be the best idea I had ever had.

By this time, Nagels had decided that hairdressing wasn't for him – a wise decision. He never had any patience with the customers. When one woman came in with a picture of Brigitte Bardot and asked if he could make her look like that, Nagels replied, 'I'm sorry, dear, I think we'd need a faith healer.'

He decided to go back to one of his previous careers as a boxer. He disappeared off down to the South Coast, moving from resort to resort, taking part in a con in which a 'member of the audience' (Nagels in a blazer and club tie), would take on the 'professional' fighter. The audience would be fooled into betting that he wouldn't last more than a certain number of rounds. They would then lose their money when Nagels managed to hold his own in the ring. That was his evening job. During the day he was holding mock auctions. He worked as the front man, giving away free gifts, or 'tut' as it was known, to lure the punters into premises which were being used as auction rooms to sell knocked-off cutlery and God knows what else.

Neither of us had the time to just hang out together as we once had, but it wouldn't be too long before he would reappear in my life and turn it upside down once more.

CHAPTER SIX

IF RAPHAEL HAD behaved badly with the clients when he was with Vidal, that was nothing to what would happen once he was his own boss. I wanted to run the best, most creative, most exciting and most professional salon in London. I couldn't do that if Raphael was going to keep seducing the clientele. If there was one rule I believed in, it was that you shouldn't mess around with the customers once you were the boss. Raphael could not understand what I was talking about. He would simply shrug and say, 'They're only women.' He looked a bit like Yves Montand, and behaved in much the same way as the legendary French lover.

Meanwhile Vidal and I drifted apart. His wife Elaine started coming to me to have her hair done after she left him for a man who ran a water-skiing school outside London. Vidal spent more and more of his time in America, where he was given a hero's welcome and went into business with Richard Salaman from Charles of the Ritz, concentrating on opening a chain of salons around the world and on the product side of the business. His explosion on to the New York scene had a dramatic effect on the way the world viewed London hairdressing. Everyone could see that we were years ahead of New York and Paris in our cutting and styling. London became internationally known as the Mecca for hairdressers, a situation which has barely changed since.

Vidal Sassoon continued to thrive and grow into a major international business. He became a household name, his products heavily promoted on television. Vidal himself, whilst becoming probably the most famous hairdresser in the world, actually stopped cutting hair quite soon after I met him. He turned into a figurehead for the brand named after him, and moved to Hollywood. He later proved himself to be a good friend to me at a time when I needed friends badly.

Because Sassoon's salon had been just round the corner from the two big model agencies of the day, Michael Whittaker's and Lucie

Clayton, I had increased the number of models that I worked with. Models were always the most willing to experiment with new looks and to trust a hairdresser they knew. Although some of the girls were well known around London, models had not yet become international celebrities. All that was still to come. They were just hard-working members of the fashion business, like the rest of us.

The most famous at the time was Jean Shrimpton, who was living with David Bailey. Bailey used to ask me to do her hair for photographic shoots and my name began to appear more and more often in the magazines. She was an incredibly natural beauty and seldom bothered to come into the salon unless it was for a job. She just brushed her hair through and it looked wonderful.

Once people knew that I was involved in creating the images which they saw on the news-stands, they were willing to let me suggest things they should do with their hair, and they always seemed to be pleased with the results. I can never remember anyone being unhappy with a haircut, but I do remember a lot of them being amazed by just how much better they could look with a good cut. It felt strange to find that women, who were usually older and certainly richer and classier than me, would ask me what they should do and would accept my advice completely.

I began to grow used to the feeling of power. I expected people to do what I suggested and I began to develop an air of authority without realising it. Because my fingers never let me down I was able to get away with it. People started to refer to me as 'Mr Leonard'. It sounded like a joke to begin with but it's surprising how quickly you can get used to a rise in status.

As far as I can remember, leaving home was a gradual process for me. I moved in with one or two girlfriends in those early years, going back home to Rene in between relationships. I'm ashamed to admit that their faces have become rather a blur now, as I'm sure my face has to them. I was certainly not looking for commitment or responsibility at that stage. Like all young men I was constantly in search of a good time whenever I wasn't at work, but I was working every hour that I could. Quite often I would still be in the salon at ten at night. I would then go for a meal with others from the salon, frequenting trattorias like Alvaro's in the King's Road, or Mario and Franco's in Soho's Romilly Street, which were the most fashionable places in London at the time. I would be back at the salon early the next morning, too excited by the work to be able to stay in bed.

I always knew that Rene and my family would be there when I needed them, and that was a great source of strength to me. They made no demands on me and I made none on them. We were simply 'family' and the house was simply 'home'. I knew that it was always there if I needed it, but I was hungry for something better. I had started out in life at the bottom of the pile and I intended to do everything I could to make sure that I didn't end up there. I wanted to enjoy my success to the full and realised that would mean moving away from home completely.

When I was still in my teens, working at Sassoon's, Raphael had a customer who was known to be demanding and difficult, always putting on airs and graces. She was a model called Ricci Wade. One day she was giving him a particularly hard time and he lost his temper. As she went to sit down after being washed he pulled the chair out from under her, sending her sprawling across the floor. It was all the rest of the salon could do not to laugh, but Vidal told me to take over and calm her down.

Ricci was a few years older than me and strikingly beautiful. She was always dramatically turned out and had blonde hair which she wore parted severely in the middle. She had a powerful personality and seemed terribly grand to me. I picked her up, dusted her off and managed to calm her down as requested. As I went to work on her hair, I was burbling away as usual, with my brain only half engaged, when I suddenly heard myself asking her out.

In years to come she would say to people, 'Can you believe I actually agreed to go out with a hairdresser? And then I married him! Can you imagine?'

It was a never-ending source of wonder to her that she had allowed her standards to fall so low. Later she was horrified to find that I described myself as a 'barber' on my passport.

'It's what I am,' I protested when she complained.

'You're a company director now,' she corrected me.

'I may be a company director,' I said, 'but only because I'm a barber.'

While I had no doubts about my abilities as a hairdresser, I had severe doubts about my abilities as a businessman. My reading skills were certainly not up to mastering contracts or legal documents, and my attention span was far too short to be able to hold in any information that bored me. I needed someone who would take a firm grip on things, someone who would push me in the direction I knew I wanted to go.

Ricci must have recognised that I filled a similar function for her. She needed a vehicle to help her to rise in society, a way of generating money and of meeting streams of influential people. I could provide her with all that. I felt sure that together we would be able to go a long way, and I was certainly right about that. Marriage seemed like a good idea for both of us. I was just twenty years old.

Ricci already had her own set of influential contacts. She had one particular wealthy friend, Donald Healey, whose family owned the Austin Healey car company. He was an older man and I guess he had been her sugar daddy. These were the days when Christine Keeler and Mandy Rice-Davies were living in London and enjoying the adventures that would later cause the Profumo scandal and help to bring down the government. No one thought anything of young girls consorting with wealthy older men before they were married.

When Donald Healey heard that we were planning to get hitched he wished me luck and warned me to be careful: Ricci could bring me a lot of trouble. But when you are young and full of yourself you don't take any notice of warnings from old men. You think you are clever enough to handle anything.

Donald was very helpful to us in advising on how to raise money for the business and later agreed to be godfather to our son, Dominic.

During our short courtship, Ricci confided that she had been married before, to a Swiss count, but that the marriage had ended. The news did not bother me. It was all in the past. She was a great support in encouraging me to set up on my own with Raphael and, soon after I left Sassoon's, we got married as planned. By this time we had both developed tastes for the more splendid things in life. After the wedding at Chelsea Register office, we held the reception at Les Ambassadeurs Club at the bottom of Park Lane. It was a famous club, very expensive and very glamorous, epitomising the sort of Mayfair life I found so enticing.

When the salon in Duke Street became too small and we needed to expand, we decided to do it in style. Rather than just find a property which was a little larger than the one we had, we decided to go looking for something that would be spectacularly different to any other salon in London. It would be somewhere that would amaze clients and journalists alike, somewhere that would reflect our clients' lifestyles, or in some cases the sort of lifestyles they aspired to. To do that we needed to raise substantial funds. We could no longer rely on Raphael's and my overdrafts.

We started out by going to the Guardian Bank on the recommendation of our solicitor. The manager seemed to see no problem with our ambitious plans and agreed to give us what we needed. The bank has since disappeared, but later, when we needed more funds, we were equally well supported by the manager of Barclays at Cambridge Circus who had helped a lot of restaurants get started and understood the way fashion-based service companies worked.

I had known from the beginning that I had to work in the heart of Mayfair. There was nowhere else to be if you wanted to establish yourself as the best in the business. And I knew that I wanted a building that would make the clients feel as comfortable as when they were at home – or in some cases even more comfortable. It needed to be as luxurious and elegant as any five-star hotel. The customers needed to feel pampered and important from the moment they arrived at the doors. I found the perfect house.

Number 6 Upper Grosvenor Street stood at the end of a terrace of grand Georgian houses, on the corner of a cobbled mews which ran down behind the American Embassy. It was an incredible stroke of luck to find a house in that area which had already been used for commercial purposes. All our neighbours were either private residences or embassies. The chances of being able to open a salon at such a select address were minute. It gave us immediate prestige.

It could not have been more central to the areas frequented by the clients I wanted to attract. The Niarchos family, one of the wealthiest of the Greek shipping families, had an apartment on the corner of nearby Grosvenor Square and offices at the bottom of Upper Grosvenor Street. They all used to come and go as if the salon was an extension of their own home. All the children of the family used to live in fear of their father and so when he came in we tried to keep him somewhere where he wouldn't see them coming and going.

Further round the square was Marion Ryan's house. Marion was a famous singer in the Fifties whose twin sons, Paul and Barry, later became pop stars in their own right (Barry was married to Princess Meriam before she married Michael Birri). Marion was a close friend of Frank Sinatra and he often used to stay at her place when he was in London. I would go there to cut his hair and sort out his wigs.

Before entering I always had to be announced by one of his minders, who would shout, in a broad Bronx accent, 'Boss, it's Mister Leonard, your hairdresser, d'ya wanna see him?'

Frank travelled everywhere with a box of wigs and hairpieces. He never let anyone else touch them. He was always courteous and generous to me and I never saw him lose his notorious temper. Just once I saw him freeze out some guy in mid-sentence who was trying to apologise for something. The guy went deathly white and looked as if he was going to keel over. Frank just turned his back on him and we all knew that was the end and he was out.

Estée Lauder used to have her office in Grosvenor Street and came regularly to have her hair done. I used to create her wigs for her as well. Later, when I had my own cologne made up to sell under the name of Leonard, she very sweetly told me that it was better than anything in her range. She was a great Jewish American character, very warm and very noisy. I always knew when she was in, even if I was on the next floor. She used to give me samples of her products to try out in the salon and liked to ask my opinion of a new fragrance or cream.

I was determined to spare no expense on doing up the salon. It had once been the home of fashion designer, Elsa Schiaparelli, the woman who discovered shocking pink, and it was full of elegant, light rooms with big windows and eighteen-foot ceilings. A distinctive circular window looked out at the embassy. It was the beginning of the Sixties by then and everyone wanted to go for the modern look. I hired an interior decorator friend, Tony Cloughly, who lived near to our new house in the heart of Belgravia, to help with the transformation. The house already had all the wonderful features of its age, like marble and wooden floors and ornate cornices. I was able to use all the most modern furnishings, mirrors and lighting to enhance the glamour of the building.

Lighting is crucial in a salon. It must be flattering to the clients, but at the same time it must be true. If you get the lighting wrong in the colouring department, for instance, you could be sending people out with colours which will look completely different as soon as they hit the daylight.

The beauty of the place was in the details. Even the front door was studded with rows of brass stars. Off the reception area was a VIP room so that the stars could be wafted out of sight of the general public the moment they entered. There was also a small boutique and changing rooms. Clients could come to be prepared for an evening out, dress on the premises and go straight to the event with their hair perfectly in place.

I wanted the reception area to be more like a hotel or a club. Too many salons had waiting rooms like dentists' surgeries. I didn't want people to have to be sitting amongst clients who were wandering around with wet hair, as normally happens in busy salons. Marie Helvin, the model, told me that when she first came to the salon it felt like walking into Claridge's.

'Marie, this is better than Claridge's,' I replied. 'And more expensive.'

Everywhere there were mirrors to reflect the light and clean white surfaces. I loved white and always used it extensively in my homes – white carpets, white walls, white curtains. It didn't matter if it got dirty, I'd just have it cleaned, repainted or replaced. After the cramped clutter of my childhood, where the dominant colours were always brown, I wanted to bring as much light and air into my surroundings as possible.

The colour scheme at the salon was grey and shocking pink, which had been Schiaparelli's colours, even down to the gowns which the customers wore. The Leonard house colours were burgundy with white writing. I refused to compromise on quality, everything had to be the best. Older, wiser voices kept telling me that there was no need to spend quite so much on the decor, that there were ways of saving money and doing things on a budget. But neither Ricci nor I wanted to hear any of it. We wanted the best of everything, and because of my client list and reputation I got whatever I demanded.

I wanted crackling log fires burning in the hearths on winter days and huge flower arrangements that would lift the spirits of anyone who walked through the doors. This was to be the Leonard House of Hair and Beauty, a place where the richest and most famous people in the world would feel at home. They would be happy to spend as much time as it took to make them as beautiful as possible.

There was nothing else like it in London. There were places in other cities, like the House of Revlon in New York and Carita in Paris, but nothing in London. Maybe it was because the rents were so high, or maybe it was because of the British upper class's supposed indifference to grooming. Whatever the reasons, there had never been an establishment like the one I was creating, and there has never been another one since. I sank £40,000, a massive amount of money at the beginning of the Sixties, into realising my dream.

The result was magical, everything I could have dreamed of. The customers must have liked it too. Some of them would come in every day, just to have their hair brushed and dressed. What they didn't know was that, even with such a generous budget, we had run out of money before we could do up the top two floors of the house. Up there, while all was calm Claridge's-style luxury below, water would be dripping through the tiles and pigeons would be flapping around the derelict rooms, able to come and go as they pleased through the many holes in the roof.

Our landlords were the Freshwater Group, owned by one of the richest orthodox Jewish families in England, who also happened to be clients. I used to do the hair for the women in the family and I also supplied them all with the wigs they wore.

Business was booming and I was living the life of a Mayfair dandy and man about town. Ricci was building a reputation as a generous hostess. We opened accounts here, there and everywhere. We would order food from Fortnum and Mason, Selfridges or Harrods, and buy clothes from the new designer shops, like Yves St Laurent in Bond Street and Piero de Monzi in Fulham Road. We opened accounts with florists and butchers, fishmongers and greengrocers, garages and interior decorators, shoe shops and restaurants, hotel bars and dry cleaners – but only with the best! The world was full of wonderful luxuries and we had access to all of them.

We told ourselves that if I was going to establish myself as one of London's great salon owners, we had to live like the people we were aiming to attract. I didn't need much convincing, I was falling in love with the lifestyle. These were boom times, each year bigger and better than the one before. There was no reason not to assume that it would continue like this for ever. If serious financiers and bankers were willing to lend me sums of money which would have seemed staggering just a few years before, and shopkeepers and restaurants were willing to allow me to run up bills, then they must all believe in me as well. It was party time from morning till night.

I've always enjoyed the feeling of being able to pick up the tab for friends in bars and restaurants. It's a habit that has made me very popular over the years but would ultimately be my downfall. I always loved to buy people presents, the more extravagant the better. I'm sure a psychiatrist could find plenty of reasons for this: low self-esteem, or a need to be loved, perhaps? Who knows? Who cares? There are worse vices than an urge to please friends. I had no interest in money for its own sake, no idea how to save it or make it grow. The thought of a pension fund or other investments never entered my head. Where I came from, a world of car auctions and fruit and veg barrows, you were rich if you had money in your pocket and tomorrow could take care of itself. I was spending more than I was earning but everyone gave me enormous credit, so I refused to see there would be a day of reckoning.

I liked being married to Ricci. She organised my social life and I provided endless interesting contacts for her through my work. She liked meeting the film stars and the titled people who came to the salon and to the house for our parties. She wasn't always as nice to those she considered to be her inferiors.

We were once going to dinner with Daniel Galvin, who ran the colouring side of the business, and his wife, Mavis. We took them a present of some antique porcelain coffee cups. As our meal was drawing to a close Ricci picked up one of the cups and looked around the room.

'You know, Daniel,' she said imperiously, 'I think these are the nicest things you have in the whole house.' I pretended not to have heard. It was always the best way to cope with her.

We had bought an elegant town house in Little Chester Street in Belgravia. It was a tiny street, more like a mews, just at the bottom of Buckingham Palace's garden, but the house was big enough for lavish entertaining. There was also a pub at each end of the street – what more could a man ask for?

Ted Heath, the politician, was a regular at one of the pubs. After he was Prime Minister he often used to be there, making new young friends. His house round the corner was heavily guarded by policemen and no guests were allowed in unless the bobbies were notified in advance, or unless they came back from the pub with Heath himself.

Living in the centre of London was almost like moving into a village, although the village was populated by the richest and most famous people in the world. Hyde Park Corner, which then had no traffic lights and was more like a racetrack than a roundabout, lay in the middle of my daily commute up to the salon. On one side was Belgravia and home, on the other Mayfair and the salon. In between stretched Park Lane with all the famous hotels where many of my international and out-of-town clients would stay and where I would often be called out to tend to their hair.

I could quite easily have walked to and from work, but of course I didn't. I bought a succession of cars, Porsches, Rolls-Royces, Bentleys, Ferraris, BMWs, Mercedes, Mini-Coopers, all the makes and models that you would expect a young man in the money to buy.

Ricci bought clothes as if they were about to be rationed, all with the best designer labels. She soon gave up modelling and became a full-time socialite. She hired a butler and a couple to help in the house and spent many hours at the salon every day having her hair and nails done.

We had a son, Dominic, and hired a wonderful old chain-smoking Irish nanny, called Nanny Maugham, to look after him. She was very patient when we bought Dominic a beautiful Afghan hound called Zorro, which he loved to share his bed with but wasn't so keen on exercising.

Ricci deserved her reputation as a lavish hostess. If she threw a party there would be plenty of champagne and caviar for everyone. I was always happy to let her do what she wanted. I was working at full speed, often not getting home until late. This could be a bone of contention between us. On the other hand I was always meeting new people and being invited to parties and clubs like Annabel's, which meant that Ricci could expand her social circle all the time. We were on the A-list for invitations to film premieres and art gallery openings, courted by all the most influential people. It was a situation which would have been unthinkable twenty years before when hairdressers were seen as part of the below-stairs set.

I was never happier than when I was surrounded by friends who were having a good time. I was happy to keep paying as long as it kept the parties going and the food and drink flowing. I loved the social life, although sometimes I would feel a slight twinge of envy for men who had wives waiting for them when they got home from work, with their tea on the table and slippers by the fire.

Who was I kidding? I would have hated it.

Raphael and I finally fell out and he left. There was an incident with a client: Raphael had apparently given her the impression he would go on holiday with her. When she turned up at the salon, white poodle in one hand, suitcase and air tickets in the other, Raphael had changed his mind and was hiding in the wig room. I was furious because the client was furious. There was a huge row and Raphael stormed out.

He later met and married a Chinese girl who had convinced him she was a fabulously wealthy heiress. The story of their romance got into all the papers. Unfortunately, he had given her a similar story, telling her that he was a rich salon owner, when all we had done was borrow some money to open a premises. It wasn't until they were married that they both discovered the other one had been lying and they didn't have a bean between them. They parted immediately and Raphael went on to live in Paris and Canada for a while. Then I heard that he had moved to Los Angeles and, after that, I lost touch.

When my partnership went wrong with Raphael I returned to the banks and asked them to back me in the salon on my own. By that time I had a reputation big enough, and a client list long enough, to keep a chain of hairdressers working full time. The banks were very helpful. Basically they said I could have whatever I wanted.

I began to gather a group of young hairdressers around me who would later become the superstars of the business. Names like Michael Rasser and John Isaacs of MichaelJohn, Nicky Clarke, Celine and John Frieda all came to me as eager young apprentices or as experienced stylists.

Another young stylist, called Nicky Butler, also joined us at the beginning as my assistant. I have to admit he wasn't the greatest of cutters but he was a genius at dressing hair. He used to disappear off to places like Bermondsey Antique Market to find interesting objects for clients like Marianne Faithfull. Marianne was still a teenager then, probably the same age as Nicky, and so ethereal and beautiful she looked like an angel. Nicky found the most wonderful combs and slides to put up her long blonde, silky hair. He made her look like Ophelia – a part she later did play very effectively on stage, shooting up heroin in the interval in order to give herself the right spaced-out look for the second act and the death scene.

Nicky was a good assistant and, like many of the others, I used to send him off to buy clothes at places like Turnbull and Asser, at the company's expense. I wanted everyone around me to have the right image. One night a week he used to leave early to be a dancer on *Ready Steady Go*, one of the first major television pop shows.

One day, he asked me what I thought his future in the business might be. I told him that he should think of some way of cashing in on his particular talent for dressing hair. So he went into partnership with a friend called Paula and started a stall in Portobello Road Antique Market. From there he graduated to the Chelsea Antique Market in the King's Road. In 1972 he started a small shop in Fulham Road with another partner, calling it Butler and Wilson, selling a wide range of costume jewellery. That shop then expanded into the next-door premises and in 1984 they opened in South Molton Street. They changed completely the way in which fashionable people viewed jewellery. He made it possible to look like a million dollars without spending it. The business became a huge success.

A salon is only as good as the people working in it, and, if you have really good people, sooner or later they are going to want to go off on their own. I was very lucky. Because the staff were so young, and because so much was happening around us, almost no one left in the first ten years. I was able to build up teams of extraordinary experience, and keep clients coming back. I found myself in the position of being able to recruit many of the rising stars of the hairdressing world. They were willing to leave salons like Revlon and Carita because of my reputation and because of the sheer scale of the salon. No one had ever seen anything like it before.

I was still in my twenties but I had become 'Mr Leonard', the man that everyone else fluttered around. My cutting hand was insured for a million pounds – just like Betty Grable's legs. I had discovered that if I strode through life with enough confidence, every door would fly open. Head waiters would automatically show me to their best tables and doormen would let me into the most exclusive clubs without hesitation.

Everywhere I went I could sign for things as if I was royalty. The more I got away with it, the greater my confidence became and the more people were willing to go along with it. I was able to talk to everyone, from the Empress of Iran to the doorman at the Dorchester, from the world's most powerful tycoons to the most junior barmen, and they all responded with equal friendliness. There didn't seem to be anywhere I couldn't go or anyone I couldn't befriend. It was heaven. I swept through London feeling like royalty.

I took this change in lifestyle for granted most of the time. But if I went back home to visit Rene and my family it would strike me just what a different world I had fallen into. The two sides of my life were like distant planets. The busier I became the less time I found to visit Roehampton. Ricci was never comfortable with my family either, which increased the gap between my old and new lives. She couldn't understand people without ambition, people who were happy with what they had in life and didn't hanker for anything more.

I was so happy to be able to cut hair all day long and to be amongst such varied and interesting people that I had no time for planning or introspection. I had no time to think about anything but hair and where the next party was.

Our proximity to the American Embassy was also useful. People from ambassadorial families like the Mellons and the Annenbergs came to the salon, and Princess Lee Radziwill, Jackie Kennedy's sister. It was Lee who recommended me to Jackie.

The first time that Jackie came she was with her mother-in-law, Rose Kennedy, an old client. There were a number of regular customers in the salon when they arrived and Jackie became impatient at being told there would be a delay before I was ready to see her. She demanded to be dealt with immediately.

'Wait your turn, Jackie,' Rose snapped. 'Remember you are only a bootlegger's daughter-in-law.'

The ticking-off worked and from then on she was as sweet as pie. I thanked Rose once I was cutting her hair. She gave a grim smile and muttered, 'All these Mafia molls are the same.'

Whenever Jackie was in London to see her sister, Lee, she would always come to me. She normally had her hair cut by Kenneth in New York and always wanted me to give her a less severe image. She loved having her hair high at the back, so I would back-comb and set it, then leave a bit at the front to fall forward, which softened the style. She never wanted to have a hair out of place which I thought made her look very plastic. I made all sorts of suggestions for ways in which she could soften her image further with a looser style.

'I'd love to, Leonard,' she said, 'but in my position it's impossible.'

When President Kennedy was in London he came into the salon as well, surrounded by security men. They would even be up on the roof, watching the road below. The view was so good the security chief asked if they could use our roof regularly in order to watch the embassy whenever the President was in town.

As he sat in the chair he looked around at the almost deserted room, with security men at every door. His face fell. I knew immediately that I had let him down.

'I thought there would be more tasty young women around here, Leonard,' he said.

'I'll make sure they're all back next time you come, Mr President,' I replied and when he was next in London I rounded up all the blondes I knew and had them all sitting around the salon.

'Christ,' he laughed as he came in and saw that I had kept my word. 'They're wonderful. They all look like Marilyn Monroe.'

Kennedy's hair was even more of a helmet than his wife's. He used a lacquer which tinted it darker – I guess to remove any grey hairs. The result was not attractive and made it feel very stiff. I told him so.

'I like it this way,' he said. 'I'm used to it.'

'But it makes you look older,' I argued.

He thought for a moment. 'Okay,' he said. 'Do what you think.'

I washed the lacquer out and cut the hair into a softer style which would flop across his forehead a little.

'There,' I said when I had finished. 'That will be nicer for Marilyn to run her fingers through.'

The words had left my mouth before I had even had time to think about them. I was always prattling on when I was concentrating on my work, never worrying too much about what I was saying. It's what people expect from hairdressers. I also had a reputation for being a bit cocky. My stomach gave a lurch as everyone around us froze, and for a horrible moment I thought I had gone too far.

'What do you know about Marilyn?' he asked with an amused smile.

'Ah,' I said, with an air of mystery. 'It's a very small world and we have friends in common.'

'We do?' he laughed. 'Who would that be?'

'Frank Sinatra,' I said. 'And Peter Lawford.'

Peter Lawford, the actor, had been coming to the salon for some years. He was the President's brother-in-law and when he was in London he used to go out with a crowd of actors including people like Laurence Harvey. Laurence, the hero of my youth who was now a regular at the salon, sent him in to me when Peter was dating some young model and wanted to feel good for a night out on the town. He was pleased with whatever I did for him.

'You should get your hands on our President's hair,' he told me. 'And his piece of fluff.'

'I already do the First Lady's hair,' I said.

'Not his wife,' Peter laughed, 'Marilyn. His bit on the side.'

Sadly, I never did get to do Marilyn's hair.

Luckily, the President laughed, appearing not to mind the teasing. He came to the salon a few more times, and I also visited him at the American Ambassador's house in Regent's Park. On the day a security man from the embassy came to tell me he had been shot I closed the salon for the rest of the day as a mark of respect.

Jackie's sister, Lee, was a regular for many years. She was one of the most snobbish people I ever met. The first time she arrived at the salon, with her husband, Prince Stanislaus Radziwill, she demanded to be seen by me immediately. I told her that I was busy at that moment but I would be happy to see her later if she wouldn't mind waiting.

'I think you forget your place,' she said.

'This actually is my place,' I replied. 'I am a hairdresser and my job is to serve the public.'

'I am not the public,' she spat. 'I am a Princess.'

'Lee, honey,' her husband interrupted. 'Forget it. He has your number.'

She burst out laughing and from then on we got on very well and she always waited patiently for her turn, like everyone else. Sometimes I would go to her in her house near Gunter Grove.

When American Secretary of State, Henry Kissinger, was the world's most famous globe-trotting politician, he also used to call me in when he needed a trim. He had the most extraordinarily powerful charisma. At the end of our first session he gazed at himself in the mirror, running his fingers through his thick, wiry hair, which he used to say only I could get to stay shaped and flat.

'You think you're God's gift to women, don't you, Henry,' I said.

'Leonard,' he replied, 'I know that I am God's gift to everyone.'

None of the beautiful and talented women he dated ever had any say in anything. He was totally dominant in any relationship. He had a girl with him on one of my visits to his hotel suite and told me not to dress her hair too elaborately because he wanted to be able to run his fingers through it.

'So, how come I'm never allowed to run my fingers through your hair?' she asked him.

'I am the only person allowed to do that,' he informed her.

Kissinger always wanted to know what famous people I had seen recently. It seemed strange that a man so powerful and famous himself should be interested in the doings of film stars and other celebrities whose achievements were nothing compared to his own. He once told me that he wished he could make better small talk.

'All I know,' he said, 'is politics. But people just let me go on. Even when I bore the hell out of them at parties they end up apologising to me.'

While he was always friendly when I was cutting his hair, he could sometimes be very snooty if I met him socially. I saw him in a restaurant in New York one evening and went up to say hello.

'Where do I know you from?' he growled.

'I do your hair in London,' I reminded him.

'Remember your place,' he snapped. 'You are only a barber.'

Such put-downs didn't worry me because, as I had told Lee Radziwill, I did know my place. My passport still said I was a barber and I was perfectly happy with that.

Many years later, however, when I was in New York to open a salon, and Kissinger was far less famous, I was tapped on the shoulder in a crowded restaurant. I turned to find the man himself standing there, greeting me as if we were long-lost friends.

'Hello, Leonard,' he said. 'What are you doing in Manhattan?'

'I'm opening a salon here,' I told him.

'Great,' he exclaimed. ' Now I won't have to fly all the way to f***ing London just to get my hair cut.'

It is amazing what people will tell their hairdressers, stuff they would never tell anyone else. Years later, after Kennedy had been shot, Jackie told me that she was seeing Aristotle Onassis, long before gossip columnists like Nigel Dempster knew about it. In fact, I already knew – from members of the Niarchos family who were intimately involved with Onassis and had told me everything that was going on. But she would have been horrified if the story had got into the papers at that stage.

One of the secrets of getting the very best clients was to gain a reputation for discretion. They have to feel confident that anything they say while they are under the dryer will not find its way into the gossip columns the following day. The writers on Dempster and William Hickey were forever ringing me, trying to persuade me to talk, but I always refused – although I am as hungry for good morsels of gossip as the next man.

Another side effect of having a reputation for discretion was that powerful men would send both their wives and their mistresses to me. Sir Charles Clore, who owned Selfridges, was one of the most blatant, but he was by no means the only one. At one stage he was going out with an Israeli model called Penina Golan who has now become a famous politician in Israel. She told me that he had given her a charge card at Selfridges which she could use to buy whatever she wanted without ever seeing a bill. His wife was at the time being seen to in another part of the salon.

One of the most notorious mistresses of the time was Christine Keeler, whose affair with John Profumo, the Secretary of State for War, would later help to bring down the Conservative government. They were hardly discreet about the affair since they all used to come into the salon together: Profumo, Keeler, her friend the voluptuous Mandy Rice-Davies, Peter Rachman, the notorious slum landlord, and Stephen Ward, the osteopath who was responsible for introducing them all to one another. They seemed a very happy crowd and the men were quite comfortable having their hair cut amongst the women, which was unusual for someone of Profumo's age and status at the time. I also used to cut the hair of Profumo's wife, the actress,

Valerie Hobson. I do remember that Christine Keeler had very bad hair, lifeless and lank. I suppose she and Mandy were attractive but neither of them was my cup of tea.

As well as doing Jackie Onassis' hair, I also used to look after Maria Callas when she was in London. All the world knew that she was Aristotle Onassis' long-term mistress, so we had to ensure that the two never met. That didn't mean, of course, that I couldn't have some fun teasing the clients when they were in the chair.

'Maria,' I said one morning while I was cutting Callas' hair, 'how's that "bubble and squeak" friend of yours?'

'Bubble and squeak?' The Diva lifted an eyebrow at me.

'You know,' I said. 'It's cockney rhyming slang – bubble and squeak – Greek.'

There was a moment's pause in which I thought she might be about to snatch up a pair of scissors and stab me to death, and then she let out an operatic bellow of laughter. 'My bubble and squeak is very well, thank you.'

These delicate arrangements meant that we had to be as trust-worthy as a family lawyer or accountant. Clients could not worry for a moment that we would make the mistake of putting two rivals in love in chairs next to one another, or would accidentally let some snippet of gossip about one reach the ears of the other. They were the ones doing the talking, we were just listening, or pretending to listen.

Sometimes I would find it too embarrassing. The late newspaper tycoon, Lord Rothermere, used to send his girlfriends to me, even though he knew that his wife, Lady 'Bubbles' Rothermere, was one of my most regular clients. There were never any scenes in the salon, but they also used to go to the same clubs at night.

One night I was in Annabel's with Tony Cloughly, the interior decorator, and Bubbles, who had one of her young men in tow. I spotted Vere Rothermere coming in with one of his girlfriends.

'Your husband's here,' I warned her.

'Christ,' she said and started trying to stuff her boyfriend under the table. It was too late: Vere had spotted her and was on his way over.

'What are you doing out with trash like this?' he indicated the young man angrily.

'He just invited me for a drink,' she protested and then changed her tack. 'He's Tony's boyfriend, we're talking about alterations to the house!'

Vere gave a snort of disbelief and stormed off. Tony was speechless with fury at being implicated and I was deeply embarrassed. Bubbles asked me what was wrong and I was frank, telling her that I didn't think it befitted her status to be behaving so badly in public. Had she still been a Rank starlet it might have been different. Our relationship became a bit chilly for a while after that and eventually she drifted off to a new hairdresser.

I was sad because I had always had a good relationship with her before and had never held back from expressing my opinions. I was round at her flat in Eaton Square one evening when she was getting ready for a night out with one of her young men. She was always enormously overweight and she had got herself up in a very flamboyant Zandra Rhodes dress and a multi-coloured wig.

'I am going to have such a fun night tonight,' she giggled girlishly. 'How do I look?'

'To be frank, Bubbles,' I replied, 'you look like a lampshade.'

She spun round to stare at herself in the mirror. 'You're right,' she wailed. And proceeded to strip the whole lot off, which was not a pretty sight.

Becoming a celebrity hairdresser is like a snowball rolling downhill. Once it is known that you do famous heads, then others will feel confident enough to call you up, and less famous people will want to be done by the same people as the major stars.

Audrey Hepburn, Judy Garland, Liz Taylor, Ava Gardner, Barbra Streisand, Gina Lollobrigida, Lauren Bacall, Faye Dunaway – they all started to call up for appointments.

Whenever La Lolla came in it was as if someone had sent a telegram to the whole of London and the phone lines would be jammed with people asking for appointments. She was incredibly popular. When she asked me if she could come into the salon after hours I thought, in my youthful arrogance, that my luck was in – it wasn't!

The big names weren't always the easiest to deal with. Liz Taylor always expected me to drop whatever I was doing and go straight to her hotel, which was hardly ever practical. Both she and Judy Garland were very bad at paying their bills. Of course it was never up to them personally, it was usually whichever husband was in tow.

Judy was married to an American bandleader called Sid Luft at the time that I knew her best. He would always tell me to leave the bill with him and he would deal with it. He never did. Sometimes Judy would be very moody and would disappear off into the bathroom, reappearing a few minutes later with a broad smile, full of chatter. I can only imagine what she did behind the closed door which had such a dramatic effect.

Her hair was always in the most terrible condition, having suffered from years of abuse by Hollywood studio hairdressers with their unnatural lacquering and setting, torturing the hair into horrible sculptured shapes. As with Princess Grace and her daughters, I got to know Lorna Luft and Liza Minnelli through their mother, and they were both good clients and friends for many years. Lorna was as gentle and calm as her sister was manic.

Whenever Lauren Bacall was due at the salon, someone would have to dash out for a bottle of Scotch. She did not consider coffee a suitable beverage while she was under the dryer. I changed her image radically by cutting her hair into a short bob and altering the colour with highlights. It was a style which I repeated later for Lauren Hutton when she became the face of Revlon.

Bacall, who preferred to be called Betty, had perfect instincts for what was appropriate for her age, which is why she has remained such a stylish figure through the years. Her drawling voice, which you could hear from one end of the salon to the other, always brought back memories of the classic Bogart movies which I had seen as a boy when I had been dreaming of meeting such women for myself.

Ava Gardner had been a great beauty but too much booze and too many 'matadors' had taken their toll. She lived in Knightsbridge at the time and usually appeared in the salon hung-over, with those gorgeous eyes invariably swollen and baggy. It was sad to see someone so beautiful going downhill. She had possibly been Frank Sinatra's greatest love and he'd always ask me how she was whenever we spoke. He would have done anything for her but she was too proud to ask.

Often meeting the stars in the flesh could be disappointing. Without the trappings of make-up artists and clever cameramen they sometimes lost some of their glamour. One who didn't was Audrey Hepburn. She was just as beautiful and charming in life as she was on the screen. I once remarked how I loved her in the part of Holly Golightly in *Breakfast at Tiffany's*.

'That's all I wear,' she replied with a smile. Audrey's jewellery was as conspicuously elegant as she was – never big or flash, just discreet diamonds.

Faye Dunaway was married to the London photographer, Terry O'Neill, and he loved taking pictures of her. She would summon me to the Savoy to do her hair so that Terry could get his shots of her looking at her best.

I did Brigitte Bardot's hair for a session with Bailey for *Elle* magazine. This was before Brigitte retired finally from film-making and devoted herself to her dogs, cats and donkeys. She had tired of being a sex goddess – you would, wouldn't you! She had very fine hair and was just as beautiful as her legend proclaimed. I would have loved to get to know her better, but I got the impression she thought I was a bit too 'rough trade' for her. And, of course, I couldn't speak a word of French.

She was brought to me again later by Régine, the rather awe-inspiring Parisian night club owner who briefly became one of London's society queens when she opened Régine's in Kensington High Street, on the top floor of the old Derry and Tom's building, which was also the last, extravagant home of Biba. Régine brought a lot of French friends into the salon, including Jeanne Moreau, Yves Montand and Sacha Distel. She was a real tough French cookie, and part of her attraction for the stars was that they could let their hair down in her clubs without too much press attention. But the venue proved as unlucky for her as it was for Biba. Despite colossal media coverage, the British scene wasn't ready for her, and eventually she split with her backers and decided that Paris and New York were where the real action was.

When Liz Taylor began to suffer health problems and came to London for operations on her back and later her head, I would visit her in her hospital room to help her with wigs to cover her shaved scalp. I could never be sure what sort of reception I would get. Sometimes she would be the warmest, sweetest person imaginable and at others she would become obsessed with privacy and security, hurling whatever she could get her hands on at anyone who tried to see her. Once, when I was there, the American singer Eddie Fisher turned up to visit her. This was after they were divorced and Liz wasn't at all pleased to see him. In fact she sent him away with a stream of abuse so powerful it quite shocked me. But throughout it all, even when she was enormously overweight, she never lost the magic 'something' which had made her such a great star. Even with her head shaved, the violet eyes would draw your gaze the moment you walked into the room.

Her own hair was very fine. It needed a lot of back-combing to create the 'big hair' effect which she liked and which was so fashionable at the time she was becoming one of the world's most famous actresses. I would rather have given her something more modern and 'wash and wear', but by then she had a successful look which she didn't want to change.

Many of our clients preferred us to go to them rather than coming to the salon. Sometimes it was because they were famous and didn't want to be bothered with people gawping at them. Other times it was because they needed heavy security or just couldn't be bothered to leave their hotels. In my case it cost them. My fee automatically trebled when I did outside work.

One morning I was asked to go over to one of the Middle Eastern princesses at the Dorchester. Since I was busy, I asked one of my top stylists, Celine, if she would go and start the job. She was very happy to. We all liked to leave the salon from time to time to clear our heads and concentrate on one client exclusively for a while. Also, this princess was known to be a big tipper.

That day Celine was wearing a black T-shirt. This was the time when women were starting to go without their bras. After an hour or so I thought I would drop in on them and see how they were doing. The door to the suite was unlocked and so I let myself in, knocking as I went. I was startled to see that Celine had removed her top and was working stripped to the waist. Apparently the princess had complained that she couldn't see her hair in the mirror against the black background.

Like many of my clients, I grew rather partial to the occasional drink. I have always been a social person. I just like being with other people, and I have always loved to eat and drink. When your social life is as glamorous as mine once was, and money is no problem, it is all too easy to keep ordering more rounds of drinks – more bottles of champagne and triple scotches instead of single ones. I could see no danger signals. I was having a wonderful time, signing away in London's fashionable bars and restaurants.

Everyone I came across told me how brilliant I was. There was hardly a celebrity in Europe or America who hadn't heard my name. Life was very heady indeed. I guess I was becoming something of a spoilt child, although I tried my hardest never to be less than charming to everyone I came across. I never found it difficult to be friendly. I have always been more comfortable being pleasant to people rather than unpleasant, but I suppose I was becoming used to getting my own way.

The tranquillity of the salon was constantly being threatened by people coming in to demand money. I was developing such a habit of signing for everything wherever I went, that I wasn't always able to meet the bills when they arrived.

Most creditors were very understanding, at least to start with, and let me put off paying for as long as possible. This was partly because they were continuing to supply my salons with hair products, laundry and cleaning services, flowers and all kinds of items which we probably didn't need. Also they didn't want to offend me in case I took my custom elsewhere. But every so often, someone would become exasperated and send the bailiffs round to see me. There was a little side door in the basement which I found very useful when I wanted to escape, leaving the poor reception staff to explain, quite truthfully, that they had no idea where Mr Leonard was or when he would be back. It gave me a perfect excuse to enjoy a long lunch with some old mates, somewhere where I could sign!

CHAPTER SEVEN

I WAS ALWAYS A great believer in supplying clients with the total beauty look from top to toe. I wanted to be able to give them everything they needed under one roof, including exciting, up-to-the-minute clothes and beauty treatments. I even installed a sauna on the premises, something which had never been done in a London salon before. I still believe it is how things should be done. At the time it was seen as a tremendous novelty.

Nor did I think that cutting and perming was enough any more. I thought we needed to do everything possible in the way of hair treatment, and I invested in the most up-to-date technology on the market for studying the hair and the scalp and ensuring that we could give people the right information for their various conditions. You can give someone the greatest cut in the world but if the hair is out of condition and limp it will still not look that good.

If someone was having trouble with their hair, perhaps with dandruff or excess grease, we would start by advising them on different shampoos and conditioners they should use. Sometimes the shampoos on the general market were too harsh or too creamy. If that didn't work I would suggest they go to see a trichologist. Philip Kingsley was the most famous in the country and was a friend of mine, another self-made man who had set up in business round the corner from the salon in Mayfair. Eventually I took on in-house specialists to help clients with particularly persistent problems. We started selling our own 'Leonard' products in the salon, mainly shampoos and conditioners but also some health treatments.

In many cases the basic products on sale in the local chemist are just as good as the most expensive 'designer label' products sold in salons, but customers like the peace of mind of knowing that whatever they are using has their hairdresser's stamp of approval and are willing to pay a premium for that. Some of the mass market 'designer' products, like the combined shampoo and conditioners, are a waste of money.

They don't do the hair any harm, but they don't bring out the best in it either.

One of my strongest beliefs from the beginning was that good colouring was as important as good cutting. At the beginning of the Sixties very few customers considered dyeing their hair. Some used it to get rid of grey hair, a few went for the bleached blonde Marilyn Monroe look or sometimes for bright reds, but they were the minority. I wanted to change all that. I thought that, just as no great restaurateur would dream of offering food without wine, we should not offer cutting without colouring. In fact I wanted Upper Grosvenor Street to have the finest hair colouring department in Europe.

I had heard of an eighteen-year-old boy who was working in Olofson, a popular salon in Knightsbridge, as a junior colourist. His name was Daniel Galvin. His brother Joshua, who later set up some highly respected hairdressing schools, had been working with Michael Rasser at the House of Revlon in New York. Joshua and Michael both decided to come back to London, Michael joining me in Upper Grosvenor Street and Joshua becoming one of Vidal's top stylists.

People who knew Daniel told me that he had similar ideas to mine and that he was actually putting them into practice. The same news must have reached Vidal's ears and we both made contact with the young colourist on the same day, asking him to come and work for us.

Daniel was developing revolutionary highlighting techniques. Highlighting goes back about 2,000 years to the ancient Venetians, who used to pull strands of hair through their straw hats when they went out into the sun and pour camomile on the ends in order to bleach them, giving them a rather stripy look. Nothing much had changed since then apart from the introduction of henna and various herbal and vegetable colours made from the bark of trees or from walnuts.

After the Second World War, the French had brought the idea of highlighting back into fashion, using greaseproof paper to separate the hair during the dyeing process. The invention of aluminium foil had been a huge step forward as it could be manipulated around the hair much more easily, but it still meant that the customer was left with plain stripes which could look rather skunk-like. I wanted highlights to look as natural as possible.

Daniel had invented a method which he called the 'brickwork' technique. Just as, when building a wall, you would never place one brick directly on top of the one below, you would always overlap and stagger them with the cement in between, so it should be with hair. That meant that whichever way the hair went it never fell into stripes. It was the answer I had been looking for.

Daniel agreed to oversee the colouring side of the business and was an instant hit. I had split the second floor between the colouring department and beauty treatments but it soon became obvious that Daniel would need a whole floor for his operation. When he joined only about ten per cent of the clients wanted colouring work. His aim was to have all of them being coloured as well as cut at Leonard's. He eventually had twenty colourists working for him and I was finally able to afford to do up the top two floors of the building and expand to give us all more space.

The colourists took over a whole floor and we opened a men's salon at the top of the house. We now had about seventy people working in the building. The only problem was that in the lease we were supposed to keep the top floor as a residential flat. We therefore designed it in such a way that within ten minutes we could transform its appearance. If an inspector from the council or a representative from the landlords turned up, the receptionists had to keep them talking downstairs while the customers were evacuated from the top floor as discreetly as possible and the 'flat' was created for them to inspect. The basins where customers had their hair washed would be instantly covered in work surfaces and a bed pulled out from a sofa.

I was starting to travel more and more, often at the behest of clients. Many of the girls who had started coming to me as models, began to get married to wealthy men and become part of the international establishment, like Sally Croker-Poole when she married the Aga Khan. She used to call me up to go and do her hair from Paris, Sardinia or wherever she happened to be. The Aga Khan's wealth is measured in billions and when Karim and Sally were married the guests showered them with pearls instead of confetti – following the tradition of Karim's grandfather, who used to be weighed in gold and diamonds every year on his birthday.

One time Sally asked me to go down to Karim's yacht in the

Mediterranean. It was the most idyllic setting. The boat was bobbing about in the sunshine of a little harbour in Sardinia, the rigging chiming gently in the breeze. There were a number of other guests on board when I arrived, all of them in swimming costumes, either lazing on the decks or eating a leisurely breakfast. We cast off for the open seas in the middle of the morning and everyone swam off the boat in the beautiful clear waters until lunch was served.

Afterwards, Sally went into her suite to wash her hair and I set myself up in the bedroom to do the cutting. As I started to work on her hair I moved around her at the dressing table. At one stage I was standing in front of her when, looking over her shoulder, I saw her husband, Karim, and one of the bikini-clad young female guests on the sun deck outside. He had his arm around the girl's slim, tanned waist and was holding her against him as he kissed her upturned face. Neither seemed remotely concerned that they were standing in full view of the whole world. I kept talking to Sally to stop her from turning around until the couple wandered off out of sight with their arms entwined around one another. I felt my reputation for discretion was being tested beyond the usual limits.

They were finally divorced in 1995, after twenty-six years of marriage, and Sally was rumoured to have received a £50-million settlement.

Clients would often ask me to come to their weddings, partly as a guest and partly to do their hair. I was always delighted to accept any invitation where I could mix my twin passions, work and socialising. At one very smart society wedding the whole day ended in disaster when the groom, an upstanding member of the British aristocracy, realised at the reception that he had made a terrible mistake. Instead of going on honeymoon, he eloped with the best man, a devastatingly handsome young army officer who had recently been doing some male modelling to make ends meet. The chief bridesmaid and I then had to spend several hours in the bedroom with the newly married and newly deserted bride, trying to stem the flood of tears.

The underworld figures I had known in my youth were also happy to frequent Upper Grosvenor Street. The Krays used to come in quite often, usually with a group of their mates like the Frazers or the Reynolds. The twins liked to have manicures, which looked most bizarre since they had hands like bunches of bananas. They always behaved immaculately when they were on the premises and we would chat about mutual acquaintances.

Reggie Kray brought his girlfriend to us. When they got married, Reggie asked if I would do the bride's hair for the ceremony and he commissioned David Bailey to do the photographs. Although it was going to be held on their own territory in the East End they wanted it to look like a Mayfair society wedding, and they did a very good job. Every heavy in the London underworld seemed to have been spruced up for the occasion. The twins' biggest fear was that one of the rival gangs might take advantage of the day and so there were minders everywhere.

There were a lot of pretty girls in attendance and the brothers wanted the family women to look like real ladies for the day. It was quite hard work. I dressed the bride's hair in a chignon which looked pretty, but this was before the days of professional make-up artists going to weddings and so the women did their own faces, which rather detracted from the overall effect. Neither Bailey nor I charged them for our services that day.

The Kray wedding was a good example of how everything in London was changing. There were no longer fixed barriers between different strata of society. You were as likely to bump into Princess Margaret at a party as Reggie or Ronnie.

I was always careful at the salon that information about clients didn't fall into the wrong hands. A number of people who I knew were connected to the underworld used to try to get the addresses of the richer clients out of the staff. They would make up stories such as Lord So-and-So was a friend of theirs but they had lost their address book – could we just help out? Another favourite was, 'We're scouting for locations for commercials. We need to find some really luxurious and glamorous places.'

I made sure that none of my staff divulged any personal details to anyone. If one client wanted to make contact with another we were always happy to pass on messages for them. They usually didn't take it any further. The link between the salon and the underworld was confirmed for me when the police turned up to interview me one day. They wanted to know why a membership card for our men's salon had been found at the scene of a robbery at the Bank of America in Berkeley Square. I gave them a list of members, knowing the card could have belonged to any one of a number of our clients.

In some cases it was the other way round, with society hostesses trying to get the telephone numbers of working-class heroes like Albert Finney, Michael Caine and Terence Stamp. People in businesses like hairdressing and dress designing held a great novelty value for the upper classes. We also had contact books crammed with the names of everyone who could make things happen. In my case I could make them look wonderful for some ball or wedding, but I was equally likely to be sitting at the next table to them at a restaurant or party.

The restaurants that were going to become the fashionable places of the future were just starting up in the early Sixties. Mara and Lorenzo Berni had opened San Lorenzo in Beauchamp Place, a small street just down the road from Harrods which was crammed with dress shops and antique dealers selling wonderful rare objects from maps to tapestries. It was a small, Italian family-run restaurant then, not much more than a bar in a basement, but I loved it. It had a scruffy little garden out the back with a couple of old iron tables.

The Bernis had come from Forte dei Marmi in Tuscany, bringing everything that was best about Italian family catering with them. Lorenzo was using ingredients like mozzarella long before any other restaurant in London, and he used to have special bread baked at a time when most British people were still happy with a loaf of sliced white.

The baker started to put the restaurant's initials, SL, on to the tops of the loaves, which was considered very smart. When the Italian ambassador took Sophia Loren there for dinner she was thrilled to find her initials on the bread and asked Lorenzo to send pasta out to her at the studio where she was filming *The Millionairess*. Peter Sellers was on the same film, and he fell for Loren in a big way. He also acquired a taste for Mara and Lorenzo's cooking. He began coming into the restaurant regularly. One evening he rang to say that he would be bringing someone special. Lorenzo said 'no problem' and set aside his usual table.

A few hours later Sellers turned up with Princess Margaret and Lord Snowdon, who were the most glamorous couple in London at the time. They both raved about the restaurant and its reputation was made. When the Rolling Stones gave their famous concert in Hyde

Park as a memorial for Brian Jones (the one at which Mick Jagger released thousands of butterflies into the air), they all went to San Lorenzo afterwards.

I continued going there for years as it grew more and more prosperous. Lorenzo enclosed the garden at the back and incorporated the large sycamore tree which grew there. The tree became their trademark and when it finally died Lorenzo had the artist Joe Tilson create a labyrinth effect with the wood which now hangs on the wall.

The restaurant became so fashionable that the paparazzi would hang around outside every lunchtime and evening, knowing that there were bound to be famous faces coming and going. Princess Diana was always going there. I once asked her why I had never had the honour of doing her hair.

'I would love to have you do my hair, Leonard,' she said, with all the coy charm she was so famous for. 'But there would be too much publicity.'

I can't imagine how she could possibly have had more publicity than she did.

Diana always skated close to the edge. I was told by some of the photographers who followed her around that she was using Lorenzo and Mara's house for her liaisons. Apparently, she was even having her most intimate mail sent there. Of course, Lorenzo and Mara are far too discreet ever to discuss such a thing.

I believe that the secret of San Lorenzo's success lies in the fact that Lorenzo and Mara are nearly always there in person, wandering around the tables, kissing cheeks, sitting down with customers for a glass of wine or a cup of coffee, exchanging gossip, putting on a bit of a show. Restaurants and hairdressers have a lot in common. There are plenty of people who can cook or cut hair, but the ones who are most successful are the ones who create a buzz and an atmosphere. You can only do that with hard work and by actually being there yourself. If the proprietors are not in evidence, you might as well go to one of the many chain restaurants there are in every city. The Bernis created a room in the heart of London which was like a terrace overlooking the Mediterranean, a light, bright place filled with trees, parasols, fans and faintly irritated waiters.

Mara still rules over 'her boys' with a rod of iron, prodding and scolding them if they drop cutlery. 'These boys,' she will exclaim, 'they think they own the place!' The waiters give slow smiles and shrug. It's just Mara's way of showing affection.

There was a part of the restaurant that was referred to by the regulars as 'Siberia' which was reserved for people who were up in town for the day and whose faces were unknown by the in-crowd. Because I was such a regular I had a favourite table which I was always able to get at short notice, and I used to do almost as much table-hopping and cheek-kissing in the course of an evening as Mara and Lorenzo themselves.

Mara and Lorenzo's children are grown up and in the business themselves now. Their beautiful daughter Marina has opened a shop, selling Italian food and wine next door to the restaurant. I often drop in if I am in the area visiting friends and she always gives me a lemonade and something to eat. It is all so relaxed and friendly we could be back in an Italian village rather than sitting in one of London's most exclusive shopping streets. They make me feel like an old and favoured uncle dropping by for a chat with the family.

Whenever I used to walk into any of the fashionable restaurants in the Sixties, Seventies and Eighties, I usually knew all the staff and at least half the customers by name. Many of them would have been regulars at the salon. If ever I was entertaining a visiting star, whether it was Robert Mitchum or Jack Nicholson, Tony Curtis or Ryan O'Neal, Albert Finney or Twiggy, I would often take them to San Lorenzo because I knew they would receive a warm welcome.

Not everyone was impressed by the food there. I was having dinner with Robert Mitchum there one evening when he complained that he could make pasta as good as the Bernis'.

'I'd like to put that to the test,' I challenged him.

'Okay,' he said. 'You're on. Your place tomorrow night?'

True to his word, the following night Mitchum showed up at my flat and cooked the most brilliant pasta dish. I had to admit that he had a real talent for it.

If ever I walk past the restaurant in the evening now the photographers who still hang around outside ask me which stars are in town, as if I am still living that same life.

I particularly liked to book lunch there for a table of friends on a Saturday, and we would spend the whole afternoon relaxing, eating, drinking and talking. As a result my entertainment bills were horrendous, but I wasn't remotely bothered. I loved to be a host and Ricci loved to be a hostess. I loved to see people enjoying themselves and I loved food. Spending a lot of time in restaurants was also good for business because I would meet all sorts of people who would then ask me to cut their hair. It was good public relations.

On Sundays I used to like entertaining people at home. I would cook a big roast. There would be log fires burning and piles of Sunday papers for anyone who cared to turn up and hang around. By the evening, of course, I was ready to go out on the town again. I could never sit still for long.

There were other restaurants which had the same magic effect on celebrities as San Lorenzo. Mr Chow in Knightsbridge was one where everyone wanted to go. It was owned by a designer called Michael Chow and became the most fashionable Chinese restaurant of the era, famous for its mirrors and flowers and Italian waiters. It was the first place in London to serve fried seaweed, which is now one of the most popular Chinese delicacies in England.

Michael ran it with his wife Tina, a beautiful Chinese model to whom he was introduced in Japan by Zandra Rhodes. As a couple they were an essential part of the London social scene and good friends to Ricci and me. Tina was also a regular client, happy to experiment with her glossy black hair. Everyone was shocked when they later divorced. Tina then became a complete jet setter and was always to be found in the hottest international scenes, modelling in the top fashion shows and even appearing in movies. She took a string of lovers, including Richard Gere, and died tragically, struck down by Aids.

The Aretusa night club in King's Road was another fashionable haunt of the time. Mimmo, who ran the restaurant at Aretusa's, had come from Alvaro's, a very popular Italian restaurant. Aretusa was, for a while, the hottest club in London and absolutely every celebrity in town went there.

Everybody knew Mimmo, with his heavy Italian accent and the even heavier gold chains around his neck. Before he came to England he had worked as a concierge in a hotel in Ischia where the Shand family used to go for their holidays. Camilla Shand, who was eleven years old when he first met her, went on to become Camilla Parker-Bowles and one of Mimmo's most faithful customers.

Another faithful customer at the Aretusa told Mimmo that they planned to open a restaurant and wanted him to run it for them. That was the birth of Mimmo d'Ischia in Elizabeth Street which was to become a great favourite of mine for the next twenty years. Elizabeth Street was the only other shopping street in Belgravia apart from Motcomb Street. It was where the people from the mansions in Eaton Square and Belgrave Square went for their meat and vegetables.

I used to book Mimmo's private rooms upstairs for the company Christmas parties, which used to draw a huge crowd. I had a birthday party there once, where Zandra Rhodes exploded out of the cake, just like Marilyn Monroe did for Kennedy.

Recently, Camilla Parker-Bowles booked Mimmo's for her daughter Laura's twenty-first birthday party. When they arrived with their party, Mimmo started doling out kisses in his usual flamboyant manner, only to find in the heat of the moment that he had come face to face with a rather startled looking Prince William. With the encouragement of the others he plonked a kiss on the Prince's cheek as well.

Like San Lorenzo, Mimmo's premises have expanded over the years, creating a covered terrace at the back with an imported olive tree, and it is his constant jovial presence, moving amongst the tables, which gives the restaurant its unique atmosphere. The walls are filled with pictures of him meeting virtually every celebrity who has passed through London in the last few decades, as well as giant paintings of himself by people like Rolf Harris and Angela Landels (wife of *Harpers & Queen*'s legendary editor, Willie Landels), all showing him looking like Stewart Granger, his face wreathed in smiles and a thick cigar between his fingers.

In the middle of one of the most crowded walls is a large photograph of me and Dominic when he was about ten. I don't think anyone seeing that picture for the first time would realise that it was the same person as I am today. Friends used to be amazed at how thin I was considering the amounts of food I consumed. If I liked a dish I would often be unable to resist ordering a repeat as soon as I had finished it. I would then set about finishing off whatever anyone else at the table might have left on their plates – much to the annoyance of some of my companions who would protest that they hadn't finished eating before I started to dive in.

I had to look good for my work and I was careful not to put on weight. I used to be sick quite often and all my friends tell me that I was bulimic. I guess they must be right, but it was an illness no one had heard much about until it was discovered that Princess Diana was troubled by it. Models had been using it as a rather drastic form of dieting ever since the skinny look became fashionable and I never really stopped to analyse what I was doing. I loved food and wanted to eat vast quantities of it. I also wanted to stay thin. What other alternatives were there? It just didn't seem to be a problem to me.

I always denied the condition strenuously to anyone who accused me, and convinced myself that the vomiting was being caused by a variety of other things from a dodgy muscle in my stomach to a food allergy. Later I blamed my medication for upsetting my system. If it didn't worry me I couldn't see why it should worry anyone else.

Because I was sick so often I also seemed to be able to drink copious amounts of alcohol without ever appearing to get particularly drunk. I was accident-prone and rather vague anyway, so who would notice the difference? Thinking back now, I probably would have killed myself from over-indulgence years ago if I hadn't spent so much time bringing up everything I stuffed down.

I knew that it was important to look good if I wanted to keep the salon's reputation. That meant always being beautifully turned out in well-designed clothes, and being tanned as well as slim. Sun beds were still something of a novelty then, and there hadn't been any skin cancer scares, so I used them copiously to top up the tan I was able to get on holidays. It was still considered unusual for men in England to pay so much attention to their appearance, but things were changing there too. This was the dawning of a new age of the peacock and I felt sure it was a trend which was going to grow and grow.

Clients were coming to the House of Leonard so thick and fast that it was hard to keep up with them. I didn't want to get a reputation for having long waiting lists. If a woman needs her hair done she wants it done immediately, not in a month's time. If you tell her she is going to have to wait she will simply take her custom elsewhere. At the same time there weren't enough hours in the day for me to be able to do everything I wanted to do. I was very reliant on my staff to keep the clients moving through the salon. I would do anyone's hair who came and asked, but in most cases I was like a supervisor, passing them on to the younger stylists to do the bulk of the cutting. I might have five or six clients on the go at any one time, which meant that I had to be concentrating hard to stay on top of everything that was happening, which added to my general air of distraction.

When I was doing Lulu one day at the height of her fame as a pop star in 1976, I passed her across to John Frieda so that I could get on with starting someone else. John was very good-looking and had always been popular with the lady clients. The next thing I knew the two of them announced that they were getting married. The family connection with the salon became even stronger when Lulu's younger sister started going out with Nicky Clarke who was working with us as a junior.

When you have so many talented young people together under one roof, sometimes for ten or twelve hours a day, there is bound to be a lot of chemistry going on. Just as I had used the lift at Sassoon's first salon as a seduction chamber, I knew that many of my stylists were conducting passionate romances around the premises with the young models and debutantes who were often with us for six or eight hours at a time, many having removed all their clothes before putting on their gowns. As long as they didn't get caught in the act or upset any of the clients, I was happy to look the other way.

We had a wig room which was particularly notorious as a venue for illicit couplings. God alone knows what went on amongst the hair-pieces in there but I frequently went in to get something, only to find some red-faced couple trying to pull their clothes together and pretending that they were looking for something. I once walked in to find Bubbles Rothermere in a very compromising position with one of her young men.

'There is a time and a place for everything, Lady Rothermere,' I said, very grandly. 'And my wig room is not it.'

One of the most notorious Casanovas was a young stylist called Gavin Hodge. Gavin was a working-class boy like the rest of us whom I met one day at Vogue House when we were both doing magazine work. He came to join us at Upper Grosvenor Street and proceeded to get into all the tabloid papers by running off with an heiress called Jayne Harries, who was dubbed Deb of the Year by the media, after meeting her at the Berkeley Dress Show. Sadly, Jayne disappeared later to Afghanistan and died of a drug overdose. Gavin now has a salon called Sweeneys almost opposite San Lorenzo in Beauchamp Place.

At around this time Barbra Streisand married her hairdresser, Jon Peters, and he went on to become one of the major Hollywood players. People no longer looked on our industry as being for poofs, as my dad had feared when I first told him of my ambitions.

Having wonderful contacts often helped to smooth my path through life. I never had as much time as I needed to go shopping, but I always liked to have smart clothes. Lady Rendlesham was a client of mine when she launched the Yves St Laurent boutique in London. She would send clothes round to the salon for me to try on, which saved me a great deal of time.

Clare had impeccable taste and a special chic, but was very frightening. She had been fashion editor of *Queen* magazine and was rumoured to have reduced the editor, Jocelyn Stevens, to tears on more than one occasion. She used to smoke unfiltered French cigarettes and drink black coffee all day long, carting a Pekinese around with her wherever she went. No one dared to cross her. Many ladies were desperate to buy at St Laurent but didn't want to bump into Clare. They would phone up to find out where she was, then quickly dash in while she was out, sometimes not even stopping to try the clothes on before buying them.

I liked St Laurent's designs a lot for myself and also used to dress the reception staff in his blouses and skirts. It was the beginning of trousers for women as fashion wear, which was going to change everything completely. Ricci was also buying the most extraordinary amount of clothes from them at that time, thinking nothing of acquiring half a dozen outfits at once, all of which were put on my account.

I heard that, much later, Clare Rendelsham died while sitting in Chelsea Library, dressed up to the nines with her beloved dog on her lap. It sounds the sort of death she would have liked.

There were a number of these very powerful women working in the fashion industry who built legends around their ferocity. Diana Vreeland, a famous editor of *Vogue* in America, was another one who could make strong men quake in their shoes. She asked me over to New York to do the wigs for a show which she was putting on as a tribute to a number of designers. I had heard terrible tales of how she could chew people up and spit them out, but I found her to be charming.

If I did go shopping I always had to take someone else with me from the office or reception to take care of the business side. I'm told

I was a nightmare shopper, going through the stock like a hurricane, trying on dozens of shirts and discarding them in my wake for other people to sort out. I was quite unaware that I was causing pandemonium, I simply wanted to get the job done as quickly as possible and find the best clothes available.

Although we were now into the Sixties, none of us in the fashion and entertainment businesses had any idea of what was about to happen. A young man from Liverpool, called Brian Epstein, had started coming to the salon, bringing one of his many boyfriends with him – although in those days most people still pretended that they weren't gay, even if they were. Some men were just starting to pluck up the courage to come to women's salons, realising that they would get infinitely better cuts there than in traditional barbers' shops.

'What are you up to at the moment, Brian?' I asked casually as I snipped away, hardly listening to the answer.

'I'm launching a new group,' he said excitedly. 'A bunch of young lads from Liverpool. I really want to change their image, give them haircuts that will make them different to all the other rock and rollers.'

'Great idea,' I said, concentrating on my snipping as a junior held up Brian's hair for me to cut. 'It's about time men started to be more imaginative with their hair.'

'They've all been off to Paris and had their hair cut by a German called Jorgen,' Brian went on. 'The idea is great but the cut needs a bit of refining.'

'How did an unknown group afford to go to Paris?' I asked. 'Did you pay?'

'One of them, John Lennon, inherited £100 from an aunt. It was his treat.'

'Bring them in, Brian,' I said, 'and I'll see what I can do.'

A few weeks later he arrived with the four boys in tow. They were all smartly turned out in suits he had bought for them. The German had cut their hair into the striking fringes which would become their trademark but he had done it in a pudding basin style, which they didn't look completely comfortable with. They were adamant that they didn't want to go for the Sassoon geometric cut with points all over their heads.

I set about softening the look for them and giving them styles that would move and always look good, even when they were shaking their heads about on stage, or being filmed on location in strong winds. The boys were very polite and respectful. They were probably a little overwhelmed by the atmosphere of a Mayfair salon, although they knew that people like the Walker Brothers and Sandie Shaw were regular clients.

The Beatles seemed to be happy with what I did, although they were nervous that they might get picked on by other men for looking too 'girly'. Brian was delighted and it seemed that as long as he was happy, they were happy. At the end they very sweetly tried to tip me.

I thought no more about them but a few months later the Beatles burst on to the scene. To the general public their haircuts looked revolutionary, but they followed my basic theory of 'sectioning' the head and letting the hair fall naturally, giving them a floppy, soft look. People talked about the 'mop tops', and there was a lot of tutting amongst the reactionary establishment about 'falling standards' and jokes about 'not being able to tell boys from girls', but a corner had been turned and men's hairstyling would never be the same again. Brian's vision had changed everything.

From then on, all the male pop stars paid as much attention to their hair as the women. Those who were close to the London fashion and social scenes invariably found their way through our doors. Mick Jagger and the other Stones took the concept to the opposite extreme, deliberately growing their hair to shock. Stars like Scott Walker of the Walker Brothers imitated and cleaned up the look. For Bryan Ferry of Roxy Music we created a sort of parody of the old nineteen thirties lounge lizard look. When Freddy Mercury of Queen burst on to the scene, glam rock was at its height and stars like him and David Bowie were changing their styles almost monthly to fit their music and their stage acts.

What all these performers had in common was a desire to find styles which suited them and which were dramatic. Looking back at those early Beatle haircuts now, they couldn't have been more natural and simple. Within ten or fifteen years virtually every schoolboy in the West had a similar cut, and in reality there was no way that anyone would ever have mistaken any of the Beatles for girls.

Within a very short time, the 'long hair' revolution had reached the high street and men everywhere started to escape from the short back and sides look which had dominated Britain since the soldiers had their heads shaved to go into the trenches in the First World War.

My book of contacts started to swell in another direction and people in the pop business began to become close friends. We were all at the same parties and restaurants. The Beatles drifted in and out of the salon and when Paul McCartney produced a film called *Goodbye to Broadway*, he asked me to oversee the hair. The last time I saw all the surviving Beatles together was at Ringo's wedding to actress and Bond-girl Barbara Bach. Barbara was also a regular customer and asked me to do her hair for the big day. I cut Ringo, Paul and George at the same time. They held the reception at Rags Club in Mayfair. Later in the evening Ringo, George and Paul all played together in a tribute to John Lennon. It was a deeply moving occasion.

Pop stars were always at the forefront of fashion and hairstyles. Years after the Beatles and Bowie, we were still creating distinctive new styles for musicians like Nick Rhodes of Duran Duran who became a very good client, asking me to do both his and his bride Julie's hair for their wedding at the Savoy. A good haircut can be a major part in the transformation of a group of scruffy lads into a professional boy-band that is going to break the hearts of millions of little girls.

As the years went past, I often found that people I had met in different situations ended up married to one another and both of them would be coming to the salon. David Bowie, for instance, appeared in a film called *The Hunger* (directed by Tony Scott who made *Top Gun*), which was partly shot at the salon. Catherine Deneuve costarred in the film, a sensual modern-day vampire story, on which I gave hair and wig advice. Bowie was someone who had very definite ideas of what he wanted to do with his hair and his image. I helped him achieve these dramatically different looks on a series of album covers.

At about the same time that Bowie was coming to the salon, I was on holiday in Africa with an American photographer friend called Peter Beard. He was a colourful character who later married super-model and actress Cheryl Tiegs and was rumoured to have had affairs with both Jackie Onassis and Lee Radziwill. He was camping on a hill above Karen Blixen's old house in Kenya, photographing crocodiles and lions and God knows what else, but still living in considerable style. He actually had her house-boy looking after him and a genuine Matisse hanging in his tent. I later visited him in a wonderful apartment on Park Avenue, and some time after that, he bought a windmill and moved it to Montana to live in.

'Come to the dentist with me,' he said one day in Kenya. 'I want you to see someone.'

Puzzled but intrigued, I went with him and he introduced me to the most beautiful dental nurse I had ever seen. She was from Somalia and her name was Iman. A few years later she burst on to the international modelling scene, with the media concocting all sorts of stories about how she had been discovered living as a native in the jungle. She ended up marrying Bowie.

Peter Beard used to keep the most brilliant diaries of his adventures, with sketches that he did himself. They would have made the most fascinating books but sadly they were destroyed when his house in America burnt down.

He flitted in and out of my life at the oddest moments. I remember once being in Manhattan with Peter Morton (the founder of the Hard Rock Café empire), and Peter was with us too. We came across a helicopter pilot in a bar somewhere. He had been in Vietnam and was a little crazed. We asked him to fly us around Manhattan and he agreed. As we were flying under the Triboro Bridge I noticed that both Peters' hair needed a trim so I got out my scissors. It was far too bumpy to do a decent job so I asked the pilot if we could land for a while so that I could finish off. He put down in Yankee Stadium and I just had time to finish the cut before the security guards sent us off.

Peter Morton was another of the young people who were changing the scene in London. His father was something to do with the Playboy Empire and Peter, with his partner, Isaac Tigrett, created the first real American burger bar in London. It was called The Great American Disaster in the Fulham Road, and was so successful that it wasn't long before he was opening The Hard Rock Café on Hyde Park Corner, almost exactly halfway between my house and the salon.

This was the city's first themed restaurant, a concept which has since spawned Planet Hollywood and dozens of others, and the first to play rock music so loudly that the customers could hardly hear themselves talk. He had people queuing round the block and even today the tourists still flock to it, even after Peter sold it for $200 million.

He lived just across the road from us in Little Chester Street and we became very good friends. I used to call him 'Mandingo, God's gift to working women'. We went on holiday together a few times with his wife Paulene Stone, a flaming redhead who had been married briefly to Laurence Harvey before he died. I rechristened her 'Red Job' for obvious reasons. Laurence Harvey had been one of the first men to start coming to the salon regularly and I had known Paulene from when she was just starting out as a model.

Peter Morton is now back in America, where he owns Morton's, a top restaurant in Hollywood and The Hard Rock Hotel and Casino in Las Vegas among other enterprises. I still hear from him regularly.

CHAPTER EIGHT

In the early Sixties I grew more and more absorbed in the whole business of photographing hair. All the glossy magazines were beginning to show an interest in the work I was doing and photographers like Clive Arrowsmith and David Bailey were keen to work with hairdressers who would create imaginative and startling looks for them.

There was one photographer in particular who had gained a reputation for photographing hair. His name was Barry Lategan and I had seen some of his work in the window of another salon near Bond Street. He had a wonderful talent for head-shots, finding angles in the girls' faces which made them look incredibly beautiful. He was also able to create a fine delineation of the girls' hair with his lighting and camera work.

He was still very young and looking to expand his portfolio, making most of his living at the time mainly by doing shots for the Hat Council. I would send girls to him sometimes to have pictures done after we had cut their hair. I would then display his prints of our models in the salon to show other clients some of our more daring ideas. Barry was from South Africa and had the softest, most gentle manner with the models, very different to Bailey, Donovan and Arrowsmith who did nothing to suppress the rougher and wilder edges of their personalities.

One day I came downstairs to reception, feeling very much the grand man of the salon as usual, and tripped straight over my own feet. I've always been rather prone to falling over and, as I pulled myself up to continue my progress as if nothing had happened, I saw a familiar face looking down at me.

'Hello, Nagels,' I cried with genuine surprise. I hadn't seen him for a few years, but he was just the same as I remembered him at Sassoon before he went off.

'What?' Nagels stared at me as the penny dropped. 'You're "Mr

Leonard" now? I don't believe it!'

I tried to quieten him down before his reminiscences got out of hand. This was not the time or place for him to be shouting about 'Old Leg-over Len'. I noticed he had a skinny little schoolgirl with him. She had been booked in for a cut with Clifford Stafford, one of the stylists who later went on to do well with his own salon. Clifford later married Joan Thring, some twenty years older than him, who was Rudolph Nureyev's manager. They met at the salon, where Clifford did her hair. He was very good with the grand dames – but I digress.

'This is Lesley Hornby,' Nagels introduced me to the girl.

I shook hands with her. She had a sweet face but didn't look any older than her fifteen years, wearing a ratty-looking fur coat. Nothing about Nagels was ever predictable. She looked like an angelic child but when she spoke she had the loudest, roughest cockney accent I had heard in years. It sliced through the hushed and decorous tones of the salon. She was obviously a bit overawed by all the heavy Mayfair money in evidence around the place. By that time I was already so used to living the high life I had forgotten what an impact it could have on people the first time they stepped into it.

'She's a model and I'm going to be her manager,' Nagels told me proudly. 'She's got a job for *Woman's Mirror*. We met Clifford at the studio and he said you might be able to use her as a house model.'

I had a feeling Nagels was telling me that there was no way he could afford to pay House of Leonard prices. I looked at the girl more closely. She had enormous blue-grey eyes and had drawn lashes on to her eyelids and cheeks with an eye pencil. In fact, I discovered later, Nagels had done it for her, imitating the look of an old wooden doll he kept on his bedside table. It was a strange effect, rather haunting. It made her look like a little doll herself.

We had about a hundred and fifty models whom we gave free hair cuts to at that time. Some of them were girls who allowed us to cut their hair in experimental styles and photograph the results. Others were top models whom we wanted to be associated with. They were not allowed to work for any other hairdresser and we could use them for shots whenever we wanted, which gave us an enormous amount of control in the modelling world.

'What do you think of her?' Nagels wanted to know the moment the girl was out of earshot.

'Very nice,' I said.

'Yeah, but what do you really think?' he insisted.

'Really, very nice.' What did he want me to say?

'She can sing,' he said, as if trying to convince me. 'Give 'im a song, Lesley!' he shouted across to her.

'Get out of it,' she replied.

'Yeah,' he turned back to me with a sigh of satisfaction. 'And only fifteen. In ten years' time she'll still only be twenty-five.' It sounded like he was thinking of buying a used car rather than choosing a partner.

This girl wasn't at all like the sort of Sloaney models I was used to. She was so young to start with, just a gawky, colt-like teenager, but she had a bony, boyish face which I thought would photograph well. Her hair was long and uninteresting and did nothing to show off her features. It was also in the most terrible condition, having been bleached and curled to death.

She had been working as a Saturday shampoo girl in a salon in Queensway, so she was obviously interested in the business. And I thought working with Nagels again would be fun – things were always unpredictable when he was around – so I agreed to give his protégée a cut.

'She needs to have some photographs done,' he told me.

'I know a great photographer she should meet,' I said. 'He's called Barry Lategan. I'll give him a ring and see if he's free. If he's interested I'll be happy to give Lesley a cut myself and get Barry to photograph her for the salon.'

I rang Barry at his Baker Street studio and he said he would be delighted to meet Justin de Villeneuve – the name Nagels was still travelling under – and his young protégée. They went straight over to meet him. Barry was always very good at putting awkward young girls at their ease, inviting them to browse through his work while he made them coffee or whatever they wanted. While Lesley looked at the glamorous blow-ups on the walls, Barry chatted to Nagels.

'Hey, Twiggy,' Nagels suddenly shouted out, 'stop biting your nails.'

'What did you call her?' Barry asked.

'Twiggy,' Nagels said. 'That's the nickname my brother gave her because she's so skinny. Sometimes we call her "The Stick". Her modelling name is going to be Princess.'

98

'Twiggy would make a great modelling name,' Barry said. 'You should call her that.'

'You think so?' Nagels said, pondering on the idea.

'Definitely.'

'Okay then,' he decided. 'That's who she is.'

Barry told them he would be happy to take shots of Twiggy when I had done the cut I was planning. From that moment on that was how she was always referred to.

Nagels was a bit on the abrasive side in those days, which led to him falling out with most of the top photographers over the next few years. He just wasn't willing to let them treat his girl as a commodity – which is how they view most models – and used to stand up for her. Sometimes he'd go over the top. He got away with it because of his personality – and because he had control of the most famous model in the world. With Barry there was no such problem. It would be almost impossible to fall out with him. He is the gentlest and kindest of men.

What I wanted to do, which I hadn't told Twiggy, was to chop all her hair off and give her what was called an Eton crop. It would make the most of her bony, boyish looks – although no boy ever had eyes or a neck quite like that. When she found out what I planned to do she was horrified, squawking like a chicken about to have its head chopped off. Like most young girls she was very fond of her long hair, using it to hide her awkwardness from the world, believing it made her look grown-up. She said she didn't want to do it – no way! I could see she was very close to tears.

'Don't worry,' Nagels reassured me, 'I'll talk to her.'

'Listen, Twiggs,' he reasoned, 'Mr Leonard is the most famous hairdresser in the world. Just having a cut by him is a chance in a million. You can always grow it back if you don't like it, but I've never known anyone dislike what he does for them.'

Nagels could win over anyone, particularly Twiggy who, at that time, was obviously very impressed by his worldly charms and ready patter. She later told me that she was overwhelmed by the grandness of the surroundings and all the staff bowing and scraping.

Twiggy stayed in the salon all day. First, my young assistant, John Frieda, shampooed her and then I did a rough cut of the hair. She then had a scalp massage and conditioning before going upstairs to Daniel Galvin, who spent about six hours highlighting her, cursing me for cutting the hair so short and giving him such a fiddly job. Once the colour was right she returned to me for the final cut. The result was even better than I had imagined. She looked completely stunning.

When we finished we gave her a mirror to look at the results and she let out a parrot-like screech of amazement, unable to believe her eyes. She had been transformed into something quite magical, like some character from a fairy tale, wearing a little cap of gold.

When she stood up in her gown and everyone looked at her the whole floor of the salon fell silent. Everyone was staring in amazement. Clients and cutters, tea boys and cleaners, receptionists and models, they all just stood and gawped. We had created something totally new. Nagels was so excited he could hardly contain himself. It was obvious that he was totally infatuated with my new creation.

'Looking in the mirror at the back,' Twiggs later told me, 'I saw all these faces staring at me, in a way that no one had ever done before.'

Although I was more than pleased with the result, I wasn't sure that the fashion world would be interested in such a strange-looking little girl, but I knew that Barry would enjoy photographing her and that a lot of clients would be asking for similar cuts once they saw the pictures.

I was right. Barry thought she was breathtaking and produced a beautiful set of pictures. I put one up on the wall of the salon, feeling very proud of myself. I phoned Nagels and Twiggs answered the phone. I told her that I'd featured her picture in the salon and she screamed with delight, nearly tearing my ear off.

One of my customers at the time was Deirdre McSharry, fashion editor at the *Daily Express*. Deirdre knew every model in London and her eye immediately came to rest on the picture.

'Who's she?' she wanted to know.

'Her name is Twiggy,' I said. 'A friend of mine is managing her.'

'Can you let me have his number?'

I gave her Nagels' number and the next thing I heard he and Twiggy had got the bus down to Fleet Street and Deirdre had interviewed Twiggy. I know for a fact that Nagels was down to his last few bob at the time. But when Deirdre asked him how much Twiggy made he said '£100 a week', which at the time was a huge sum. Deirdre duly wrote down everything they told her and produced a two-page spread of photographs, including Barry's head-shot. The headline was 'I NAME THIS GIRL THE FACE OF '66'. Without realising it, Nagels, Barry and I had created one of the milestones of the Swinging Sixties.

In those days the *Daily Express* was one of the country's most popular newspapers, with a circulation of over four million. That made Deirdre probably the most influential fashion editor. If she wrote something everyone sat up and took notice. If she needed a helicopter to get her to a shoot she just had to pick up the phone.

She had gone to the paper from the *Evening News*, a rival to the London *Evening Standard*, which was when she first came to me to have her hair done. I was always happy to have journalists as clients because I knew they were talking to other people, recommending us. Deirdre came to me every week for twenty-two years and I never charged her a penny. If she was going off to a media event I was always happy to furnish her with hair pieces, which were becoming all the rage, just as the clothes designers were happy to lend her frocks. People like Deirdre were style setters for the rest of fashionable London.

My biggest quandary was knowing whom to charge and whom not to charge. To start with there were all the models. We needed them for photographs. We also wanted them to come to the salon and be seen there by other clients. The problem was there were just so many of them. Then there were the journalists – not all of them as helpful to us as Deirdre. Finally there were friends. If a friend came to the salon I could never quite bring myself to charge them. Some of them were taking advantage and coming in for the full works several times a week. As a result we were often working half the day for no money – not a good position to be in for the long term, although it created the most terrific buzz at the time. Deirdre used to love to hear the gossip. She always wanted to know who was in town and who was looking wonderful.

I have always found it difficult to let other people pay for things, particularly meals. Deirdre was one of few people who used to ask to take me to lunch.

'Once a year, Leonard,' she used to say, 'I take my bank manager out to lunch. At least let me do that much for you. It's all on expenses anyway.'

I know it makes no sense but I just wasn't comfortable allowing other people to treat me. Of course now my position is rather different, but I still don't find it easy. Deirdre has moved to Bath and I recently went down to visit her. We had a lovely time over lunch and she finally bullied me into allowing her to pay. We then spent the afternoon wandering around in search of a cake shop so that I could bring some cream buns back for Rene.

Twiggy's arrival on the scene changed everything in the modelling business. Her look was a complete contrast to Shrimpton and the other girls at the top. Her shape influenced every designer and every model from then on. The whole business of fashion photography was undergoing a revolution at the same time. Photographers were starting to use 35mm cameras instead of the big glass plate ones, which meant they had much more freedom to move about and capture spontaneous, zany moments. Bailey always believed that the motor drives which these new cameras had, gave off a sexual rhythm that the models subconsciously reacted to.

In 1972 *Cosmopolitan* was launched and Deirdre, after a couple of years on the *Sun*, was recruited as fashion editor under Joyce Hopkirk. About a year later she became editor. These days, when new magazines are being launched every few months, it is hard to imagine just what an impact *Cosmo* had on everyone. This was the beginnings of women's lib and the burning of bras. *Cosmo* was the first women's magazine to discuss sex openly.

One of their greatest gimmicks was to print the first nude male centrefolds. The first one, if my memory serves me correctly, was Burt Reynolds, followed by Germaine Greer's husband, Paul de Feu, who was a builder by profession. Then they used Vidal. He looked amazing. He was one of the first celebrities to become a 'gym rat' and to bang the drum for fitness and body building. It would be at least twenty years before most men started to catch up and gyms sprang up in every town around the country, but in the beauty business we were all becoming very self-conscious about exercise, vitamin supplements and diet.

Deirdre did suggest that I should think about following Vidal's example, but I wasn't too sure that it would be the right image for a Mayfair salon. I was working with women every day and I needed to keep my distance. A picture of me in the nude might have under-mined my image of complete authority. I used to work a lot with Deirdre on *Cosmo*, particularly with her favourite photographer,

Norman Eales, and models like Patti Boyd and Paulene Stone.

'Get Leonard, Deirdre,' Eales used to say, 'he always does big, fat hair.'

Deirdre could never understand why the models were always so giggly at the sessions. I could have told her – they were constantly stoned! This was the time when cannabis was arriving in London by the sack-load.

Years later, Deirdre confided to me that she had felt twinges of doubt about launching Twiggy into the big time when she was still only fifteen, but she thought she would be safe with kindly, avuncular figures like me and Barry Lategan around her. I noticed she didn't include Nagels in that description.

In the end I felt rather sorry for Twiggy. She obviously wanted to progress and develop but Nagels was very keen to keep her just the way she was. She was always anxious not to upset him and didn't really know how to go about changing her career without his help.

CHAPTER NINE

'JOHNNY IS OPENING a club in Jermyn Street,' a model called Jan de Souza told me just before Christmas in 1969 as I worked on her hair. She had been a customer of mine for many years and I had met her boyfriend, Johnny Gold, on several occasions. He always seemed a very charming man.

'You must come to the opening,' she said. 'And bring all your friends.'

I duly went along to see what it was all about. The premises were surprisingly tatty for a West End club but from the first night Tramp had the right atmosphere for the Seventies. Johnny's business partner was Oscar Lerman, who later married Joan Collins' sister, Jackie. Jackie then went on to write *The Stud*, which was based on the club and was turned into a raunchy film for Joan. It was directed by Quentin Masters who was so upset by the way the producers had it edited that he asked for his credit to be removed and wouldn't have anything to do with the film afterwards. It went on to be a big box office success and made a fortune for everyone else. Quentin was understandably livid. Johnny married Jan a couple of years after the opening and is still happily with her today.

If Annabel's, which had opened its doors six years earlier, was aimed at the upper class and big business establishment, Tramp was aimed firmly at the show business glitterati. Joan and Jackie were both at the opening, as was Roger Moore, who became a regular, and Natalie Wood. From the first night it became *the* club. Paparazzi hung around outside in the hope of snatching a picture of someone going home with someone they shouldn't be.

Johnny ran the place in just the same way as Mimmo and the Bernis ran their restaurants, with the force of his personality. Every night he would be there, at his regular VIP table just on the right as you went in, making sure that everyone had what they wanted and was happy. He was an expert at creating a pleasant, relaxing atmosphere. The restaurant used to specialise in 'horoscope hamburgers' where there was a different sauce for every sign of the zodiac.

Journalists were banned from entering, unless they were members (*Sunday Times* Editor, Andrew Neil, later met the House of Commons 'researcher' Pamela Bordes there). Consequently, rumours abounded in the press about what went on behind the closed doors, making this exclusive establishment more and more famous. From then on I divided my nights almost equally between Annabel's and Tramp.

At the beginning of the Seventies a client of mine, the film star, director and famous womaniser Warren Beatty, made a film called *Shampoo* with Julie Christie about a hairdresser who slept with all his customers. I was sent a script during the development period and asked if I would become involved as an adviser. It seemed to me that it had a lot to do with sex and almost nothing to do with the business of hairdressing, so I declined.

Warren used to come to the salon whenever he was in England, which was quite often when he was dating Julie Christie. Julie had been a customer of ours for years. She always arrived with her Labrador. Several clients used to bring dogs into the salon. Sarah Miles, the actress, used to have an enormous Pyrenean mountain dog which Nicky Butler used to take out for walks in Hyde Park while Sarah spent hours having her naturally curly hair straightened. Nicky would come back bright red in the face and gasping for breath after the dog had dragged him for miles.

Warren Beatty was one of the most conceited men I have ever met. He loved to be pampered with haircuts and facials and massages. He always seemed very false to me, and I had the impression he saw himself as the perfect all-American Mr Immaculate. I'm not surprised that he has ended up wanting to run for President.

On one trip he brought Julie to London to have a breast enhancement with the celebrated plastic surgeon, Philip Lebon. I had known Philip since the early Sixties when he used to socialise, water-ski and work with Vidal. He told me how devoted Warren was while Julie was recovering from the operation. He would sit beside her bed for hours on end just stroking her hair and holding her hand. No wonder he had such a brilliant track record at pulling the world's most beautiful women.

When Warren came to the salon soon after the release of *Shampoo*, I told him my reservations about the movie.

'From what I hear,' he said with a twinkle in his eye, 'you will have a much more interesting story to tell one day.'

A lot of the big American musical acts used to drop by, or would call for me to go to their hotels. Many of the black singers at the time used to wear wigs. The Afro style took some time to catch on. Groups like the Supremes (which was where Diana Ross started), still wanted to have hair like white singers and didn't want to go through all the performance of having their own hair straightened. It was much easier for them to have a selection of wigs made up which they could pull on for a show or a personal appearance, then pull off again as soon as they got back to their hotels. I persuaded them to move away from the very false, sculpted look which they had, and made them look more natural.

I was developing a reputation for being able to create good wigs. I used to work closely with the client, doing sketches for them and deciding the sort of style they wanted. I would then take the pictures to the wig makers who would turn them into a reality. Once the basic wig was made I could then cut it, wash it, curl it, colour it and do whatever else was needed to make it look completely natural and suit the client's face.

The best wigs were made from the hair of Italian nuns who would have their hair cut off when they joined their nunneries and sold to the trade. I always liked the idea that some of the most notorious women in the world were wearing hair from the heads of Italian virgins.

Shirley Bassey was another performer who relied a great deal on wigs and came to me to try to attain a more natural look, rather than the fierce, helmet-style of the Fifties and Sixties. But it wasn't just the women. Frank Sinatra tried everything to cover his baldness before finally having to admit that a wig was the most effective answer. He was one of the first celebrities to try a transplant – a technique which Philip Lebon and other surgeons were experimenting with in London with varied success. Quite often the transplanted hair didn't take and the patient was left with a cluster of little holes in his scalp. Frank was one of those. He was very philosophical about it.

'You gotta try everything, Leonard,' he said with a shrug when I surveyed the damage. From then on he covered the problem with a toupee.

The other alternative to a wig was the 'hair weave', which meant fixing a wig or toupee almost permanently to the head by weaving it into the existing hair. I was never a great fan of this method, believing that it was better for the scalp if you could take the wig off at night and allow the skin beneath to breathe. I hear, however, that Elton John is very happy with his.

Because I was in business for such a long time, many of the stars that I knew changed dramatically during the times that I knew them. When I first met Michael Jackson he was a sweet-faced little boy singing with his brothers in the Jackson Five. Their songs were played all the time in the clubs. Because they knew I had worked on Bob Marley's dreadlocks and helped Jimi Hendrix to create his explosions of black curls, they sought me out as soon as they landed in London.

Many years later I was in Los Angeles when a film-producer friend of mine, Allan Carr, told me that he had been invited to dinner at Michael Jackson's house.

'Tell him Leonard sends his regards,' I said.

The next thing I knew Allan rang me at my hotel and told me that Michael wanted me to go to dinner as well. I was due to see Tony Cloughly, the interior decorator, who was also in town, and so he was invited along too.

Allan was always amusing company, and prone to eccentricity himself. The word 'camp' might have been invented for him. He liked nothing better than to wear voluminous kaftans to hide his portly figure. But his showy, flamboyant exterior hid an astute mind. He worked on numerous films and shows and produced *Grease* and the Broadway hit *La Cage Aux Folles*. At one stage he decided that he was too fat and had his jaw wired up. Just in case he was offered anything too tempting to eat, however, he carried a pair of wire cutters in his pocket and was known to snip through the wires at the dinner table, having them refixed the following day once he had eaten his fill.

I thought it would be a fun evening and I hadn't seen Michael for quite a while, so I agreed. At this stage there had already been a fair amount of press coverage saying that Michael was barmy. There was talk about his plastic surgery and artificially whitened skin, his affection for a monkey and various other crazy stuff. I had never taken much notice of it, knowing the press often made these things up and that people who were supposed to be completely mad turned out to be perfectly sane when you actually met them.

On arriving at the house I was asked if I would like a tour. A sort of moon-buggy was provided so that I could be driven around the estate which was like one giant fairground and zoo.

I assumed that there would be a number of other guests at the dinner. Indeed, Michael assured us, as he came down to greet us while we were having drinks, that there were.

'Come through,' he said, directing us towards the dining area, 'and meet my friends.'

I could see about a dozen figures already seated around the table, waiting for us to join them. But none of them made any effort to greet us as we came to the table. In fact none of them moved at all.

'Please excuse my friends if they are a bit quiet,' Michael said in his little piping voice, indicating that we should sit down in the only chairs that remained vacant.

The other guests were dummies, all dressed in the height of fashion. For a moment I thought I was being sent up and then Allan winked at me. As the truth dawned on us, both Tony and I started to giggle. The butler, his face a picture of seriousness, requested that we refrain from laughing.

Throughout the meal, which came complete with footmen and silver service, Michael kept up the charade that we were amongst friends. The staff served food to everyone at the table, removing the untouched plates from in front of the others after each course, and filling their glasses with wine. At one stage I thought I might try making conversation with the dummy next to me. I reasoned that it could be a robot and might answer back. I said a few words and the butler leant down to whisper in my ear.

'Please don't talk to the other guests, Sir.'

By the end of the meal I was keen to go. They ordered me a limousine to take me to my hotel and Allan stayed behind. I never found out what happened once I had gone.

When he came to England for one of his big tours, Michael took a floor at the Inter-Continental on Hyde Park Corner, where I had a salon at the time. He asked if I would do his hair before he left for the shows and I was happy to agree. He wanted to be done last thing before leaving and no one except his own people was to be in the salon. Before he arrived, however, I had to do all his doubles. There were half a dozen of them, young men who were used as decoys in order to protect him from the fans, the paparazzi and anyone else who might try to get to him. My job was to make them look as much like Michael as possible, which wasn't hard as they already looked like his clones. Some had travelled with him from the States and some had been recruited in London. All of them worshipped the ground that Michael walked on.

Once they were done the other staff would leave and I would wait alone in the salon until Michael appeared. I would then have to wash and dress his hair without any assistance. Once I had finished I would go up to his suite to check that his hair still looked all right once he was dressed for the show. The limousines waited downstairs to spirit him away to Wembley Stadium.

World-famous eccentrics come in all shapes and sizes. When I had a salon at the Inter-Continental Hotel, a woman came in to have her hair done. We got talking and she asked if I would do her friend's hair.

'He's staying at The Inn on the Park,' she explained. 'He wouldn't be willing to come to a public salon, but would expect you to go to him.'

'Sure,' I said. 'That's not a problem.'

I was used to cutting hair in hotel bedrooms and suites. Sometimes I would even be called to establishments which had their own salons. The clients would go down to the salon to have their hair washed and come back to their rooms for me to do the cut.

That evening I went across the road to The Inn on the Park, one of the most expensive hotels in the world, now known as the Four Seasons Hotel. I gave the name which I had been told to ask for and discovered that my new client had actually booked the whole top two floors of the hotel for himself and his entourage.

I was shown up to the mysterious client's floor. There were a lot of heavy-looking bodyguards loitering in the corridor outside the room where my client was waiting, their jackets bulging with walkie-talkies and, I guess, guns. They asked me if I would mind taking off my shoes and putting empty tissue boxes on my feet.

'Our employer is very concerned about the spread of germs,' they told me.

Inside the suite I found the billionaire recluse, Howard Hughes. He was quite an old man by then and his hair, which was filthy, hung down his back in long, greasy rats' tails. He didn't use my name once and I wasn't sure what to call him. He kept staring at me intently in the mirror, as if waiting for me to say the wrong thing, and the bodyguards kept coming in to see what was happening.

'Do you ever wash your hair with shampoo?' I asked eventually, trying to sound conversational as I worked.

'No,' he seemed shocked at the very idea. 'I just wet it and get one of the maids to towel it.'

His fingernails were as long as a Chinese mandarin's, curling at the ends, as thick as horn. He only wanted me to trim the tips of his hair, which I was happy to do, but he insisted that I use sterilised scissors and combs and change them between each snip. Luckily I had four sets with me. I was worried he might suddenly become angry at what I had cut off and ask them to take me away. As soon as the hair was cut off he had it put into another empty tissue box and I wondered whether he was planning to keep it or burn it.

'I'm surprised you let your hair get into this state when you are so keen on hygiene,' I said.

'Don't be rude!' he snapped.

'Well,' I muttered, 'it needs washing.'

'I'll be gone before this hair is ever washed again.'

I changed my tack. 'Was that your daughter I met at the salon?' I enquired.

'No,' he growled. 'I am not into that kind of thing. When you get to my age you appreciate pretty young women more than ever. Maybe I should send some of my other girls to see you.'

I kept snipping and changing the scissors for a while in silence. I then asked him about the famous flying boat which he had designed which had never taken off.

'I'll be leaving this earth long before that thing ever does,' he replied.

The bodyguards kept coming and going from the room, bringing us anything we needed, walking slowly like astronauts in their tissue boxes. After a few minutes I realised I wanted to go to the bathroom. I asked him to excuse me.

'Sure,' he said. 'I'll get them to bring you some more Kleenex boxes.'

'Why?'

'You could pick up germs in there.'

I clumped my way across the room, trying not to laugh, and, on emerging, found a fresh pair of boxes waiting for me.

I can't say that I was able to make much difference to his scruffy appearance. But he must have been happy because he asked for me again next time he was in town.

In the early Seventies, the designer Barbara Hulanicki created the Biba empire. Her partner and manager was her husband, Stephen Fitz-Simon. Biba was the most extraordinary phenomenon. It started out as a boutique in Kensington Church Street. Within a few years Barbara had expanded it into an entire department store, taking over Derry and Toms in Kensington High Street. I doubt if any designer has ever had such colossal premises all to themselves. In a way it was the precursor of the Ralph Lauren and Calvin Klein stores of today but on a much wilder, wider and more decadent scale. The whole Biba style was typified by Twiggy's Twenties flapper look, and Barry Lategan and I worked hard with Barbara to create her distinctive advertising shots. She always became totally involved in the shots herself, practically taking on the role of hairdresser to get the look exactly as she wanted it. She encouraged me to do just what I wanted and always seemed happy with the results.

Twiggy and Barbara became great friends and Twiggs was allowed free range in the store. Barbara's idea was to continue the same intimate cosy atmosphere she had had in the boutique, but it didn't work out. People came to look and to have fun, but they didn't buy in the quantities needed to cover the huge overheads she had landed herself with. Also with the dim, coloured lighting effects it became a Mecca for shoplifters.

The pace of work was always frantic and eventually the whole business collapsed just as dramatically as it had arisen. It was a lack of business skills which brought it all down, although Barbara also had difficulty adapting her styles to suit developments in public taste. Once she had an idea or a look in her head she absolutely wouldn't change it. She wanted the shows to be the same each year and the public became bored. The final days were very sad, like a gigantic jumble sale, with people stealing everything they could lay their hands on.

Several years later, I met Barbara again in Brazil where she was attempting to do the whole thing again. I was out there working on a

Sunsilk commercial and we had a long, leisurely lunch in the shade of an umbrella in a boulevard café, reminiscing about the days when it seemed as if the 'Biba look' might take over the world. The South American business didn't work out either and, after a brief spell back in London, she and Fitz moved to Miami. Barbara now designs hotel interiors for clients like Chris Blackwell, the head of Island Records.

I was always very bad at giving staff warning when they were going to be asked to do something special. I would agree to do a fashion show for Zandra, Barbara, Ossie Clark, Bill Gibb, or one of the other big names at the time, and completely forget to tell anyone at the salon until a few hours before. This increased the pressure and the buzz around the place.

In the early days, people like Daniel Galvin and John Frieda were always as keen as I was. We would all rush around in a permanent state of last-minute panic trying to get everything done on time for these extravaganzas. Bill Gibb, for instance, a brilliantly romantic designer who died of Aids and is largely forgotten by the public now, took over the Royal Albert Hall one night and had virtually every celebrated beauty in London modelling his extravagant Pre-Raphaelite clothes in aid of a charity. We had to create hairstyles to match the mood of the clothes on the night with virtually no notice at all.

As time passed and my top stylists became more established themselves, they were less willing to drop everything and rush off to do a show. On the other hand, things were becoming more structured and businesslike at the House of Leonard. My financial adviser was a wise chartered accountant, Neville Shulman, who time and again saved my businesses from collapsing through my endless overspending. Neville introduced all kinds of financial and bank controls in an effort to curb my constant drawings of cash, buying of expensive presents for staff and clients and heavy entertainment bills. All were to no avail as I seemed to have a compulsive need to spend and refused to save for a rainy day. It was as if I was insisting on sailing the *Titanic* straight into a giant iceberg. The ship was the House of Leonard and the iceberg was yet another looming liquidation.

I had met Neville through my contacts in the film industry. I liked him immediately and started asking his advice. Pretty soon I was relying on him to handle every deal I was involved with.

I had always been a fan of the seat-of-the-pants sort of

management. I preferred to go out for a long lunch rather than think about plans and systems. Neville was endlessly patient with me and very supportive when everything went wrong and the money finally ran out.

If only I'd listened to him early on I might have put something away for a rainy day. But I thought the money would always keep rolling in and tomorrow would take care of itself. When everything finally came crashing down, Neville was still willing to help out with free advice and support, sometimes even financially, which really proved his friendship and loyalty. He's continued to help out right up to today and if I need to discuss something or just have some letters typed he's always there for me.

As well as experimenting with wigs, Daniel and I were also becoming more and more bold in our uses of different colours. I used to use a lot of coloured wigs for pictures with Barry Lategan, Clive Arrowsmith and others, and there were a few fashionable people who were beginning to want to change their colour regularly. Daniel and I both felt the only way we could get the public to be aware of colour was to shock them with something so outrageous that they would have to sit up and take notice. We wanted women to think, if the professionals can do that for models, what might they do for me?

Daniel was messing around with things like nylon and poster dyes. He would bleach the hair and then apply them. The effects would be very eye-catching, although they weren't all shiny and fluorescent like the colours that were to come later. There was another young colourist at the salon called Harry, who came from the Middle East. His mother used to send over this wonderful henna which Daniel would mix up at the salon. It was much better quality than anything on the general market.

Zandra Rhodes, the fashion designer, was one of the most flamboyant and creative figures around London at the time. She had first come to us because she was having her naturally black hair cut by Vidal's top stylist at the time, Christopher Brooker, and she wanted to bleach it and dye it green. This was when her designs were just starting to get her noticed by the media and the public. Her style would eventually be taken up by the punk movement and she would become a household name for her wild looks and eccentric use of materials and colour. Vidal was creating 'Isadora' green wigs at the time, but no one had ever contemplated actually dyeing their own hair such an out-rageous colour. Zandra found the wigs uncomfortable and, being a textile designer by training, couldn't see why you shouldn't be able to colour hair just like material.

'The colourists here would never agree to do that for you,' Christopher told her. 'The only person who will do that sort of thing is Daniel Galvin at Leonard.'

She went to see Daniel, who was happy to do as she wanted, excited at the prospect of having a client who actually wanted him to experiment. Zandra had clear ideas of the sort of effects she wanted to achieve with her hair, usually to go with some new design concept or other – Red Indian, Japanese, Ukrainian peasant, Mexican, African, Chinese, she tried everything over the years. We would talk for hours about how we would achieve the different looks for her.

I would come up with some suggestions based on her designs and do the cutting. Then we would go to Daniel and his colourists and explain what we wanted. Poor Daniel used to despair at the tasks we set him. One Thursday night, Zandra and I decided that for the climax of her fashion show on the following Saturday night, Selina, a black girl who was going to be modelling a wedding dress, should have a sugar almond pink Afro. But we had to test it first. There was a very camp young black colourist at the salon called Neil who was always game for anything. Daniel persuaded him that it would be great publicity for him if he had hair the same colour as the model at the show. Luckily, Neil agreed and Daniel was able to get to work to create a new colour in record time. The result was stunning.

'What we find ugly today will be beautiful tomorrow,' Zandra told us. 'I'm tired of good taste. I want to do everything wrong.

'Have you ever thought of using the dyes that I use for my silk prints?' she asked. Daniel confessed he hadn't and she sent some samples over for him. The colours completely knocked us out. They were so different and so vibrant. We got in touch with the chemist who was formulating products for us, to find a way of turning the dyes from the fine powders which Zandra used for her silks to some sort of emulsifying wax. This would be easier to handle and would not end up flying all round the place and staining the salon floor. We also didn't want to poison our clients with anything toxic.

Zandra and I kept bumping into one another at *Vogue* fashion

On Top of the World (Mont Blanc in the background)

OVERLEAF: Some simple and elaborate hairstyles

LEFT HAND PAGE: *Top left*: Twiggy. *Top right*: Ingrid Boulting.
Bottom left: Sarah Miles and son, Ben. *Bottom right*: Maudie James.
RIGHT HAND PAGE: *Top left*: Louise Nordell. *Top right*: Jean Shrimpton.
Bottom left: Twiggy. *Bottom right*: A *Vogue* shoot in the Pre–Raphaelite mode

On one of Dodi Fayed's yachts.
Dodi took the picture

With Petra and Greta Morrison
in India

Top left: Marella
Oppenheim with
Peter Morton and
one of his girlfriends
in the Bahamas

Top right: *Mutiny on
the Bounty*. On location
with Anthony Hopkins
(centre), Mel Gibson
(left) and Daniel Day
Lewis (right)

Centre: My one-
second 'starring' role
as a hairdresser in
Stanley Kubrick's
Barry Lyndon

Bottom left: With Anna
Roberts in Kenya.

Bottom right:
Loadsamoney, which
you needed at the
Colombe d'Or in St
Paul de Vence

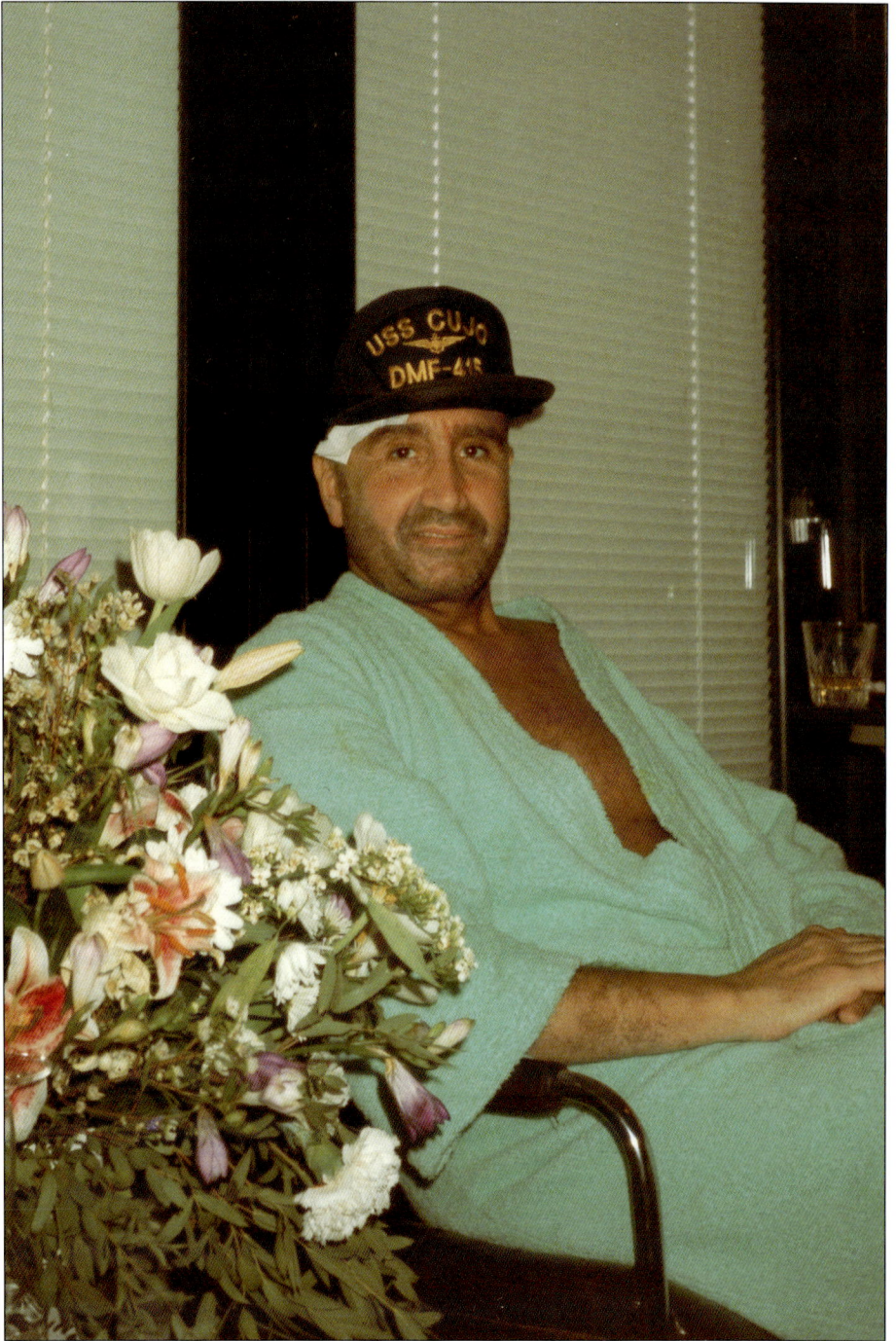

After my operation for a brain tumour.
Photograph, flowers and baseball hat courtesy of Dodi Fayed

With Michael Rasser, Nicky Clarke and John Frieda at the Hairdressers' Benevolent Ball given in my honour

With Vidal Sassoon

The old Mayfair salon

shoots and parties, as well as at the salon. I loved the colourful, romantic way in which she was using materials in her designs. It seemed a very similar approach to my ideas for hair. It wasn't long before we were working together on her shows. We also created some stunning posters for her work, featuring actresses like Anjelica Huston and Marisa Berenson. Last time I saw Zandra she had bright pink hair.

I used to become so excited by the drama and glamour of fashion shows that I preferred to be out the front. I would be watching the action on the catwalk, when I should really have been behind the scenes checking the details of each model's hair before she emerged into the lights. Zandra was always very sweet to me, but I think this began to annoy her. In the end she started using people whom I had trained, for the actual show work.

All through the Sixties the promotional pictures for hairstyles, including Vidal's, had been in black and white. Most hairdressers were happy with this because it was the cut and the shape that they were primarily interested in. I wanted to move forward and show people just what beautiful effects were possible with colour. In 1967 Daniel and I decided to launch 'Crazy Colours'. We went to see Felicity Clarke, the Beauty Editor at *Vogue* who used my services a lot. We also discussed the possibilities with photographers like Barry Lategan and Clive Arrowsmith and with Barbara Daly who was just coming to the fore as an exciting new make-up artist with some wild concepts.

They all loved the idea and we set it up as a photo-shoot for *Vogue*. We couldn't believe our luck. We were actually going to be able to launch our new product, free of charge, in the most prestigious fashion magazine on earth. The resulting pictures were so dramatic that they appeared in English, Italian and American *Vogue*. There was no one in the fashion world now who hadn't heard about the House of Leonard and the exciting work that was going on there. The *Vogue* pictures were a sensation and are now collectors' items. I made sure that even if the pictures were eventually printed in black and white, Daniel would still get a credit for the colouring and highlights. His work was crucial to the overall effect.

We never actually expected the public to wear the colours we were creating for the magazines. It was like the haute couture clothes that appear on the catwalks in Paris and Milan. Only the very rich and fashion-conscious would ever wear that stuff, and then only to film premieres or parties. But the ideas filter down to the shops in more practical, less outrageous forms. It may take a few years before the woman in the street is wearing anything that even resembles what is photographed on the catwalks.

We expected the same to happen with the colours but an Italian company based in London, called Rembow, actually launched Crazy Colours on the retail market. To celebrate the launch, on Guy Fawkes night, Barry Lategan took a picture of model Patricia Roberts' head, in all the different colours, with a lit sparkler on the top. Another classic image had been born, but I never predicted the punk explosion.

Zandra Rhodes had a rather more sophisticated approach to fashion shock, and a trickle of other strong-minded women were starting to come through the doors of Upper Grosvenor Street with ideas of their own. Janet Street-Porter, a friend of Zandra's who was then making a reputation for herself as the outrageous fashion editor of *Petticoat* magazine, was one of the first to explore the possibilities. She was immensely tall and we had to ask her to sit on the floor of the salon so that we could work on the top of her head. I decided to cut the top of her hair into a star shape, which Daniel then dyed blue.

People like Zandra and Janet set a style which the whole world would be following ten years later. But it took a lot of courage for those first pioneers to walk out into the street looking like nothing anyone had ever seen before.

Not many of my customers were brave enough to be so radical. Sometimes they might be willing to allow us to do something very subtle for them. If, for instance, I was cutting a perfect bob for someone, they might agree to have a tiny feather cut into it, the top half of it coloured to their birth-sign and the bottom half to their partner's birth-sign. The result would look like the tiniest fly-fishing feather caught in the hair.

We actually started to use real dyed feathers in some of the shots for the magazines, working them into the hair itself – something which I have noticed certain hairdressers have started doing again. It was all connected to Zandra's 'Red Indian' period.

To get feathers of exactly the right colours, I went to see a lady called Mrs Rule just off Soho Square. She supplied feathers to film companies, but her main business was to supply all the decorations that the Soho strippers used for their costumes. Her shop was on the first floor and there were always hookers around the entrance and on the stairs, hoping for business. Mrs Rule was an older woman who seemed quite at home amongst the girls. She wanted to introduce some of the strippers to us for hairstyling but I balked at that: I didn't want us to gain a reputation as that sort of Mayfair salon. Instead I gave her hair pieces and hairdressing tips.

Once Crazy Colours had been launched on the general market we moved on to using henna seriously for the first time since the turn of the century. If you are working amongst the most fashionable and creative people in the world you have to stay one step ahead of your competition. By now about thirty per cent of our customers were having colouring done as well as cutting, and we were moving towards our goal of a hundred per cent. Ten years later every punk in the King's Road had his or her hair done in the most outrageous colours possible.

When kids first started to wear the spiky punk hairstyles they used to make them stand up stiffly with sugared water, like candyfloss. It worked well but the problem was that when the sugar dried it attracted all the flies and bees, which we didn't want in the salon. We had to think of a better way to achieve the same effect. That was when we started to experiment with the various gels which are now so popular in the general market.

In the late Seventies Zandra was asked to be 'Queen of the Punks', which involved travelling down the King's Road on a carnival float. She loved the idea and asked me to go with her. I didn't think it was quite my scene.

Nagels was busy with Twiggy's career, and with his own new career. Just as he had decided to make himself a hairdresser with no real vocation, he now decided to become a photographer. There wasn't anything that Nagels couldn't do if he wanted to. He simply told people that he was now a photographer and no one thought to question it. He took to photography like a duck to water and his work was surprisingly good. He was even getting covers for *Vogue, Harpers* and *Queen,* mainly with pictures of Twiggy but also of stars like Raquel Welch and David Bowie.

I first met Bowie when Nagels was photographing him with Twiggy for *Vogue.* Both Nagels and I had strong ideas on what we wanted to achieve, and Bowie was very happy to go along with every-thing we suggested, just like a model. He was so pleased with the results that he used the picture for the cover of his album, *Pin-Ups*.

Everything was changing in London. The hippy musical, *Hair,* had opened to great controversy in the West End because of its explicit treatment of drugs and nudity. Marsha Hunt was adding to the notoriety of the show by having an affair with Mick Jagger and bearing him his daughter, Karis. Elaine Paige, who later became a star in Andrew Lloyd-Webber and Tim Rice musicals like *Evita*, also started her career on the stage in *Hair*. The whole idea of expressing yourself and doing something different with your hair was being talked about everywhere.

After the Beatles' breakthrough into America, Twiggy followed and became an international star. I travelled with her and Nagels to New York and watched as he arranged ticker-tape processions down Wall Street and stirred up mass hysteria on the same scale as Beatle-mania. We did hairdressing demonstrations on national television shows and to packed crowds in massive stadiums. Swinging London had been born in the eyes of the world. Now it wasn't just me on a roll, Nagels was going too, and the three of us became a team. Whenever Twiggy was being photographed Nagels was there and I was doing the hair.

On one trip Twiggy was given a live baby duck as a present and took it with her everywhere. One terrible day one of the huge minders employed to protect her sat down without looking and squashed the duck. Twiggy was devastated and to this day still can't eat duck. After that, Nagels decided she needed her own bodyguard and asked Teddy the Monk, who had a flower stall outside Harrods, to come as our minder. It all added to the illusion that we were something very important indeed, and the media believed us.

Nagels was in seventh heaven, socialising with people like Fred Astaire in Hollywood and Noël Coward in Jamaica. Twiggy was amongst the most famous people on the planet and he was milking it for every bit of fun he could.

Telling Deirdre McSharry they were making £100 a week had turned out to be an understatement. Nagels was now into the Rolls-Royces and Lamborghinis (at least three), and was looking around for ways to increase their earnings.

Before Michael Chow started the Mr Chow restaurant in Knightsbridge with his second wife Tina, he was married to a hairdresser. He had created a salon for her in Sloane Avenue, very state-of-the-art, with under-floor lighting. Nagels took a liking to it and, hearing that Michael was separating from his wife, took it over, without really having any idea what to do with it.

'Why don't we call it Leonard and Twiggy?' he suggested to me over lunch one day.

I had been wanting to have another salon nearer Knightsbridge, and so I agreed. It was my first venture outside Upper Grosvenor Street. The idea of opening branches all over the place was already working for Vidal, and it seemed logical that I should do the same. But where would I find the time actually to be there? There were so many things I wanted to do. Having been to New York I now wanted to open a salon there so that I could service my regular clients on both sides of the Atlantic, rather than make them come all the way over to London. I also wanted to open in Los Angeles so that I could be there for the stars when they were working at the studios. I wanted to launch my products to a wider audience and do more work in magazines to promote my ideas. I wanted everything and I wanted it immediately, no matter what the cost.

Even if I had opened in Los Angeles, I doubt if I would have spent much time there myself. It is not a city I have ever felt quite comfortable in.

Once, when I was staying at the Beverly Wilshire Hotel, the actress Sharon Tate heard that I was in town and rang to ask if I would do her hair. I had known Sharon for some time. She had often come to the salon in London and we had done some photographs with Barry Lategan. I had also met her with her husband, Roman Polanski, whom I wasn't too keen on. I agreed to go out to her house in the Hollywood Hills to see her.

Sharon was always very glamorous in a rather false, Hollywood way, and I liked her. I hadn't realised she was pregnant until I saw her that day. She was very bubbly and full of life.

'Do you like LA?' she asked as I worked on her hair.

'No,' I said.

'Nor me.' She gave a little shiver. 'I'm sure I'm going to be killed here some day.'

We chatted on, as hairdressers and clients do, and she told me they were having a party at the house that evening. 'Will you come, Leonard?' she asked.

'Sure,' I said.

But when I got back to the hotel I went off the idea. For some reason I just didn't fancy going back to the house. I rang to make my excuses.

'Oh, Leonard.' She sounded so disappointed. 'Please come, we'll have such a great time.'

For a second I wavered, but I really didn't feel like it. I have always been quite shy and I find parties full of people I don't know difficult. Instead, I spent the evening at the Jockey Club and then went back to my hotel to sleep.

The next morning the television informed me that Sharon and some of her guests had been brutally murdered. It was the night Charles Manson and his gang came to call. I have never in my life been so glad to have missed a party.

CHAPTER TEN

DANIEL GALVIN HAD become an indispensable part of the business, not only because of the reputation he had created for the colouring department, but also because I knew I could trust him in every aspect of my life. Each night he used to convey the day's takings to my house in Little Chester Street. At that stage we were making an enormous amount of money, much of it in cash. The idea of credit and charge cards was very new and the concept of a cashless society was still something from the world of science fiction.

I was usually still working or socialising when Daniel turned up at the house and so he would have to deal with Ricci. She was merciless. If the money was short by even a few pence she would call him to account for it. Sometimes he would make up the difference out of his own pocket rather than get into an argument.

Daniel often got me out of mundane difficulties as well. At one stage I was driving a Porsche which, if I wanted to take a bunch of people to the country for the weekend, was completely impractical. So I used to persuade Daniel to let me have his Rolls in exchange. He would grumble that there was nowhere in my car to put his kids' fold-away pushchairs, and that our Afghan Zorro's claws scratched his leather upholstery, but he would let me borrow it nonetheless.

I was very proud of all my staff at that time, because I knew they were the best in the world. We were all so obsessed with our work we would talk of little else when we were together, which was most of the time. We would meet for breakfasts in an Italian restaurant around the corner from the salon most mornings to discuss what we were going to do that day. We would often still be together in the evenings, chatting about ideas and plans and exchanging our experiences of the day.

It was only later that I realised that some stylists were resenting my total dedication to the salon and my assumption that they felt the same. They wanted to spend less time in Leonard's and more time with their friends and families. They started meeting in secret, planning to move away and start up rival salons. But to me it was like one long, non-stop party. A golden period. We were young, ambitious, successful and feeling very rich. I always made sure that all the staff did well from commission and tips. I wanted to ensure that they were rewarded fairly for their hard work and I thought they would therefore be happy to stay with me.

It is the same in most successful salons. Hairdressers generally love their work and enjoy the company of their colleagues. The long hours mean that they often don't have time for much social life outside their salon. A fair number of partnerships and marriages were hatched in the House of Leonard over the years.

I had heard that Michael Rasser wanted to be made a partner in the business, but I didn't feel ready to take on another partner after my experiences with Raphael. When Michael and John Isaacs, another stylist at the salon, asked me and Daniel to join them for a working breakfast at The Inn on the Park one morning, I thought there must be something up. John's was one of the first marriages within the House of Leonard when he married Susan, a junior who was becoming a fully fledged hairdresser.

The news they had to break over breakfast was worse than I had expected. Not only were Michael and John planning to leave and set up on their own – something which I guess was inevitable – they were going to take with them nine of my best staff, including the chief receptionist, one of Daniel's best colourists and the top manicurist.

When stylists join a salon they have to sign an agreement which says that if they leave they will not start up a rival business within a mile's radius of the salon they are leaving for a certain number of years. In reality it is an almost unenforceable condition and would also be pretty unfair. All the best London salons are within a few miles of one another and to stop newcomers setting up within the area would virtually stop them from going into business on their own. I never felt able to insist that they stuck to their agreements.

We were a huge business by then, employing around seventy people. It was inevitable that some of them would branch out on their own, but I felt John and Michael should not take so many of my other staff with them. Never mind, it was done, and we remained on good terms. But it was the end of the first golden age of the House of

Leonard. It showed that we had become a mature business and now there would be other, newer salons snapping at our heels.

Soon after Michael set up in business, Princess Anne started going there, and asked him to do her hair for her wedding to Captain Mark Phillips. That one event put the MichaelJohn salon well and truly on the map. The Duchess of York became a client and Tony Blair went to them when he first became known in politics, triggering a lot of talk in the media about 'the Blair cut'. They opened another salon in Beverly Hills and continue to flourish today, with their own range of products. They have managed their success well and built on it. John and Susan have since left the business and run a coffee shop in St John's Wood.

It was hard, when things were going so well and clients were constantly demanding that I go to them or see them after hours, to spend as much time as I should have with Ricci and Dominic. Marriages need constant care and attention, as much as work.

Dominic was growing up and had become a prep school boy. Ricci put him into Hill House, a school where the young Prince Charles went for a while. The Hill House pupils are a well-known sight around Belgravia and Chelsea, walking crocodile-style from one building to another in their brown corduroy breeches and mustard-coloured jumpers. It was a little bit of traditional London, like red telephone boxes, black cabs and policemen in helmets.

When I was around at home, Dominic and I got on well. I bought him a go-cart, which he was really only meant to use in Gloucester-shire, where we had bought a weekend house called Paradise Farm in the village of Kempsford. For a while the cart was kept in the garage in London. One day Dominic disappeared from the house. We searched everywhere, getting more and more worried. We rang his friends, the hospital, but he had vanished into thin air. Eventually he was discovered by the local police using Belgrave Square as a racing track. Once we got the go-cart to the country we used to attend go-cart meetings and races together.

I tried to get to Kempsford at weekends but I would nearly always be working on Saturdays, when many of the stars liked to come because they were not at the film studios. I would then have to dash to the country in the evenings and return the following night. Ricci and Dominic spent more time there and I know Dominic loved it. It had several acres of garden, including a lake.

We put a lot of effort into restoring the house to its original glory. We decked the bedrooms out in Colefax and Fowler fabrics and made it the sort of house that all our friends would want to come to for relaxing country weekends. It had been my dream, when I was living in the concrete jungle of White City and glimpsing the flowers at Covent Garden Market, one day to live in the heart of the countryside. But I always found it hard to adapt to the slow, rural pace of life.

While I remained a city boy at heart, it was pleasant to have somewhere completely different to go to, where we could entertain the people we really cared about, as well as people who were good for the business. We would nearly always stock up in London before driving down, arriving with the car stuffed with haunches of lamb and panniers of strawberries and raspberries. At that time we used to shop for groceries in Fortnum and Mason, the legendary store in Piccadilly, because I cut the owner's hair, Galen Weston. I also used to use it as a place to meet friends like Terence Stamp and Michael Caine. Terence always loved to take tea in the restaurant because he had a flat in the exclusive Albany opposite.

Gloucestershire was an area that Ricci knew well from her past and was comfortable in. We would often have people down for dinner and to stay and we were all looked after by Jean and Rose and George the gardener. I can't imagine what they made of us as we swept in and out of their lives.

I'm sure I must have taken Ricci for granted in those days. She was a marvellous hostess, happy to entertain my ever-expanding social circle. No guest's glass ever stood empty for long in our houses. She loved the social whirl as much as I did and was right at the centre of it. It was she who introduced Prince Andrew to Koo Stark, the photographer who became his girlfriend for a short and highly publicised period.

Although I was surrounded by beautiful women from the moment I arrived at work in the morning to the moment I went to bed at night, it never occurred to me to be unfaithful to Ricci. However she was becoming more and more discontented and was starting to lead her own life. She was being seen with a number of different men, some of them mutual friends and most a lot younger than she was. I guess it was her way of trying to hang on to her youth and beauty.

Although I knew that not all my friends were too fond of her, I was very happy with the marriage and assumed she was too. I didn't want to do anything to disrupt it. I realised that I was not the easiest man to be married to, being as wrapped up in my work as I was, but then she wasn't an easy woman either. We had a lot of rows, but what married couple doesn't?

Dominic had left Hill House and gone to Harrow when I discovered that Ricci was having an affair with a handsome but much younger man called Charlie Young. He was an old school friend of Prince Andrew's.

By that time Ricci had started to travel a lot on her own, disappearing off to Cannes for the film festival, or St Tropez for 'a few days' break'. I was always so busy I didn't stop to think what was actually happening during these trips. She had always been fond of young men and often brought them back to London, convincing me that they were just good friends, even bringing them into the salon for free haircuts. We started to have more and more fights about stupid little things, but it was money and who was spending the most that caused the most aggro.

I was determined to make an effort to patch things up and, in my usual way, decided to throw money at the problem by buying Ricci a very special present for her birthday. There was a gold and diamond necklace at Cartier which I knew she particularly wanted and I decided to buy it for her as a surprise. I phoned to make an appointment and discovered that she had been in with one of her young men and had already bought the piece. I was devastated. We were having a party that night and I know it was all very uncomfortable for the guests, with neither of us speaking to the other.

I hired a private detective to find out exactly what was going on and was horrified by the evidence he brought to me. I tried for a while to keep the marriage together but it soon became obvious that Ricci and I now wanted very different things.

I had always wondered if she was ever completely honest with me. Soon after we were married I met her former husband. He looked surprised when I addressed him as 'Count' and I explained that Ricci had told me he had a title. He assured me that not only did he not have a title, there weren't any to be had in his home region in Switzerland anyway. I had found these sorts of deception quite harmless at the time, even oddly charming in a way, but things were now entering a new, much darker phase.

I could see that I exasperated Ricci just as much as she exasperated me. She didn't like my closest circle of friends, thinking we were all a bunch of working-class louts. (There were times, of course, when she had a point.) There was a group of us who used to socialise regularly and in the late Seventies, the artist Peter Blake and Nagels formalised the arrangement by calling us 'the Percy Boys'.

Peter first came to the public's attention in 1961 when Ken Russell made a documentary for *Omnibus* called 'Pop Goes the Easel', which featured him and several other young artists. The *Sunday Times*, which was launching its colour supplement, then wrote an article about him and he was away. I bought a set of prints off him called 'Wrestlers' and hung them on the walls of my gym in South Audley Street.

An association with the Beatles led to his designing the famous cover for their 1967 album, *Sergeant Pepper's Lonely Hearts Club Band*, in which he lined up lots of famous faces, many of them waxworks from Madame Tussaud. In fact, it was at a party in Madame Tussaud that he met Nagels and Twiggy. They were celebrating the opening of a new section, containing the first animated waxworks, which Peter had been involved in setting up.

Peter came up with the idea of calling us the Percy Boys' Club, after an amateur boxing club in the East End which had produced a number of great fighters. The main objective of our club was to get completely plastered in restaurants where we wouldn't be asked to pay the bill. It was a sort of early version of laddism, involving a lot of drinking and shouting and improbable story-tellings.

To be a member you had to have a working-class London background, to have done well, and to be fond of your food and drink. The core membership included me, Nagels, Peter and David Essex, who had made his name in *Godspell* in the West End and become a teen idol. A number of others then joined in, including Kenny Jones (from The Who and Small Faces), Gary Glitter, Brian Aris the photographer, Tommy Roberts the founder of the Mr Freedom shops, Mikey Stevenson the assistant film director who was to become one of my very best friends, Ian Dury, Pete Townshend and Peter Langan the restaurateur.

Langan wasn't strictly speaking from London but he and Michael

Caine owned Langan's, one of the smartest restaurants in Mayfair, which we all liked to go to because he hardly ever remembered to give us a bill. He could also out-drink the lot of us. He later died tragically by accidentally setting light to himself in a drunken rage.

There was one night when Langan was with us and he had imbibed particularly heavily of some South American fire water. The following day Richard Shepherd, the other partner at Langan's, rang me at the salon and asked me to go over to the restaurant.

'I'm very busy, Richard,' I said, aware that I already had several clients waiting.

'I really think you ought to see this,' he said.

I dashed over to the restaurant and Richard was waiting for me. He took me through to the kitchens without a word and pointed to the giant ovens. One of the doors was standing open and Langan was curled up inside, peacefully sleeping off his hangover.

When Langan was drunk he could make himself extremely objectionable to women. I never wanted to take a date to Langan's because I knew that he would lurch over and start making embarrassing remarks about her anatomy. I remember at one Percy Boys' dinner in Mr Chow's, where Peter Blake had almost unlimited credit because he had provided artwork for the walls, Jacqueline Bisset, who was a big film star at the time and a client of the salon, came over to the table to say hello. As I was talking to her Langan leaned across.

'I've always admired you,' he slurred at her. 'I think you're wonderful.'

We all waited with bated breath for what might come next.

'In fact,' he went on, 'I think the sun shines out of your arse.'

Jacqueline gave a frosty smile and asked one of the waiters to bring the sweet trolley over, as if attempting to change the subject. When it arrived she picked out a very creamy cake and smacked it neatly down his trousers. We were all deeply impressed.

Jacqueline featured on another of our nights as well. We were all at Langan's when Peter Blake spotted her sitting at the other end of the room and confessed that he fancied her something rotten. Nagels and I thought we should effect an introduction and so we loaded Peter on to the cheese trolley and wheeled him the length of the restaurant to present him formally to the star. We then left him to talk to her and he returned to the table half an hour later, glowing with satisfaction and wondering why we were all creased up with laughter. Once he had sat back down we owned up that when we had reached the table with the trolley we had realised that it wasn't Jacqueline at all.

On another occasion in Langan's a small dog at a neighbouring table kept yapping at us. Langan, who had sat down with us, eventually couldn't stand it any longer, and he fell on to his knees and bit the dog, which then disappeared under its owner's chair, whimpering pitifully.

Despite the fact that he ran one of the most famous restaurants in London, Langan was forever telling customers that he couldn't understand why they ate there because the food was so appalling. He sometimes used to order in takeaways for himself rather than eat from the kitchens. He had a favourite Greek restaurant called Rodos, underneath Centre Point, which only opened at ten o'clock at night and was always full of hookers, doormen, taxi drivers and villains. Langan loved to go up there and spend the night eating their houmus and kleftiko with piles of chips, and drinking.

We invented a call-sign, a sort of two-note yodel, which we could make to one another so that one Percy Boy would always recognise another. When David Essex was appearing in a rather serious play at the Old Vic, we all went along to watch. As he appeared on stage, and the audience fell silent, I let out the yodel, just so that he would know we were there to support him. To his eternal credit he managed to keep going without so much as a flicker of surprise.

The Percy Boys were all men who liked nothing better than to spend time in one another's company telling and listening to stories, eating a lot of good food and consuming a great deal of drink. No doubt it made us very boring to everyone else around.

It certainly helped to put an end to my marriage. I moved out and rented a house in nearby Chester Row, which was close enough for Dominic to come round to visit me whenever he felt like it, which seemed to be quite often.

Just after Ricci and I had split up, Bob Marley came in to have his dreadlocks sorted out. Dreadlocks are a bit of a nightmare for hairdressers. They are basically very tight plaits which take a long time to create and even longer to take out. One of the main reasons people have them is to save time on washing their hair, just giving them a wipe over with a damp cloth every now and again. They then leave them in for weeks or even months until the hair has virtually matted together. Marley used to come into the salon to have his undone and his hair washed and trimmed and then to have the plaits redone. I would always need to set aside a whole day for the job.

He was the most delightful man, and very easy to confide in. He was one of the first people in the public eye to smoke dope openly. I was always a little nervous that the police would come storming in and search him while he was on the premises, earning us the sort of reputation that might frighten away our more conservative clients.

That day he must have got me talking about my troubles during the hours that I was working on his hair. A couple of days later, I was at a friend's house for a party. The radio was on because Bob was being interviewed and they were playing his music. I was shocked to hear him say, 'I want to dedicate this next tune to a friend of mine in London called Leonard, who always looks after me so well and who's feeling a little down today. This is for you, Len, listen to the lyrics, man.' He then played 'No Woman No Cry', which was all about how much better off a man was without a woman.

Ricci and I had bought both our house in Little Chester Street and Paradise Farm in Kempsford, and now I was renting the house in Chester Row from my friend Tony Cloughly, the fashionable interior decorator. I had to consider my outgoings at Upper Grosvenor Street with the rent and massive staff costs. Then there were the restaurant bills which I had got into the habit of footing for everyone, and the clothes bills which both Ricci and I ran up everywhere. I also had to pay Dominic's school fees at Harrow and the general running costs of our extravagant lifestyles.

The money was flowing out in every direction, completely out of control. But then it was pouring in at an equally extraordinary rate, as far as I could see. I worked constantly and there were clients queuing to come to the salon. I was surrounded by people telling me I was the greatest hairdresser in the world and I could see no reason why I should make any adjustments to my lifestyle.

When I was away from work I was living amongst my clients, many of whom were either films stars or had enormous inherited wealth. They were relaxed about spending money because they knew that they had plenty of it. I thought I had plenty of it too, but it was an illusion. I had a high cash-flow, but no reserves to fall back on.

The lifestyle we led seemed normal to me, but it was far from normal. I should have known better, coming as I did from a simple background. I guess, in many ways, I had lost touch with reality. But at that time, it didn't seem to matter. I lived for the day and the days were very good indeed.

I had no wish to argue about money with Ricci when we divorced. I never wanted to argue about money with anyone. I preferred to ignore it and hope it would sort itself out. I was as careless about signing the divorce papers as I was about signing the bills at San Lorenzo or Mr Chow's. Ricci got everything. She even got an allowance for food for Zorro, Dominic's beloved Afghan hound. Still, I was hardly going to starve, not when I could keep on signing the restaurant bills.

Dominic seemed to be enjoying Harrow. Coming from an ordinary background, I was not in a position to know much about our grander public schools. I knew the Niarchos family and they had been there, and I had met the headmaster once on the set of *Young Winston*, and that had given me enough confidence in the school to send Dominic there. I think initially he got a bit of teasing about having a hairdresser for a father, but once the other boys went home and told their parents, it was explained to them that Leonard of Mayfair was no ordinary hairdressing salon.

I suppose in many ways I was in the perfect position for a newly divorced man. I knew many of the most beautiful and wealthy women in the world. Not only did they come to the salon, but they were always at the parties, clubs and restaurants which I attended. Models, actresses and heiresses were everywhere.

There was a group of them I saw a great deal of, which included socialites like Sir James Goldsmith's nieces, Dido and Clio, and Rachel Ward. Rachel was a particularly beautiful, aristocratic girl who starred in *The Thorn Birds*, an incredibly popular television series based on a best-selling book of the same name, set in the outback of Australia. During the long nights we spent in places like Annabel's and Tramp I found myself drawn more and more to this leggy brunette with her enormous brown eyes and devastating smile. Rachel was like every man's fantasy of a high-born actress. Dancing and drinking with her soon led to a passionate fling. But her career was just taking off and she was about to star in *The Thorn Birds*. Down Under, she met and married the Australian actor, Bryan Brown.

During my relationship with Rachel, I got to visit some of her family members. She had uncles who were Earls and God knows what else. By then I was already very comfortable weekending in the stately homes of England. I loved spending my time in houses that were full of Old Masters and beautiful furniture.

Once my marriage was over, I had several affairs with high-profile women which would have made excellent fodder for the gossip columnists. There was Georgiana Russell, the daughter of Sir John Russell, the British ambassador to Spain, who had an affair with Richard Compton Miller at about the same time. She later went out with Prince Charles and Richard ended up being featured in his own William Hickey column when one of his colleagues rang Richard's mother, Lady Compton Miller, to ask how he felt about being upstaged by the heir to the throne. Then there was meat baron Lord Vestey's wife, Kate. The Vesteys owned all the Dewhurst butchers' shops.

Kate had a flat in Egerton Crescent in Knightsbridge, next door to David Frost, who was a regular customer at the salon, having his hair blow-dried and waved virtually every day before going into the studios or heading for the airport. He complained to me one day that Kate and I were keeping him awake at night with the noise of our love-making. I suspect he was just teasing me, but Kate was always very demonstrative and from then on whenever we made love I couldn't help visualising David listening on the other side of the wall.

I had a brief dalliance with a model and ski instructor called Ivana. She was a stunning-looking girl but had the heaviest Yugoslav accent, which made it almost impossible to make head or tail of what she was saying half the time. When I did start to understand her I realised that she actually had only one topic of conversation – herself. Ivana was determined to be a huge success in the world and believed that the way to do it was to meet and marry a wealthy man. She was completely single-minded in her campaign. In clubs and restaurants she would keep asking who this man was and who that man was. What did they do? How much were they worth?

Our relationship was very short-lived and in 1977 I heard that she had married a young property millionaire in New York called Donald Trump. Over the following decade the pair of them became some-

thing of a legend in the city as his deals became bigger and bigger and
Ivana grew more and more beautiful, with the occasional help of
plastic surgeons. Donald was another one who fancied the idea of
running for President.

She told me that she went into modelling simply because she knew
that it was a way in which she could meet rich and powerful men.
Many of the models I knew ended up, either by luck or design,
married to great fortunes. These days, of course, they can become
wealthy in their own right.

The Miss World competition was another opportunity I couldn't
resist. Eric and Julia Morley, who organised the event, asked me if I
would judge it, two years in a row. I knew them because all the
contestants came to my salon to have their hair done. The Morleys
had strict rules about who was allowed to go near the girls socially. But
for some reason, when one or two of the young women asked if they
could be escorted round town, Julia said it would be all right as long
as I was their escort. I couldn't believe my luck, and nor could any of
my friends when I turned up at Tramp with the girls. It happened both
years, and both times the evenings out led back to the Grosvenor
House Hotel. Very convenient indeed.

The hotel was closely guarded and I couldn't just waltz up to the
girls' rooms without the door staff immediately getting on the phone
to Julia. So I would drop them at the door and make an elaborate show
of saying goodnight. I would then make my way round to the service
entrance, where I could always find someone on the staff whom I
knew, and I would be smuggled up to their rooms in the service lifts.

I think I must have given people the impression of being a harmless
sort of a chap, perhaps even a little asexual in my vagueness, someone
to whom they would entrust their daughters and charges.

One of the girls in the social group that I saw a lot of was Marella
Oppenheim. She was from a wealthy banking family based mainly in
Paris and was very well connected. Her godfather was Sir Marcus
Sieff, Chairman of Marks and Spencer. She was moving around the
London social scene with girls like Rachel Ward and Clio Goldsmith.

Marella was small, dark and very pretty, a bit like a younger version
of *Gigi* star, Lesley Caron, with a face like a Siamese kitten. I fell
deeply in love.

I wanted desperately to impress her. One day, she told me that she had been searching for years for a book called *Tales of Beelzebub* by Gurdjieff. She could have said *Tales of Peter Rabbit* by Beatrix Potter for all I knew the difference, but I immediately rang Heywood-Hill, a book dealer in Curzon Street I had an account with. Miraculously they managed to find me a copy. I sent it round to her by hand and I think it did the trick.

Once I met her I became a one-woman man once more. In fact Richard Compton Miller nicknamed us 'the Bunnies' because he complained that we were always at it, which made us late for everything. I think he may have been exaggerating. I was always late for everything anyway, regardless of whether I was in bed with Marella or not.

Marella's French mother seemed to be as horrified that their daughter was going out with an older hairdresser as Ricci had been to find herself going out with a younger one. Alas, I have never been the sort of man that women relish having as a potential or actual son-in-law. Her father however, Charles Oppenheim, was always very pleasant to me. Although they spent most of their time living in Paris, they also had a house in Mayfair, decorated in a lavish 'Jewish Renaissance' style, like a sort of mini Versailles of chandeliers and gilt.

Marella was very demanding and I did everything she asked of me. When she said she wanted to be a journalist, I rang Richard Compton Miller, who was then running the William Hickey column in the *Daily Express*, and he arranged a job on *Tatler*. She gave it up quite quickly when she realised it would mean she would have to get out of bed in the mornings. When she decided she wanted to be an actress, I introduced her to my good friend, Mikey Stevenson, who was assistant director on all Kubrick's films and knows everyone in the business. When she said she wanted to model I put her in touch with photographers I knew like Clive Arrowsmith and Barry Lategan. They were all the best contacts in each field but none of it really worked for her. I think probably she was just not hungry enough to put in the necessary effort to succeed at these difficult careers.

I always loved putting friends in touch with one another. I enjoy people more than anything else in life and to be able to help someone out by introducing them to someone else is the greatest of satisfactions. I spent half my life on the phone fixing up parties and meetings, making introductions and assisting people's paths through London society.

So many famous people met through the salon. Lady Londonderry was in for a cut when she met pop star, Georgie Fame. She had just had her hair done and was looking absolutely gorgeous when he spotted her as he came out of the VIP room. She was equally smitten with him. They started a notorious affair, although Georgie continued to play the field. Jimi Hendrix's girlfriend, Kathy Etchingham, tells a story of how she was in bed with Georgie one night when Nicolette came banging on the front door. Kathy had to remain hidden in the bedroom while their rowing went on downstairs.

When Nicolette became pregnant, Lord Londonderry assumed the baby was his first-born son and the child duly became the Earl of Castlereagh. Georgie and Nicolette's affair continued and her marriage eventually broke up. It was later proved that Castlereagh couldn't possibly be Londonderry's son and he lost his title to his half-brother. Many years later Nicolette tragically ended her life by jumping off the Clifton Suspension Bridge in Bristol.

These sorts of high society intrigues were going on all the time across London and, since most of high society regularly passed through our doors in Upper Grosvenor Street, much of it was bound to take place there.

Ricci was furious when she heard I was seeing someone new. She might not have wanted me for herself any more, but she was damned if anyone else was going to have me. One weekend Marella and I were at Paradise Farm having lunch with a few friends, including Richard Compton Miller and Clive Arrowsmith.

Richard and Nigel Dempster on the *Daily Mail* were the two main gossip columnists at the time, but both had given up trying to prise information out of me about my clients and acquaintances. Richard was to become one of my closest friends and often had the agonising experience of coming across some really worthwhile story while we were together and not being able to use it because of our friendship.

Clive, who was completely mad, had also become one of my best friends. He was living the Swinging London dream up to the hilt. I think I was best man at five of his weddings, but it may just have been four – it was certainly a lot. I know he asked me to do another one and I said I thought enough was enough. At one of them we had to keep waving the bride's car round and round Chelsea Register Office because Clive hadn't turned up, having been on something of a bender for several days before. After about five circuits we spotted him rolling up the King's Road towards us and we all went inside to watch him get hitched once more.

If Clive threw a party it could easily last for three days and, by the end, you had no idea how long you had been with him. When the madness was channelled into his photography, however, he produced beautiful work, and still does. He has become a Buddhist and has now given up drink and drugs completely. The only problem is that whenever I phone him now, he's always 'meditating'.

Anyway, back to that fateful weekend in the country. We were all sitting round the lunch table, enjoying ourselves, when there was a screeching of brakes and a crunching of gravel as Ricci's car came to a halt on the front drive. The next thing we heard was the slamming of the front door, heavy footsteps in the hall and then the sounds of things being broken. I made my excuses and left the room, carefully closing the door to the dining room behind me.

In the bedroom I found Ricci smashing the place to pieces. She was in a roaring fury, yelling abuse at me and describing Marella in terms that I wouldn't care to repeat. Several picture frames hurtled past my head and exploded against the wall. The television and the record player were sent spinning on to the floor. It took me some time before I managed to calm her down and persuade her that she should leave the house. Once she had gone I returned to my lunch guests as if nothing had happened. Richard, to his eternal credit, never breathed a word of the incident to his readers.

CHAPTER ELEVEN

Nagels and Twiggy broke up in 1973 when Ricci and I were still together. Twiggs was co-starring with an American actor, Michael Whitney, in a thriller called *W*, directed by Mel Ferrer. The story called for the two stars to be very much in love and I suppose they carried on their romance off camera as well. Twiggs and Michael then embarked on a long love affair which eventually led to their marriage and the birth of a lovely daughter, Carly. She was named after the songwriter, Carly Simon, who wrote 'You're So Vain', which was actually about Warren Beatty although Mick Jagger and many other Lotharios liked to imagine it was about them.

Nagels was absolutely devastated. He told me when he came back to London, 'Len, you've no idea what it was like. I could see them every day, romancing in front of the camera and falling more deeply in love, and I could do nothing about it. It was terrible. I felt like topping myself.'

His rise to the top with Twiggs had been extraordinary. It is hard to imagine today, when so many celebrities cram the international stage, just how few big stars there were in those days. Twiggy was famous all over the world.

Twiggy and Michael then came to London and tried to hide their relationship from the press, but it soon leaked out. Mara Berni at San Lorenzo was Twiggy's confidante, just as she would be to Princess Diana many years later. My accountant Neville Shulman also looked after Twiggy and Nagels and had been involved in their more recent deals and negotiations. Twiggy asked him to manage her career as well. First he asked Nagels if it was okay and Nagels agreed, provided that Neville continued to represent him as well. Neville agreed to that. They were both hoping that perhaps Twiggy would take Nagels back at some stage in the future. But she had been unhappy for some time with Nagels. He spent so much of the money she earned on expensive cars and clothes, mostly for himself, and she never forgave him.

Nothing, however, could ever dampen Nagels' spirits for long. As always he had plans, big plans, for the future. He was looking for somewhere to base himself so that he could get on with the dozens of new projects that were buzzing around in his head.

'I just need somewhere to base myself, Len,' he confided. 'A nice address in the West End.'

I had a spare office at the top of Upper Grosvenor Street, next to mine, and, without thinking, I suggested he should use that. Naturally he liked the idea and moved in the next day. It was just like the old times, except that now we were both famous in our own ways. My office was decorated in grey flannel and his in green flannel – lots of steel and glass. In some ways it was great for me to have a friend around all the time, although it distracted me even further from my business. It was perfect for Nagels to have somewhere to make phone calls and meet people, somewhere in the heart of Mayfair where he could hang his hat. The problem was that I was picking up all the bills.

A number of the stylists I had trained had begun to follow the example of Michael Rasser and John Isaacs and set up salons of their own. Things were no longer quite as crowded in the house, which meant there was room for Nagels. Without Ricci to go home to we would spend most evenings together with friends like the Percy Boys. Once again I was mostly picking up the tab.

Just as great rock bands tend to split up when they are at their height and go off to create new combinations and do their own things, so it is with hairdressers. It is always sad and disruptive to the business to have your senior stylists disappearing. But in the long run it keeps the industry alive and creative with everyone struggling to make names for themselves. When key staff that I had recruited and trained first left it was a bit of a shock. I tried never to take it personally, although I was always upset if they took a lot of other people with them.

I was particularly sad to lose John Frieda. He had been my personal assistant and had managed to build a good reputation doing all the magazine work which I didn't have time for because I was concentrating on films and other things. He went off with Clifford Stafford to form Stafford and Frieda just off Marylebone High Street. They later went their separate ways, both with tremendous success. A couple of stylists called Keith Wainwright and Leslie Russell also went off and started Smile in the Brompton Road, just opposite Scotch House. It is still going strong over twenty years later although it has now moved to World's End in Chelsea. Leslie was married to Cathy McGowan, who was one of the earliest television disc jockeys, fronting *Ready Steady Go* and starting the trend for informal pop shows. Leslie had a number of clients from the pop business, including Cilla Black, who was another of Brian Epstein's discoveries, the late Dusty Springfield with her enormous blonde beehive and Sandie Shaw who used to pad around the salon in her bare feet.

I also lost Celine, Colin and Karen when they went off to start Colombe in Motcomb Street in Belgravia. All three of them were exceptionally good hairdressers who had been incredibly important to the salon, as well as being good friends, and most of their clients followed them. The media became very excited by the new salons. Word spread quickly, so, even if the stylists did nothing to actively poach clients, the clients would soon seek them out if they valued the way they did their hair.

Colombe has gone now and they have all moved on to new enterprises. Karen runs Colin and Karen in Lower Belgrave Street with Colin Glassman, who used to run the Leonard and Twiggy salon for me. They have a tremendous reputation with a lot of the royals coming in to them – although Karen is far too discreet ever to gossip about her client list. About once a week I drop in on them when I am passing and she always gives me a cup of coffee and something to eat. She also does Rene's hair for me. I like Rene to go up there to have her hair done every so often, otherwise she would never leave Roehampton at all.

Most of all I was sad to lose Daniel, who decided, after more than ten years with the House of Leonard, that it was time to set up on his own. He was very honourable and asked permission to take his assistant with him but gave his word never to hire anyone else from the salon. He stuck to his promise, which was good of him because I think virtually all the colourists would have left with him if he had asked. We parted on very good terms and I have felt proud to see how well he has done since. He is now the world's pre-eminent expert on colouring with a client list which includes Tom Cruise and Nicole Kidman, Faye Dunaway, Richard Gere, Catherine Zeta-Jones, Mel Gibson, Cher and the late Princess Diana. His son, Daniel Junior, also joined his business but briefly defected to MichaelJohn after some highly publicised management conflicts, which caused a lot of family worry. Happily, they have been reunited and are working together once more.

As a result of these defections, I eventually had to move all the stylists from the Leonard and Twiggy salon in Sloane Avenue and close it down to fill the gap. It wasn't making any money, anyway. It was too small an operation, really just a way of getting publicity with our combined names. Nagels wasn't too bothered, except that he had been rather keen on dating the receptionists from Sloane Avenue, who always seemed to be leggy Scandinavian blondes. He used to roar up once a week in his Lamborghini, help himself to some cash from the till and whisk the receptionist off to lunch. He always felt that I owed him for closing down the business. But he didn't ever contribute anything, and I often found myself subsidising it from the main salon. I felt that I was compensating by giving him the office in Upper Grosvenor Street with all the back-up facilities.

Nagels and I were right on the same wavelength. We'd had the same training in ducking and diving from the barrows and we were both more comfortable with cash in our pockets than in financial planning meetings. After years of happily signing for things, I had started to have a few problems with settling bills and a few people were less inclined to accept my signature by the mid-Seventies. So then I had to start carrying cash around for those who were not prepared to hand out credit quite as generously as they had in the past. There was always plenty of cash in the till at the end of the day, so that didn't seem to be a problem to me. It was my salon, after all.

Nagels was playing the field among the girls with all his usual verve, sometimes getting through several in the course of a single day, but hadn't met anyone who could replace Twiggy in his affections.

One evening we went with Peter Blake to see mime artist Lindsay Kemp perform in a theatre in Shepherd's Bush. As we came out we met Malcolm McLaren, who went on to become notorious for living with Vivienne Westwood, dressing the punk movement from Tommy Roberts' old shop in the King's Road and founding the Sex Pistols. I remember he looked like a little boy in a huge, belted raincoat. As we emerged into Shepherd's Bush Nagels looked up and saw an illuminated poster of a top American model called Jan Ward. He stopped and stared. She was stunningly beautiful.

'I'm going to marry that girl,' Nagels announced. Apparently she had always been Twiggy's favourite model.

'I know her,' I said.

In fact Jan had been coming to the salon for some time and we had been doing her hair for free. I had met her in 1966 when she was doing a job for the photographer Norman Parkinson in Jamaica and came to me to have her wigs cut. Until then she had been having her hair done in Paris in a style which has become fashionable again thanks to Rachel in *Friends*. I talked her into changing to a new cut, a precursor to the shaggy look that people like Rod Stewart and Linda McCartney would later adopt. The new style attracted lots of publicity, not least because I turned her from dark to blonde. It was a pretty cut which required someone to have a well-shaped head, which Jan certainly had. When cut right the hair would move beautifully in the wind.

I knew she wasn't a real party animal like most models, but quite a serious person, more likely to be spending her evenings in discussions with R.D. Laing than dancing at Tramp. She had studied architecture and design at university and only took up modelling to make some money – very different to Twiggy's background.

'She won't be interested in a spiv like you,' I warned Nagels.

'I want to meet her,' he insisted.

Jan had been to several of my parties and I was pretty sure that she would come to another one if I asked her. I did, and she agreed. I didn't bother to tell her that it would just be a dinner party for a select few. I invited one other couple, and Nagels.

Determined to impress her, he arrived with a bunch of roses and all his usual charm. But this time Nagels had to pull out all the stops. Jan was no fifteen-year-old schoolgirl who was going to allow herself to be bowled over with a bit of patter on the first date. The more Nagels gabbled on, the more superficial he managed to appear to her. By the end of the first dinner it seemed obvious to me that he should give up and direct his energies elsewhere, but he was absolutely not going to be beaten. He pursued her for another date, and another and another and eventually, through sheer persistence, he wore her down. The more she played hard to get the more determined he became.

To my astonishment, when he asked Jan to marry him she said yes and I was back in my best man suit.

As a couple they used to come to the country with us a lot. It was a strange marriage but produced two beautiful daughters, Daisy and Poppy. Even though they are divorced now, Jan and Nagels are still best friends and I'm glad that I was instrumental in bringing them together.

I never needed much sleep, which was just as well considering how hard I was working – and playing. Many of my best clients were international people. Stars were quite likely to phone me in the middle of the night from Los Angeles, San Francisco or Florida to say they were having a problem with their hair, blissfully unaware that I was trying to grab a few hours' sleep in another time zone. These people obviously couldn't visit me every time they needed a trim. Instead I used to recommend them to stylists in other cities who I knew had the same basic hairdressing philosophy as me.

I was not willing to take on anyone as a client just because they had money or influence. When public relations gurus Tim Bell and Gordon Reece were trying to improve Margaret Thatcher's image before she got into Downing Street, they brought her along to the salon. I guess they hoped that I could perform some sort of miracle and turn her into a cross between Twiggy and Lauren Bacall.

She looked like a middle-aged housewife, even though it was already obvious she was a formidable personality. I studied her very suburban perm for a while in silence, trying to visualise how we could change it to flatter her face more and make her look younger.

'There is a lot we can do,' I told her, aware that she was looking round at the models' pictures on the wall with some trepidation. 'I would need to change the cut completely,' I went on, 'to complement your face. It needs to be softer and more natural.'

I knew this was exactly what her advisers were trying to persuade her to do, but they were having trouble convincing her.

'No, Mr Leonard,' she said in a voice which suggested argument would be pointless. 'I think the voters are more comfortable with me the way I am. I just need a wash and perm.'

I took a deep breath and looked at her again in the mirror. I was disappointed.

'We will do it this once,' I told her. 'But if you want to come back regularly you will have to let me cut it properly.'

She didn't come back again. I know I could have made her look better, but she didn't do too badly in life, so perhaps she knew what she was doing when it came to getting her own image right.

Every day seemed to be a rush and I was having trouble fitting everything into the hours available. Part of the problem, of course, was the social life that I was leading with Marella as well as my working schedule. Clients would often invite me to social functions and I was hopeless at saying no. Marella also had a packed social calendar. When Maria Niarchos, a member of the Greek shipping family, got married to a Frenchman in Deauville, Normandy, Marella and I were invited to the wedding. Marella had been to school with her, I think, and Maria's father, Stavros, had invited me.

The day before was my birthday and I had celebrated it by taking a group of friends to Nikita's, a Russian restaurant in Chelsea. We left the party in the small hours of the morning and drove straight to Normandy in the Porsche. We went to the wedding and then on to another family party afterwards. They had flown Maria's favourite Spanish group in to play all night.

During the party Stavros invited me to see his horses back at his château. By then I was something of a zombie. Once Stavros had finished showing me round I crept back to the stables and found myself a nice bed of hay to lie down on and fell asleep till dawn. The next day there were more parties arranged, which Marella wanted to stay for, but I knew I had to get back to the salon. So, after just a few hours' rest, I was driving back to the ferry and into Mayfair, where the clients were all waiting to be pampered and cut.

When I got back home I wrote Stavros a thank-you note. He rang me a few days later to say that I was the only person in the whole wedding party who had thought to thank him.

On another trip to France with Marella, we went to a very fine vineyard in the Loire Valley. As we strolled along the walkways between the vats, inhaling the wonderful aromas and listening to the guide explaining what was going on, I noticed a man leaning perilously close to the edge. I stepped forward to warn him and my feet slipped from under me, sending me into a neat head dive into the wine. The owners were very nice about it, hauling me out and drying

me down. When I got back to London several of my friends uncharitably suggested I might have done it on purpose. But I was never that
desperate for a drink.

In retrospect it never ceases to amaze me how willing clients were
to accept what I said as gospel. Despite the impression of calm com-
petence that we liked to project, we always had far more customers
than we could comfortably handle. Therefore, if anything went
wrong, like a basin or a dryer breaking, we immediately had a backlog
of people waiting. Sometimes I would be halfway through cutting
someone when I would simply run out of time. Even if the hair was
six inches longer on one side than the other I would always be able to
think of some excuse why I shouldn't finish that day.

'I would like to leave that side for a couple of days to see how it
hangs before I cut the other side,' I would say and they would agree,
thanking me for my trouble.

'It must be your time of the month,' I would suggest if their hair
seemed a little out of condition. 'We'll finish it off in a few days.'

You can get away with all that sort of thing as long as word of
mouth still has it that you are the best hairdresser in London. As soon
as there are others, like my trainees who were now becoming famous
in their own right, clients begin to be less patient, particularly those
who drove into Mayfair from the country specially to get their hair
done. As the years went by it became harder and harder to park
around the salon and people became less inclined to spend hours
waiting for me.

To my face everyone continued to treat me with respect, but,
unknown to me, a number of people were beginning to lose patience.
Some clients asked for other stylists to look after them. Staff did their
best to juggle the appointments around to ensure that no one was left
sitting fuming because I had double-booked myself or agreed to do
something at the last minute which didn't fit into the diary.

Nagels was having a go at the rock and roll business by then,
inspired by his past friendship with Paul McCartney and George
Harrison. He formed the Jack Bruce Band with the ex-lead singer
from Cream, which had recently disbanded. He was also managing
Tim Hardin, a songwriter who had created such classics as 'If I Were
a Carpenter', but whose drug habits gave Nagels no end of
headaches.

For my part, I liked the idea of having a mate in the building. He was someone I could sneak out for a drink and a meal with whenever my mind started to wander from my work. I don't think the staff were quite so thrilled. They spent most of the time trying to guard me from distractions, spiriting Nagels past the door as quickly as possible, before I could see him and wander off for a chat.

Although he and Jan often used to come down to the country at weekends, neither of us was a natural country dweller. Actually we were a right couple of poseurs. One year we decided to take up shooting and went to the royal gunsmiths Holland & Holland in Mayfair to have shotguns made. I got one for Dominic as well because he was big enough by then to join us. Nagels went totally mad and ordered up a Norfolk suit complete with plus-fours, tweed hat and leather patches, a cravat and a bandoleer of cartridges. He looked like something out of the pages of P.G. Wodehouse.

The three of us got up early and made a great deal of fuss about getting ourselves ready. Jan, Marella and the other house guests, all sitting around in their dressing gowns with steaming cups of coffee and the Sunday papers, watched our antics with amused expressions. Once we'd breakfasted and got all our gear on, we set off into the woods, feeling very pleased with ourselves. The autumnal air was clean and invigorating and we kept telling one another we couldn't imagine why we hadn't started doing this years before.

As we reached the woods we stopped and listened to the silence and realised we hadn't got a clue what we were supposed to be shooting. We walked a little further and Nagels gave me a nudge, pointing at the ground a few yards ahead where an unsuspecting wood-pigeon was rummaging around in search of breakfast.

Knowing we had to return to the house with something after the song and dance we had made, we spread out and crept forward to surround our prey. As soon as we all had it in our sights I issued the command and we simultaneously blasted the poor thing to pieces.

We felt so remorseful as we looked at the poor, broken little creature, that none of us wanted to pick it up. It was all horribly unsporting and from then on we stuck to potting clay pigeons.

During this period of my life I didn't get back to see Rene and my family in Roehampton as much as I should have done. Our worlds had drifted apart. When I heard that Dad was ill in hospital, I suggested that Nagels and Mikey Stevenson come down with me to visit him. He had always been fond of them both. He had known Nagels ever since the days when we used to roll home late at night and share his bedroom. Nagels gave us a lift in his Rolls and Mikey went up first to find Dad and bring him to the window. We parked the Roller and gave a loud toot on the horn.

I could see him looking out the window and pointing 'his boys' out to the other old chaps in the ward. I was grateful to Nagels and Mikey for doing that because Dad died a few days later and I would like to think that he was proud of me at the end.

Once the divorce from Ricci was finalised I started to look for a new home and found a beautiful apartment overlooking the River Thames at 11 Chelsea Embankment. From my bay window I could see to my left directly into publisher Lord Weidenfeld's apartment. This occasionally gave me a bird's eye view of his affair with my good friend Zandra Rhodes, something I was very happy to tease her about whenever I saw her. She didn't seem bothered that I had seen her standing at the window opposite the Buddhist temple on the other side of the Thames without a stitch of clothing on.

My apartment had enormous rooms, one with a minstrels' gallery, and gave me all the scope I needed for decorating and entertaining. I was becoming a pretty good cook myself now and loved throwing dinner parties. The trouble was I could never resist trying the food while I was cooking it. One evening Nagels came round and I cooked us both some beautiful steaks, but I kept testing little mouthfuls as I went along until there was hardly anything left. I decided to serve it up to Nagels anyway and hope he didn't notice.

'You've given me a bleeding Oxo Cube, Len,' he complained when I served him what was left of his portion.

Neville Shulman was forever nagging me about spending too much money. I was constantly having to promise to be a better boy and always failing to keep my promise. He was very enterprising in finding new ways to keep me out of financial trouble. But, to my regret, I just wouldn't conform.

Nagels continued to use Neville as his accountant too. He was also spending more than he was earning, and losing his income from

Twiggy made him very bitter. He wanted to share some business with me but I refused to include him.

Although to the outside world the House of Leonard still seemed the most prosperous salon in London, our finances were actually very dodgy indeed. We had about ten bank accounts going at one time, with money being juggled by my bookkeeper from one to another whenever the bank managers complained too loudly. We had to liquidate several companies in order to get rid of some of the debts. But they still seemed to keep piling up. Neville did his best to keep me away from the cash, asking other people in the company to bank it at the end of the day. But I usually found a way of getting hold of it whenever I felt hungry. I couldn't shake off the habit of living for the day and hoping that tomorrow would take care of itself.

My lawyers were constantly giving me complicated-looking contracts and agreements to read and sign. I became very adept at holding them in front of my face just long enough for everyone to think that I was studying them carefully, when actually I couldn't make head or tail of them. I was always more than happy to allow my lawyers and Neville to take care of all the legal and accountancy matters, leaving me to concentrate on my one skill, cutting hair.

One of the bonuses of closing down the Leonard and Twiggy salon had been a girl called Sue Maxwell, who had been on reception there and had moved to Upper Grosvenor Street with the rest of the staff. She proved to be so organised and efficient that I asked her to be my personal assistant. Before long she was more or less my nanny, organising every part of my life – as long as I didn't forget to tell her what promises I had made to everyone. She used to come to work with her wire-haired dachshund which didn't like men and barked at us from under Sue's desk at every opportunity.

I remember she had the tiniest little yellow Fiat 500, one of those things that looked like miniature Beetles. When my Bentley needed to go into the garage in North London one time, she offered to drive behind me and bring me back. Needless to say, she had the dog with her. Unfortunately, I had forgotten to warn her that I also had Dominic and Zorro in the car with me. Somehow we managed to cram both dogs and the boy into her tiny back seat and make our way back across London with Zorro's nose practically touching the windscreen and the dachshund grumbling and snapping from beneath the Afghan's feathered haunches.

Sue married Oliver Bond, who was one of the first stylists at the salon and my main assistant before John Frieda. When I was having my not so secret affair with Kate Vestey, Sue and Jeffrey Lane, the salon's publicist, used to join us for dinner to provide a cover. Sue was in a good position to do this because her father was a racehorse trainer and had looked after horses for the Vesteys. Oliver was a great party-goer too, often staying out for days on end. Eventually Sue grew tired of the whole lot of us and went to work for Clare Rendlesham at Yves St Laurent. The dachshund went with her and managed to strike up a working relationship with Clare's Pekinese.

I loved having friends round to the apartment in the evening. I would tip a bottle of Pimms into a jug, fill it up with fruit and lemonade and spend the evening at home cooking, eating and drinking until it was time to go out to the clubs.

For a while, before meeting Marella, I went out with an American model called Deniece Lewis. She was very beautiful but I don't think either of us was particularly serious about the relationship. I was with her in Tramp one night when Dodi Fayed came in. I didn't know him very well at that stage. He spotted Deniece and started asking questions about her. When someone told him that she was with me but that I wasn't really interested in her, he approached me and asked if he could dance with her. I had no problem with that and they went on to have an affair.

From then on Dodi and I became firm friends. He realised that I was always surrounded by beautiful women – he was at Tramp the first night I turned up with a Miss World contestant – and obviously thought he had struck gold. If there were two things Dodi loved it was beautiful women and cocaine. He had nothing else to do with his time.

He started turning up at the flat unannounced and hanging around until the small hours of the morning. He would usually be driving something like a Ferrari, with a Mercedes following with his various friends and hangers-on. We often used to go out for meals, although Dodi would always be jumping up to go to the loo to do another line of coke. He loved mixing with the film stars. He used to get very jumpy if Richard Compton Miller was there, worried that Richard would write about him in the William Hickey column. I assured him that when Richard was with me he was off duty, but he could never really relax.

Dodi was always good company and great fun to be with, but his twin habits of girls and coke caused him a lot of trouble. At one stage he went into the film business and, together with David Puttnam, produced *Chariots of Fire*. I had got to know David in the days when he was a photographer's agent. It is hard to imagine now that the grand Lord Puttnam was ever that cheeky, smiling lad who used to come into the salon, showing his portfolio and trying to persuade me to work with his clients.

When Dodi became a producer he asked me to do the hair on the film, which I was more than happy to do. Dodi would be there every day. He would hang around the set making a nuisance of himself with all the women, saying that he had just come to visit me. Eventually Puttnam had to ban him. The male actors all complained that Dodi was distracting the actresses, keeping them out all night and making them late to work in the mornings. I think they were probably jealous.

Dodi was the most generous of friends. He was always offering to lend me his father's yacht or one of his villas around the world. Mohammed seemed to be pleased that I was his son's friend. When I eventually had to tell Dodi that he had to stay away from me – the coke habit was becoming just too embarrassing – Mohammed contacted me and asked me to reconsider.

I told him how fond I was of Dodi and how I had begged him to give up the habit but had failed. There just wasn't anything I could do about it. I was sad that we drifted apart for so long; in fact he was one of the few people who came back to see me once everything had gone wrong. Through me he formed a number of strong friendships, particularly with Tony Curtis, who shared both his tastes.

Of course Dodi went on to become a star of the tabloids when he started to date Princess Diana and finally died with her in the crash in Paris. It was just the sort of death anyone who had known Dodi would have predicted for him. He always lived too fast and too dangerously. He was a special friend and a kind man. But I certainly wouldn't have wanted him to have been dating anyone in my family.

Another big influence on Swinging London during the late Sixties and Seventies was Hugh Hefner and his British representative, Victor

Lownes. The Playboy Club created a major revolution in the London social scene. There had been hostess clubs practically since the time the city was founded, but never before had there been such a slick, heavily promoted and marketed operation. The premises were housed in a modern block on Park Lane, not far from the salon, and it wasn't long before the bunny girls started to find their way through our doors.

In the end it was a bit like a corporate contract, with us going to the club to get them all ready before an evening's work. Both Hefner and Lownes used to come to the salon themselves from time to time.

The House of Leonard had officially become the first 'unisex' hairdresser's in London. It had started when I noticed that men were frequently sitting around in the reception area waiting for their wives or girlfriends to finish being cut. Now and then, if I knew them, I would suggest that we give them a trim while they waited. As they became less self-conscious about being in a ladies' salon and grew to like the atmosphere, they started to make appointments for themselves. We then turned the top floor into a men's salon and I began to think about opening gyms and health clubs to cater for men's other 'beauty' needs – a revolutionary idea at the time but commonplace now.

The idea of the 'bunny club' caught on all over the world. Through Victor Lownes I became friends with a man called Bernie Cornfeld, who had made a huge amount of money out of an insurance company which later went broke amidst a lot of scandal. The first time I went to Bernie's house off Belgrave Square and he invited me to 'his room downstairs', I was amazed to find that he had equipped the whole place out as a miniature bunny club, complete with the beautiful girls.

Best of all, however, was Stocks, which was Victor's house in a former girls' public school in Hertfordshire, where he used to hold weekend parties. Late at night anything went, and his pet chimpanzee used to sit at the dinner table with the guests. When an unattached male VIP like Peter Cook or a well-connected socialite like Dai Llewellyn arrived they would be assigned a girl to 'look after' them. Most evenings, once the girls had had a few drinks to loosen them up, there would be at least one orgy going on somewhere in the house. It would often be in the huge jacuzzi, where young and willing Playboy models and bunny girls would fulfil all the male guests' wildest fantasies. One evening Tony Curtis was in the jacuzzi, cavorting with several of the young ladies. They ducked him playfully under the water and his toupee floated away like a large rat swimming for its life.

'Why don't you take a dip, Leonard?' Victor asked me one evening.

'Because I'm frightened of what I might catch in that water,' I replied. It was always safest to have a shot of penicillin after a weekend at Stocks.

Wherever I went it was a standing joke that I would have my scissors with me and I would be more than happy to cut anyone who asked. My scissors were my passport to go anywhere I wanted in the world.

I met Andy Warhol in Studio 54 in New York. I think I must have gone there with Bianca Jagger. He always used to wear those extra-ordinary white wigs. They had become a sort of trademark with him but they were terribly low quality. In fact, they were something of an embarrassment but, just like Margaret Thatcher, Andy knew exactly what he wanted to achieve with his own image and he was right. He asked if I would make some new wigs for him in the same style but with better quality hair. We became friendly and he came to the flat whenever he was in London.

On one of his visits he very sweetly did a sketch of me, to say thank you for the wigs. Francis Bacon was also in the room at the time and, when Warhol had finished, Bacon snatched the paper away from him, turned it over and did another sketch of me on the other side. I couldn't believe my eyes. I must have been the only person in the world to own a piece of paper which had portraits of me by two of the world's most famous artists on either side.

Once my name was established I was given a free hand to do pretty much whatever I wanted for the magazines, particularly *Vogue*. I worked in conjunction with the photographers who had become my friends, like Barry Lategan and Clive Arrowsmith, and make-up artists like Barbara Daly who wanted to do the same sort of wild, glamorous pictures as I did.

When I first met Barbara she had only been out of Leeds College of Art a couple of years and had been working in the make-up department of the BBC. She was trying to get into films and, while she waited for a break, she had approached some magazines and photographers about doing session work. At that time most of the make-up in magazines was either done by the models themselves, or by make-up artists from the big beauty houses like Max Factor and Revlon, who were willing to work for free in exchange for a credit in the magazine. It took Barbara some time to persuade editors that they should actually pay for a make-up artist.

She had started by getting some advertising work, during which she met Barry Lategan and Helmut Newton. They quickly realised her potential and sang her praises to the magazine editors. Once she had started to work, it wasn't long before everything that had gone before looked dated and boring. She was brimming with imaginative concepts. She and I immediately hit it off. We would sit around with the beauty and fashion editors and the photographers and just dream up wilder and wilder ideas. Our professional lives were to become more and more entwined as the years went by.

We scored front cover after front cover and many of the pictures have now become collectors' items, viewed as works of art and symbols of that period. The ideas came to me from every angle. There was a famous model and heiress called Penelope Tree (she lived with Bailey for a long time after he broke up with Jean Shrimpton), whose name encouraged me to dream up the idea of building her hair up into a tree on the top of her head and creating a bird's nest on top. It looked like an atomic explosion of hair and became one of the most enduring images of the period. Artists like Barry, Clive and Barbara sparked me to think more and more creatively. We were a team producing exactly what the fashion world wanted to see.

The names of Leonard and Barbara Daly were now appearing regularly in the media and the general public were becoming aware of our existence. Barbara finally found big-time fame when she was asked to do Princess Diana's make-up for her wedding to Prince Charles.

Even in these egalitarian days it still pays for people like hairdressers, dress designers and make-up artists to have royal patronage. Just as doing Princess Anne's hair for her wedding helped the MichaelJohn salon, and Princess Diana helped Barbara, Sarah Ferguson helped to establish Nicky Clarke on the social scene and to make him a star in the hairdressing firmament. It is by no means essential, as it might once have been, to be associated with royalty in order to prosper, but they still have enough prestige to bring in other customers and to impress newspaper editors and television producers.

Although Nagels and I had beautiful offices at the top of the house, we often used the basement for our meetings – partly because we couldn't be bothered to schlep all the way to the top, and partly because it was closer to the kitchen which produced refreshments for the clients and staff. I liked to have easy access to food and drink at all times.

One day he and I were taking a break down there, chatting about this and that. He was sitting on one of the bins and I was on top of a pile of towels, tucking into a sandwich or two, when the phone went. It was Jeffrey Lane, a publicist who worked for the Hollywood show business agency Rogers and Cowan, and also advised the House of Leonard. Every time a big star was in London he would bring them to the salon and, of course, the press would always find out.

Jeffrey had first come into my life in 1968 when he was not even twenty years old, but he was already going bald. He was working in the publicity department of Columbia Pictures at the time on a film called *Marooned in Space*. The two most striking things about him were that he was very small and very charming. He doted on his mother and was tremendously supportive of his family as he became successful. He had read about me in Nigel Dempster's column and thought it would be a good idea to ask me to design some space age hairstyles to promote the film. He brought along six models and we created some crazy styles for them which got into all the papers. Jeffrey and I then became good friends. I asked if he would do my personal publicity, even though he was still working for the film company, and I became his first private client.

Jeffrey very quickly worked out that I was completely incapable of turning up to anything on time and he developed a method of telling me that every meeting or press function was actually an hour or two earlier, just to make sure that I was there at the same time as everyone else. He realised that I was very bad at giving interviews, being far too vague and unable to concentrate for more than a few minutes at a time, so he set up all sorts of fashion and beauty features instead, pro-jecting the image of the House of Leonard without requiring me to talk to journalists too often. He then worked for Rogers and Cowan for a while, before disappearing off to Los Angeles in the Eighties. He became a freelance Hollywood publicist looking after people like Burt Reynolds and Joan Collins, both of whom were equally fond of their wig collections, and the perma-tanned George Hamilton.

'Listen,' Jeffrey said as Nagels and I tucked into our snacks. 'I've got this client flying into England tomorrow, an actress called Lynda Carter. She's made a television series called *Wonder Woman* which is coming to Britain. The World Beauty Council have voted her the most beautiful woman in the world. I'm just doing the press release.'

'That's nice, Jeffrey,' I said and told Nagels what he had said.

'Who the hell are the World Beauty Council?' Nagels enquired from his perch on the rubbish bin.

'Nagels wants to know who the World Beauty Council are, Jeffrey,' I said, trying to get bits of the sandwich off my tie.

'It's you two,' Jeffrey said. 'So be ready for some calls from the press.'

'Right you are, Jeffrey,' I said and, sure enough, the next day the papers were full of how the Council, led by Leonard and Justin de Villeneuve, had voted this actress the most beautiful woman in the world.

Nagels, like many of my close friends, did not approve of my relationship with Marella. There was a feeling that she was taking a lot from me and not giving much back. One evening we went out to dinner at Scott's in Mayfair and he gave me a long lecture on how I should end the relationship. I made all the right non-committal noises to give him the impression I was taking notice of him.

'Are you planning to eat your way through the whole bleeding menu, Len?' he said after I had been munching for a while. 'The waiters are beginning to get a bit tired. I think it might be time for us to go.'

'Right you are, Nagels,' I said and he drove me back to the flat.

When I got inside I found a message from Marella saying that she wanted to go out for a meal. Since I had already been into the bathroom and brought up all the food from Scott's, I felt I could just about manage another meal. At midnight we set off to another restaurant and I started to stuff my face all over again.

Unfortunately for me, Nagels was having lunch with this particular restaurant's owner the following day. They were both comparing notes on the enormous quantities of food that I was able to stash away and they soon realised that both of them had seen me go through hearty meals within a few hours of one another the night before. It took me a while to live that one down with Nagels.

CHAPTER TWELVE

'Y OU ARE A good friend, Len,' Nagels once told me while we were having a peaceful drink together, watching the world go by. 'If I was hanging over the side of a cliff and you were holding on to my wrist to stop me falling to my death, I know that you would do everything you could to haul me back to safety.'

'Cheers, Nagels,' I said, but he held up his hand to indicate he hadn't finished talking.

'But if Jack Nicholson drove by at that moment I know for a fact that you would let go of me in order to wave.'

A slight exaggeration perhaps, but I could understand what he was getting at. Stars held a terrible fascination for me.

One of the great joys of being a hairdresser has been that it has allowed me to work on film sets and befriend some of the world's biggest names.

I started my film hairdressing career in the Hammer House of Horror, one of Britain's most successful and prolific studios in the Sixties, which produced an endless stream of vampire and monster movies with stars like Christopher Lee, Vincent Price and Peter Cushing. Vincent was nothing like his screen image. He was cultured and warm, a fantastic cook and a major art collector. Christopher was an extraordinary man, a gifted linguist, so tall he towered over everyone. His typecasting in the Dracula role frustrated him as he was a very fine actor and desperately wanted to play romantic and comedy parts. He always wore a serious wig but had no problems with it, as no one could ever look down on him. Peter was a shy man, but also a terrific actor who should have been allowed to show his full range of talents.

The two Carreras brothers, Michael and Jimmy, who ran Hammer used to come to the salon themselves to have their hair cut, long before we actually had a dedicated men's department. One day, Michael suggested that I should do some film work for them. At the time they were making movies like *She* with Ursula Andress, who had become famous for her role as James Bond's girl in *Doctor No*, and I gave her a very glamorous Grecian style. She was going out with John Derek (she later married him, before Bo Derek), and I used to do his hair as well. Not surprisingly, John found it very hard to cope with his girlfriend being half naked on a film set surrounded by handsome actors.

The Hammer Studios were a strange world of their own. There were actors there who never seemed to do anything else and some of them actually believed they were vampires and werewolves. It was all rather unnerving.

I very quickly discovered that the down-side of film work was all the waiting around for the crews to get set up and the light to be right. I couldn't be doing with all that, I was much too anxious to be off and busy with something else. So I used to come in and set everything up at the beginning and only return for major scenes, to make sure they were doing everything right.

Once it was known that I did film work other offers started to come rolling in. It was unusual for a hairdresser with a salon to be able to get work on films as well, since the two worlds had traditionally been very separate. Barbra Streisand, for instance, was a client at the salon and also asked me to do her hair for *Yentl*, which she was producing as well as starring in. She had to look like a boy in the film so I created a wig which she could sweep her hair up into. A lot of people have told me they found her difficult to work with but I never had a problem. She was certainly very loud, but never any trouble.

'A friend of mine would like to meet you,' Michael Carreras' wife Jo told me one day while I was cutting her hair. 'She's married to a film director and they need some ideas about hair for a science fiction film he's planning.'

The director in question turned out to be Stanley Kubrick and the film was to be *2001: A Space Odyssey*. A meeting was arranged and Stanley and I chatted for several hours. He was amazingly scruffy with wild, curly hair going in all directions, heavy glasses and dishevelled, baggy clothes. I offered to cut his hair. He agreed, but he wanted it to look scruffy even after I had done it. It was an image he cultivated deliberately.

I had never met someone with such a range of thoughts and ideas bubbling in their head. It seemed as if he wanted to know everything I had ever learned about hair, and more particularly how I thought people would look by the year 2001.

'So,' Kubrick said when it seemed as if there was nothing else left to say. 'Have you got any ideas how to help me with this movie?'

'Well, to start with,' I replied, 'I could get my wig makers to create the ape hair suits you need.'

Stanley's eyes glittered with amusement. 'Can you handle that?' he asked. 'And can you do designs for all the other hairstyles as well?'

I couldn't think of anything I would like to do more. To start with the idea of working with Kubrick, the director of the wonderful *Dr Strangelove*, was very exciting. Secondly, I would be able to put all the ideas I had been working on over the years into practice, and develop some of the themes which I had started on a smaller scale with *Marooned in Space*. I would have a free hand to show just what I thought hair should be like in the future, which meant that Daniel (who was still working with me at this stage) and I could really go to town on the colours and I could do some experimenting.

Many of the predictions we made in the film have been shown to be remarkably accurate. The wig-styles we invented were totally futuristic and contributed to the impact the film made, but reality has caught up and you can now see equally outlandish designs in the clubs or even on the streets. Every science fiction film or television programme since has come up with pale imitations of those styles.

It was when I started working on Stanley's films that I met up with Michael Stevenson. Mikey was one of Stanley's directorial assistants. This meant that he was in charge of keeping the talent happy and making sure that everything happened when and how it should. The great director could then concentrate on making his film. Mikey was another East End lad who used to hang around the dance halls in sharp suits at the same time as Nagels and me. We became instant mates and he has stuck by me through thick and thin ever since.

The working relationship with Kubrick went well and, as soon as he was starting to plan *A Clockwork Orange,* he got in touch with me again. Once more we were looking into the future together. This time, however, Stanley wanted the hair to look more authentic. He didn't want wigs, he wanted actual cuts. All the ideas that I had been working on with Zandra, plus the futuristic ideas in the space films and the colour ideas I had worked on with Daniel came together. For some of the characters we created the forerunners to the punk Mohican, with the sides of the head shaved and the middle part spiked up and brightly coloured. I created an intense, painful hairstyle to add to Malcolm McDowell's frightening demeanour.

Clockwork Orange became one of the most controversial films ever made, with its depiction of violence allegedly leading to copycat killings in the USA. This concern caused Stanley to withdraw it from screens in this country and also to refuse to allow it to be shown on television. Only after his death were cinemas able to show it again.

When Stanley died recently everyone wrote about how difficult he was to work for, how he always insisted on hundreds of takes and never accepted anything less than perfection. All that was true, but I never had any problems with him. He was a cinematic genius and an incredibly intelligent and imaginative man who drove everyone around him hard. But as long as you did the job you were paid for he was fine.

He was undoubtedly eccentric. He never wanted to give interviews, refused to fly on planes, and exploded at people who didn't produce the results he wanted, but he never interfered with my work. He asked me what my ideas were, I told him and he said 'Go ahead and do it.'

After *Clockwork Orange* I worked for him on *The Shining,* during which I became friendly with Jack Nicholson. It was a very scary film both on and off camera. Nicholson really got into character as a maniacal crazy and, with whatever he was on, he would spend his time leering at us all with that twisted grin of his and trying to frighten the young girls working in production. There were screams echoing all round the set and many more coming from Jack's caravan.

During the filming of *The Shining* Jack was going out with Anjelica Huston. I had first met Anjelica when I had done her hair for magazine pictures. She had also done some modelling for Zandra Rhodes, who was good at getting unusual people to do shows and photographs for her. Jack started using me as an alibi whenever he didn't turn up on set, telling everyone that he had been out with me all night when in fact we had parted company in some bar in the small hours of the morning and he had disappeared off somewhere with a girl under each arm and a happy smile on his face. Because I had known Anjelica for many years, this put me in an embarrassing position.

Jack and Anjelica made a great couple. They were always rowing but they were very good together. The problem was that Jack simply couldn't keep away from the ladies. In the end Anjelica lost patience and stormed back to America. Once she had gone Jack got completely out of hand.

'Ah, don't worry, Leonard,' he assured me as we set out with yet another car full of young girls. 'Anjelica and I will get back together again. You'll see. We're destined for each other.' But he underestimated her determination and they didn't get back together, at least not at the time of writing this.

The *Shining* was followed by *Barry Lyndon*, one of the greatest hairdressing challenges imaginable. It was an eighteenth-century period piece and was a highly stylised and somewhat camp film with hundreds of high-piled intricate wigs to match the dandified costumes. I seemed to be working from early morning to very late at night, but I loved it.

The film starred Marisa Berenson and Ryan O'Neal, both of whom became good friends. Marisa was particularly intrigued by the salon in Upper Grosvenor Street because Elsa Schiaparelli was her aunt and she remembered coming to the house as a small girl.

Ryan used to stay with me when he was in London, both at Little Chester Street and later at the flat on the Embankment. At the time when I saw most of him, he was having an affair with Bianca Jagger. This was a little embarrassing, since he used to meet her at the basement gym that I had opened round the corner from the salon in South Audley Street. Other clients started to complain about how intimate Ryan and Bianca were with one another in public and I had to ask them to cool it. Neither of them took offence but they found it hard to keep their hands off one another.

One evening, when I was still married to Ricci, I threw a dinner party and invited Michael York and his wife Pat, Bianca and Ryan

and some others. After dinner Mick Jagger rang from his house in
Cheyne Walk, just a short distance from Little Chester Street. He
wanted to know where Bianca was. I told him she had already left.
When I went to the bedroom, however, I found her canoodling
with Ryan. I was not too thrilled since Dominic was still little and I
didn't think he needed to stumble across this sort of scene.

Bianca had been a customer at the salon for many years and
always insisted on having Daniel wash her hair. Since Daniel was
often colouring as many as thirty people a day, he didn't really have
time to wash hair, particularly as Bianca always insisted on having
her hair rinsed for fifteen minutes at a time. She was a big name in
those days, however, so Daniel just had to bite his tongue and do as
she wanted.

Ryan used to bring his daughter Tatum with him on his trips and
I was shocked to see her, at the age of nine, smoking and partying
away with the adults. When Ryan and Bianca wanted some time
alone, however, Tatum was dispatched to the park with Dominic
and Zorro to keep her out of the way. She went on to become a
child film star in her own right, making *Paper Moon* with her father
and a remake of *National Velvet,* with her in the role originally played
by Liz Taylor. Tatum later married the tennis star, John McEnroe.
She was such an enchanting child and seemed to have such a
promising future but something went wrong and her life seemed to
collapse around her.

While Ryan was working on *Barry Lyndon*, Stanley supplied him
with a nanny to look after Tatum. The nanny was Sabrina Guinness,
a fun-loving heiress, who had been helping around the film set.
Sabrina was already making a reputation for herself through her
friendships with stars like the Rolling Stones and she became very
friendly with Ryan. She and I started an affair during the filming and
she took me to meet a number of her relatives in their grand Irish
country houses. After she finished with me she was reputed to have
gone on to have an affair with Prince Charles.

Entertaining stars was undoubtedly good for business, but it was
also hideously expensive. It wasn't the stars themselves who cost the
money, it was all the hangers-on. If I took Ryan out to dinner, for
instance, he would come with an entourage of six or seven people,
all of whom were happy to eat and drink into the small hours of the

morning at our expense. At the time I didn't mind because I had the money in my pocket and I loved having a lively crowd around. Looking back, I can see that it was all madness.

The other stars of *Barry Lyndon* were, of course, the wigs. Stanley asked me if I would fly over to Ireland, where he was planning to film, taking the wigs with me. I guess he was going over by ferry himself, since he hated flying. When I boarded the flight, with my first-class ticket, I discovered that he had booked a first-class seat for each of the elaborate hairpieces. I sat in solitary splendour throughout the flight, surrounded by a sea of giant wig boxes.

Stanley had also given me a suitcase to take out with me. 'It's something for the crew,' he told me.

Unfortunately, when I reached customs, they asked me what was in the case and I didn't have a clue. When they opened it I was horrified to see that it was packed solid with condoms. Apparently, the crew had been finding it hard to buy any in Catholic Ireland. I felt myself turning the colour of beetroot as the customs man looked up at me.

'What's this?' he enquired.

'I'm planning to have a good time,' I replied weakly.

'It looks as if you are going to have a fucking good time,' he said, snapping the case shut. 'Go away and enjoy yourself.'

I was always meticulous in my research for any film project, which was something Stanley was also keen on, right down to using the right combs and hair ornaments for the period. I used to buy piles of expensive art books and then take them along to show Stanley pictures from the period. I would reverentially open up the beautifully printed pages and lay them out in front of him. Stanley would then rip out the pages that he liked and pin them up on the office wall in front of him.

'You have no respect for art, Stanley,' I complained.

'You can always buy more books, Leonard,' he replied.

He had asked for some of the wigs to be 'salt and pepper'. When I arrived with them he insisted I had got them the wrong colour. I stormed off to the canteen and fetched some salt and pepper shakers. I returned, emptied them on to the table in front of him and mixed them together. They were exactly the same colour as the hair. He didn't argue with me again.

The eighteenth century was an interesting time for hairdressers. The enormous wigs worn by fashionable and powerful people ensured that hairdressers and wig makers became very important figures in high society, just as was happening again in the nineteen sixties and seventies. In the eighteenth century, men who would never normally have been admitted into society were able to gain access to the top if they could dress or beautify those who were already there. There seemed to be many parallels with our own time.

While researching the period, I discovered that there had been a famous court hairdresser at the time called Leonard. I told Stanley this and he insisted that I make my first and only acting appearance in front of the camera, as a hairdresser, fussing over Ryan's hair.

In those days the film industry was strongly unionised. Although I was designing the wigs and advising the on-set hairdressers, I was not allowed by the unions actually to do hands-on work during filming. The majority of my work was done before filming actually started, checking how hair had looked at the time and deciding how to reproduce the effects. I would then go to the filming to make sure they were doing it right. One day, watching one of the hairdressers adjust a wig on one of the actresses, I could see that it just needed a tweak to achieve the full effect.

'Like this,' I said, giving it the smallest of tugs. The next thing I knew the whole film set had been closed down as everyone walked off. I had broken a golden rule. I had touched the hair without a union card. It took them a full day's negotiation to get everyone back to work. How Stanley persuaded them later to let me stand in front of the cameras without an equity card I will never know.

Marisa was a wonderful friend. She was always a little uncomfortable if she had to wear a new wig and I wasn't around to help her. After we received some calls from the IRA threatening to disrupt filming, the production moved from Ireland back to England, to Wilton House near Salisbury. The place was owned by the Earl of Pembroke who was an old friend of Marisa's. Meanwhile, I had to go back to the salon to deal with my backlog of clients.

The following day Mikey rang me in a panic. 'You've absolutely got to come down to Salisbury,' he told me. 'There's a problem with the wig and Marisa has fallen out with the hairdresser. She's refusing to come on the set until you get here to oversee things.'

'What does Stanley say?' I asked.

'Stanley says it's fine by him.'

I quickly rescheduled my appointments, passing my clients on to the more than capable staff who were running the salon during my increasing absences, then hurtled down to Salisbury in record time in the Porsche.

Stanley was always very generous with his entertaining, although he never wanted to spend too much time on it himself. He was a very reclusive man who was so focused on his work he could think of nothing else. He did not want to spend long evenings in restaurants with the rest of us after filming. Whenever I was called out to work for him he would tell Mikey and my other chum, Associate Producer Brian Cook, to look after me.

'We'll need expenses,' Mikey warned him.

'Take whatever you want,' Stanley said. 'Just put it down to "entertaining Mr Leonard".'

They took him at his word and we had some wonderful nights. One in Salisbury was particularly good. We started with dinner at Wilton House with Marisa and the Earl and then went back to the White Hart Hotel for champagne afterwards. Realising that I had drunk far too much to drive, I decided not to take the car back to our hotel and left it where I had parked it at the beginning of the evening. The next morning we were all on set early as Marisa and the other actresses were being plastered in white make-up. I was taken straight to the set and didn't have time to go and look for my car, which I knew I had left in the town centre somewhere. Halfway through the morning a policeman turned up enquiring who owned the Porsche. I confessed it was me and asked him why he wanted to know.

'The mayor would like to know because it is parked on the front steps of the town hall,' the policeman replied solemnly.

'You parked it on the front steps of the town hall?' Mikey asked me incredulously.

'I remember parking it somewhere,' I admitted, 'but I wouldn't know where. It was dark.'

I collected the car later in the morning, and the police didn't give me any trouble. Like the mayor, they were happy to have so many people bringing good business to Salisbury.

The crew were always looking for new ways to get expenses past the producers. At one stage during filming someone noticed that there were a lot of items being charged to Room 13 in the hotel, including meals, champagne and even a few hand-made shirts. When the producers made some enquiries as to who was occupying this room they discovered that it was in fact being used as storage for wigs and costumes. They were not amused.

At one stage in the film Barry Lyndon had to lose a leg. 'You know, Ryan,' Stanley said to him over lunch one day, 'if you were to cut your leg off for this part you would undoubtedly get an Oscar.' Ryan didn't seem to share Stanley's confidence and they had to find a one-legged double for him.

After he had stayed at my London flat for a while, Ryan gave me an exquisite hand-carved box as a thank-you present. Inside it I found two perfectly rolled joints. It was a kind thought but I never did touch drugs, so I kept the box and passed the contents on to Nagels. He decided to smoke them on the night of the Berkeley Square Ball.

By the time I drove him and Tony Cloughly to the ball, Nagels was so high he could have flown there under his own steam. He spent the whole evening proposing to people, including the models Amanda Lear and Paulene Stone, and Tony too – all of whom turned him down. Ryan later told me that the joints had been filled with a mixture of finest Lebanese weed and elephant tranquilliser.

Funnily enough, Paulene did accept Nagels' proposal later on and they became engaged for a while. They made an odd couple because she towered over him.

After *Barry Lyndon* came *Full Metal Jacket*, a Vietnam picture which for many of the takes Stanley shot on waste ground on the Isle of Dogs in East London, complete with imported palm trees and American war planes. He wanted to have a scene in which the recruits had their heads shaved by the army barbers.

'We need some of those clippers they used,' he told me.

'They didn't just use clippers,' I replied. 'They had suction machines to take the hair away as they cut it.'

'Great,' he said. 'Get some.'

I managed to track down some machines in America and had them sent over.

'What do you do with the hair that you cut off in the salon?' he asked next.

'We sweep it up and throw it away,' I said.

'Can you collect it and bring it down to the set?'

For the next few days we had to collect up all the hair that landed on the salon floor, sort it into colours, bag it up and deliver it to the set so that it could be filmed being sucked up into the machines.

Barbara Daly, who was fast becoming the most famous practitioner of her trade in the world, created the make-up for Stanley's films. The team of Leonard and Barbara, which had produced so many magazine covers and model spreads, was now in the movies together, working to create memorable images in just the same way as we did for magazine and fashion shoots.

My friendship with Barbara had been cemented through many long nights of fashion shoots together in Rome with Barry Lategan. Twice a year we would go out to work our magic on the fashion collections for Italian *Vogue*. I would be carting suitcases full of wigs and hairpieces with me, my head crowded with ideas.

The photographic studios were a strange nocturnal world during the fashion shows. The clothes would be brought to us during the evenings, when the shows finished. All the top photographers would then beaver away, shooting the models wearing outfits from the different collections, desperately trying to get their pictures done before dawn arrived and the designers' runners came to take the clothes back to the catwalks for another day of live shows. Models, hairdressers, make-up artists and editors would all be closeted together, adrenaline pumping as the night hours ticked away, and we developed a strong team spirit during those trips.

There was never any room for modesty on those shoots. The most beautiful girls in the world would be dressing and undressing in full view of anyone who cared to look, but no one had time to think about sex, we were all so frantically busy. That was for afterwards.

Sometimes the beauty and fashion editors could not understand what it was I was trying to achieve. My ideas sounded too fantastical when put into words and I was never good at explaining myself, so I would have to do the cuts in order to demonstrate. I could always envisage what I wanted and was confident that my hands would produce the results I wanted. Sometimes I would do the cutting myself, otherwise I would oversee as one of my juniors, like John Frieda, took over.

'Where's my developing fluid?' Barry asked in the middle of one of these hectic nights. 'It was in here,' he pointed into the open fridge, 'in a bottle in the door.'

'A bottle in the door?' I was beginning to feel stirrings of unease. 'That was developer? I thought it was mineral water.'

'You drank it?' Barry looked aghast and I wondered for a moment if I would survive the night. Surprisingly it seemed to have no ill effect on me. Equally surprising, when I returned to London and told the story to my friends, none of them seemed to have any difficulty believing that I could drink a bottle of neat chemicals and feel no ill effects. Most of them laughed heartily and said it was absolutely bloody typical.

There were new models arriving on the scene all the time, some of whom would become good friends. When Marie Helvin first arrived in London she was only able to stay for three months at a time because of needing a work permit. She originally came from Hawaii but had based herself in New York.

She was lovely to work with. She had amazing wavy hair which we used to wrap around her head and pin in order to straighten it out and achieve the look of the moment. To begin with, she worked a great deal with Barry Lategan and me, then she met and married Bailey and he monopolised her for a few years.

During the days in Rome I would work on shows for designers like Valentino and Karl Lagerfeld, preparing the models before they went out on to the catwalks. Tensions and tempers always ran very high behind scenes at these shows. This was particularly true of Valentino, who was as worried about the way he and his boyfriend would look when they went out to take their bows, as he was about the models. I would try to give him the attention he was demanding at the same time as checking the girls.

I also used to work with Yves St Laurent on his shows in Paris. With him I had a free hand to do whatever I thought best. If ever he had a comment to make about anything I had done I invariably found that he had taught me something valuable.

The parties thrown by the designers at their villas after shows were some of the greatest and most extravagant in the world, full of their rich and famous clients. Sometimes it used to feel as if they put more thought and imagination into their entertaining than into their designing.

I first met Tony Curtis when he came to the salon to have his hair cut. In those days he still had his own hair, although it was beginning to thin a little. He still wore it in the distinctive bouffant style that had made him a role model for every fashion-conscious young man in the Fifties and early Sixties. We hit it off immediately and he asked Ricci and me to dinner at his house with Rex Harrison and his latest wife, Elizabeth. She had previously been married to Richard Harris and told me one of the benefits of marrying Rex was that she didn't have to change her monogrammed towels. A few days later Tony rang and asked if I would like to go to the cinema with him.

'Sure,' I said. 'What shall we go to see?'

'Don't worry about it,' he said. 'I'll meet you outside Simpson's in Piccadilly this evening. Wear a raincoat.'

'Wear a raincoat?' I protested. 'It's the middle of summer.'

'Just wear one,' he said and hung up.

I duly turned up but I couldn't see Curtis anywhere. I felt a tap on the shoulder and came face to face with a man in a hat and dark glasses with the collar of his raincoat turned up.

'Why are you dressed like that?' I asked.

'I'm in disguise,' he explained.

He then led the way towards Piccadilly Circus and a cinema showing a film called *Deadly Weapons* starring Chesty Morgan, a woman whose only claim to fame was the size of her immense breasts.

'I don't want to see this,' I said.

'Of course you do,' Curtis said, pushing me forward, his head down and collar round his ears.

'Mr Curtis,' a woman's voice made us both jump, 'may I have an autograph?'

We both quickly ran away. Tony was annoyed to miss the film but I was relieved.

Over the following years I met a succession of Tony's girlfriends and wives, each one younger and bustier than the last. Eventually, when he asked me to meet him and his latest amour off a plane at Heathrow, I suggested it might be an idea to book a forklift truck to help the young lady get to the car.

He was also very keen on his disguises, which became increasingly elaborate and eye-catching. On one of our evening outings we were stopped by a policeman. The copper thought that Tony might be the missing Lord Lucan, who was wanted for the murder of his family nanny, trying to sneak back into London. Funnily enough, Lord Lucan had been into the salon for a haircut not long before he disappeared.

Ricci was thrilled that such a big star had become a close friend and used to invite Tony down to the house in the country so that she could parade him in front of the locals in the pub. Tony was impressed by the size of the garden and said he would give me some plants for the gardener to put in. Sure enough, next time I saw him, he brought bagfuls of seedlings. He gave George the gardener strict instructions on how to plant them out. I left them to it.

Tony then went back to America and I didn't see him for a few months. The seedlings took root and began to grow . . . and grow. They were not particularly pretty and, when George complained to me that they were taking over the garden, I suggested that he should pull them up and burn them. I was sure that Tony would have forgotten he had ever given them to us.

The next week George did as I said and started a bonfire which sent a thick plume of smoke drifting through the village, putting mysterious smiles on all the villagers' faces for several hours. Next time Tony came down he enquired after his plants and I confessed that they had run amok and had to be burnt.

'You burnt them?' His face fell. 'That was the best cannabis money can buy. I was looking forward to sharing the harvest with you.' Oh well, at least the villagers had a good time, and, I guess, so did George.

Tony wasn't the only big star with a taste for cannabis. When he was filming *Ryan's Daughter* in Ireland, Robert Mitchum grew his own crop. He then smoked it through a strangely shaped bone pipe which, legend had it, was the kneecap of his best friend.

As his hair became thinner Tony made the decision to start

wearing wigs and hairpieces to maintain the famous Curtis look. As the years passed the wigs became more and more extravagant and noticeable, like a mad parody of the original style, but Tony was blissfully unconcerned, continuing his way through life as if he was still twenty years old. I copied the idea of his quiff for one of Zandra Rhodes' models and dyed it electric blue. His enjoyment of life was always highly infectious.

The only problem was that he allowed his girlfriends to carry on as if he had real hair. I once received a panicky and puzzling phone call from him when he was staying in London and I went round to find out what was going on. Knowing that his current squeeze was keen on gripping his hair at moments of intense passion, Tony had decided to stick the wig on with super-glue rather than tell her the truth. He must have been performing particularly effectively that night, because she had pulled so hard on his hair she had taken off the skin of his scalp and all the natural hair underneath. He was a mess. There was nothing I could do. I had to take him along to a doctor before his whole head went horribly septic.

On another occasion he summoned me to Mario's restaurant at Brompton Cross late at night, telling me to come and rescue him from his date.

'What for?' I wanted to know.

'Just come for God's sake, Len!' he hissed and hung up.

When I got there I could see the problem. The woman's breasts were so enormous they were actually resting in her plate of spaghetti.

'You've got to go now, Tony,' I said. 'You're filming in the morning.'

Tony shook his head in mock disappointment and his wig, which he had not attached properly this time, slid off into his plate. He started to fish it out but I stopped him.

'Just leave it, Tony,' I said. 'Let's get out before anyone with a camera turns up.' We ran for our lives, leaving the poor girl gaping at the wig in the plate next to her.

Tony was a good friend to me for many years and used to try to tempt me to accompany him to the Cannes Film Festival each year. He was one of the people who stuck by me when things started to go badly wrong, but he was sometimes too eccentric for his own good.

When I remarried he used to come and stay with us on the Embankment. On one visit he was between marriages and kept bringing home a succession of the most unsuitable girls. Eventually, I pointed out to him that he was treating my place like a knocking shop. He was very apologetic and, as a gesture of his contrition to my wife (I had married for the second time by then, to Petra), he did a painting in lipstick on the rather expensive guest bathroom mirror, sealing it with lacquer so that it was impossible to remove. Both Petra and I suffered something of a sense of humour failure at what I am sure was meant to be a kind gesture, and the mirror had to be replaced. I have since discovered that original Tony Curtis works of art sell for thousands of pounds in places like Florida and Hawaii.

Once, when I was in Las Vegas to do Helen Reddy's and Barry Manilow's hair for their stage shows, Curtis invited me over to Caesar's Palace to have dinner with Frank Sinatra, whom I had known for some time. Sinatra kept telling everyone we had the same middle name and introducing me as 'Leonardo Alberto', just as he was 'Francisco Alberto'. My old dad would have been pleased that at last the name Albert, which I always hated, had come into its own.

The other guests were Sinatra's cronies, all of whom looked like Mafia hard men. At the end of the meal Sinatra gave me a fond hug and told me that he and Curtis had arranged for a gift to be waiting for me back at my hotel.

When I returned to my room I found three women there, 'courtesy of the management'. All three were showgirls, with legs which seemed to go on for ever; one was blonde, one was black and one had the most stunning red hair I had ever seen. Whoever had hired them had told them not to take no for an answer and to ensure that I had the best possible time. I shall never forget it.

Sinatra seemed to like being part of a crowd, especially if there were a number of villains present. One evening at dinner I was sitting next to a man everyone referred to as Maxi. He told me his girlfriend was dead.

'I'm sorry to hear that,' I said. 'What did she die of?'

'Crabs,' he grunted.

'I didn't know someone could die from crabs,' I said.

'They do if they give them to me,' he replied without blinking.

While I was in Las Vegas Frank invited me to drive out to Palm

Springs with him to see his house and meet his old mother. He was planning to introduce her to Barbara Marx who was going to be his next (and final) wife. I had done Barbara's hair and she was pleased with the results so she encouraged me to go with them. Maybe she felt she needed some moral support.

The house was like a film set of a palace in the desert. Dolly Sinatra was a real Italian mamma, completely in charge of the house, and had no illusions about her son, who reverted to being a naughty schoolboy around her. When Frank introduced Barbara, Dolly sniffed and said, 'I hope this one will see me out.'

Tony seemed to know everyone in Hollywood. Having dinner with him at the White Elephant Club in Curzon Street on another occasion, I was startled when he suddenly hailed a man who had just walked in.

'Hey, Duke,' he shouted, 'over here.'

John (Duke) Wayne swaggered across the room and sat down to join us. We ordered more food and, as we chatted, the Duke asked if I would like to give his hair a trim. I said that would be fine.

'Me too, Len,' Tony chipped in.

Once we had eaten our fill and sunk a couple of brandies, we made our way back to Tony's house for a late night hair cutting session and off came both their wigs. I was surprised just how ancient Wayne looked without his.

When I first met Jack Nicholson he introduced himself to me by saying, 'I hear we have tastes in common.'

As I knew he had a terrible reputation for illegal substances I immediately became defensive. 'What's that then?' I replied cautiously.

'We both like the same girls,' he said. From that moment on we were the firmest of friends. It seemed we had both been out with several of the same people. I questioned him carefully about dates and discovered that I had been with them first.

'Thank God for that,' I said.

'Why?' he wanted to know.

'I'd hate to come after you.'

His lip curled up in a wicked grin. 'I was once told I was a cut above the rest. I guess I know what they meant now!'

Like me, Jack had come from the wrong side of the tracks and, like me, he was determined to enjoy the fruits of his success to the full. Whenever he was in London, he would join me for long evenings at San Lorenzo and Tramp and there was always a surfeit of beautiful young women hovering around us. To me he seemed to be exactly like the devil he played in *The Witches of Eastwick*. He made for delicious and dangerous company.

The first I would know of his visits would be a phone call.

'Hi, Lenny,' I would hear the familiar drawl down the line. 'It's Jack. I'm in town. Do you fancy a little partying?'

'Sure,' I would reply.

'Know anyone who would like to join us?'

'Maybe,' I would say, knowing that there would be any number of beautiful women in London who would be more than happy to spend an evening in Jack's company. I would make some phone calls and his limousine would pick us all up.

He would always stay at the Connaught in Carlos Place, between Grosvenor Square and Berkeley Square. It is one of the most exclusive and conservative hotels in the world. The force of Jack's charm, however, meant that he was always able to fill his room with nubile young women at the end of a night's revelries and the management never complained.

One of the great joys about film-making was getting to go to exotic locations. The most magical of all was Moorea, a small island off Tahiti where *The Mutiny*, starring Mel Gibson, Anthony Hopkins and Laurence Olivier, was filmed.

I had done Olivier's hair in London, where his sequences were being filmed.

'This is a great honour for me,' I babbled like a schoolboy fan in front of his hero, arguably the world's greatest living actor.

'Nonsense,' Olivier corrected me. 'It is an honour for me to have my hair cut by the great Leonard.'

That, I think, has to be the ultimate lesson in humility and charm for anyone. The words have glowed in my memory ever since. While I was cutting his hair the director Roger Donaldson came in and they started talking about the scene. Olivier wasn't sure how he was going to end it.

'Why don't you pull your wig off and throw it to the floor in exasperation,' I suggested. They both looked at me for a moment in silence.

'I think that would work,' Olivier said and that was exactly how he played it in the film.

On location there was a young Tahitian beauty cast as the female love interest. She wasn't on the island when I arrived and I was told that she was still at home. On the weekend that she was due to be collected I was the least busy person on the set. The Assistant Director suggested that I be the one sent to fetch her. Everyone seemed to think this was a good idea – believing, I guess, that her virtue would be safe with someone they thought was a camp hairdresser.

I spent three days with her in Tahiti, during which time we struck up a very affectionate relationship which lasted until I eventually had to return, regretfully, to England. I could see that every man in the company had been hoping to impress her as soon as she arrived and all of them were deeply disappointed to see that I had already staked a claim.

Anthony Hopkins was very strictly on the wagon at the time and used to drink tonic water. One evening I noticed that one of the assistants had accidentally added vodka and that Tony was raising the glass to his lips. I jumped forward, knocking it out of his hand. For a moment I thought he was going to hit me, but I quickly explained. He swung his glare round on to the person who had poured the drink.

'Can you swim?' he enquired.

'Yes,' the young man said.

'Good,' Anthony purred, 'because if you ever do that to me again you are going to be swimming back to England.'

Gene Kelly was holidaying there while filming was taking place and he used to go jogging on the beach in the early morning. Mel Gibson objected because he had his family with him and thought Kelly's colostomy bag would frighten the kids.

Other films that I was proud to work on included *Dr Zhivago*, *Rollerball*, *Flash Gordon*, *Ragtime* and *The Sicilian*, which I did for Michael Cimino. This film, which starred Christopher Lambert and Terence Stamp, was about the Mafia, who are notoriously powerful in Sicily. The real-life gangsters took great pleasure in looking after us and advising Cimino on technical details. It was at a time when the mayors of Palermo kept being murdered, and our new friends made no secret of the fact that they had not just read about it in the papers.

'Anything you want, Leonard, just let us know,' a senior figure of the family told me over lunch one day in a family restaurant in Palermo.

'Oh, thank you,' I replied politely. 'But I am being looked after very well.'

'No,' he growled, shaking his grizzled head. 'You misunderstand. Anything you want, anywhere, at any time. Just get in touch.'

'Right,' I now understood exactly what he meant. 'Thank you very much.'

When James Cagney was brought over to England to film *Ragtime* he asked to be put in a country hotel rather than the Connaught, which was his usual haunt. There must have been some administrative mess-up because when I was told where to go to do his hair it was one of those dreary international hotels at Heathrow. I was even more surprised, on walking into his room, to see that he had idyllic views of the English countryside from his window. I sidled over to have a closer look, and I realised that the film company had erected scenery on the balcony outside to hide the airport runways and service buildings. The elderly Mr Cagney appeared to be quite happy with the arrangement.

In the film of *Flash Gordon* the hero was played by a dark-haired actor called Sam Jones. It was produced by Dino de Laurentiis, who had already fired one director. My instructions were to make Sam look as much like the hero from the comic books as possible.

'We'll have to dye you blond,' I told him and he agreed.

Later that day Dino came on the set and saw the lead actor for the first time. 'We can't have a super-hero played by a blond poof!' he roared for all to hear, including Sam.

Someone had to fetch a copy of the comic to show the legendary producer that we were in fact making his star look exactly right.

'Just beef up his muscles an extra inch or two,' I suggested.

There is a famous scene in *Dr Zhivago* where a white stallion cavorts in the snow. The problem was that the horse they wanted to use was brown. I came up with a method of dyeing it which I thought would work. Unfortunately, the wetness of the snow meant that filming had to be continually interrupted so that the animal's coat could be retouched as patches started to appear.

I seem to remember that some of the crew stuck a ram in Omar Sharif's bedroom one evening, and there were a number of complaints about the banging. I suppose that made a change for Omar. People didn't usually complain.

Another source of work for me at that time was advertising. I used to be hired by advertising agencies to help promote products like shampoo and conditioner. The idea was simply to make the models' hair look as gorgeous as possible. The commercials always had to be shot in glamorous locations like California, the West Indies or Brazil, because the agencies would say the 'light had to be right'.

Arriving in Rio for one of these shoots I was horrified to discover the local managing director of the company had hired a model with the most terrible hair.

'But she has a great bunder!' he said in a thick South American accent when I complained – at least that was what it sounded like.

'What's a bunder?' I asked.

'A great bunder,' he repeated, slapping his backside.

'A great bottom?' I burst out laughing. 'I'm sorry, but she hasn't got any hair on her bottom. We'll have to recast.'

So the whole film unit spent a week sitting in the sun sipping cocktails at the client's expense while I set off in search of the right girl. I was told that if I went up to the towns in the north of the country, along the Amazon, I would find the prettiest girls in Brazil. They certainly were very pretty, and the Amazon was just as primitive and mysterious as I had always imagined it would be. Also, they were all dark-haired and the client specifically wanted a blonde.

I returned to Rio and confessed that I had been unable to find anyone who would fit the bill. We then contacted an agency in New York and flew another girl down from there.

To achieve the wonderful effects shampoo ads needed, we could almost never use the actual products that were being advertised. To start with, I would use my own shampoos and conditioners, and then we would employ tricks like soaking the hair in beer to give it more body and movement. Beer is the most wonderful thickener for hair, although it isn't the most attractive of smells for a girl.

Although I was now part of the marketing machine for a multimillion pound industry, I was still being asked to employ the same sorts of tricks that Nagels and I had first learned in our youth, when he was relabelling dodgy wines and I was flogging fruit and veg or tarting up used cars.

It is surprising what different ingredients are used to make hair attractive in different cultures. When I was in Bali, for instance, I discovered that they use bananas and the rotten bark from trees to wash their hair. The resulting mixture gives their hair a wonderful sheen. When I was in Japan I wanted to find out how the Kabuki dancers achieved their elaborate hairstyles. I visited one of their theatres to learn how to pin the hair up over pads in order to create the beautiful shapes.

The more I travelled the more ideas I got for styles which I could copy and adapt for fashion pictures in the West.

CHAPTER THIRTEEN

MY RELATIONSHIP WITH Marella Oppenheim lasted a few years, but in the end her wild personality became too much for me. She was happy to live out her life in the gossip columns, whereas I wanted to avoid appearing in them most of the time. I didn't mind publicity for the salon and the talents of the stylists and colourists, but I was savvy enough to know that clients didn't want to read about their hairdresser living it up till all hours of the morning. I was very sad when the relationship ended, although I know that many of my friends thought that I would be better off without her.

If you have a reputation for being sociable and reasonably gentlemanly in your behaviour it is surprising what invitations you will receive once it is known that you are unattached. When the first Superbowl was held in England, the film star Darryl Hannah flew in and was staying at the Mayfair Hotel, part of the Inter-Continental Group.

I was very involved with the hotel at the time because we had plans to open another salon there. The manager Patrick Board, a great and loyal friend, asked me if I would be willing to escort Miss Hannah to the game. What red-blooded, unattached male would be able to turn down such an invitation? She was considered one of the hottest and most beautiful stars at the time. We had a wonderful afternoon and, after the game, we went out to dinner at San Lorenzo and then on to dance at Tramp. In the small hours of the morning, having danced ourselves to a standstill, we made our way back to the hotel and up to her suite. It seemed the most natural thing that we should undress one another and slide into bed. It was as if we had known one another for years. The following morning she was due to fly off on location and we parted the best of friends, our paths never crossing again.

Neil Zarach was a good friend of mine who owned an exclusive furniture and design shop in South Audley Street, next to my gym. He and I spent a great deal of time wandering back and forth between our two premises, behaving like a couple of shopkeepers in some drowsy little Mediterranean village and going off for long lunches at Scott's and Harry's Bar. Zarach was a very modern shop, full of glass and glitter, and very successful, particularly with the Arabs. Just the sort of stuff I liked at the time.

Neil had started his career in the early Sixties with a shop in the Fulham Road in partnership with my friend Tony Cloughly and Count Albrizzi, Tony's boyfriend. Whereas Tony was from working-class northern roots, Albrizzi came from a wealthy family with a palazzo in Venice which had its walls lined with original Canalettos. He was also a designer.

The three of them started with a glass and mirror company and then Albrizzi invented coffee tables made from cubes of perspex. The idea caught on and they moved to Sloane Square. The shop became highly fashionable, with people like Ossie Clark holding fashion shows on the premises and everyone strolling around with bells round their necks and flowers in their hair, smoking pot. This was the very heart of Swinging London in the Swinging Sixties, the sort of life that was celebrated in films like *Darling, Blow-Up* and dozens of others. Neil and I crossed paths in restaurants and at parties everywhere, although we didn't become close friends until later.

Neil then fell out with his partners and went into business with interior decorator David Hicks. Both Tony and Albrizzi died of Aids and I still miss them and their wonderful glass and mirrors shop.

Hicks had just married Mountbatten's daughter, Lady Pamela Mountbatten, which meant that he was practically royal and used to invite the Queen to tea. Those were the days when everyone was still very impressed and reverential about anything to do with the royal family, the days when someone like poor old Dodi wouldn't have been allowed through the service entrance at Kensington Palace, let alone the front door.

When Neil parted company with Hicks he opened a shop in Sloane Street, in the premises which now houses Versace. It was the late Seventies by then and the Arabs had arrived in London with barrel-loads of oil money. The antiques and interior decorating world is horribly snobbish and nobody wanted to deal with these arrivistes with more oil money than they knew how to spend, but Neil had no such inhibitions. He happily set about designing and furnishing their new royal palaces which were springing up all over the world, including two homes for King Hussein of Jordan. The film stars also kept coming to him and his reputation soared.

When Neil moved to South Audley Street he started coming to the salon to have his hair cut, always bringing a bottle of Dom Pérignon with him so that we could party as we worked.

A young German heiress called Petra Arzberger got talking to Neil one day in his shop and said she was looking for a good hairdresser. Neil suggested she go down the road to see me. He offered to ring ahead to make sure I looked after her.

Petra was in her early twenties, a small blonde, bubbling with fun. I was very taken with her, and she seemed to be equally taken with me. I invited her out on a date and suddenly found that I was in a serious relationship. I had never met any woman who treated me with so much sweetness and respect. In fact she spoiled me rotten and seemed to have unlimited supplies of money with which to do it. I had never met someone who bought me so many presents.

To begin with I found it unnerving. I liked to be the one doing the buying and the spoiling. I wasn't sure how to respond to someone who was determined to lavish on me everything I could possibly want, even things I didn't want. Not only did she come back from every shopping expedition with new designer clothes for me from shops like Piero de Monzi in Fulham Road and Armani and Versace in Mayfair, she would bring them for my friends as well, for people like Mikey Stevenson. She would return with bags full of wonderful jackets and shirts, silk ties and cashmere jumpers. All my friends took to her immediately. Mara and Lorenzo organised a dinner in her honour at San Lorenzo, inviting all my closest friends. They served up fish and chips in newspaper, which was rather a shock to Petra, and to some of the guests, like Dodi.

Petra seemed to be completely happy to sit around in bars and restaurants with us, never nagging me to come home to spend time alone with her. Even though she never drank herself she didn't mind hanging out with me and my male friends as we poured it down for hours on end. She was so nice I asked her to marry me, despite the twenty-year difference in our ages. I had no qualms at all, she just seemed to be the sweetest person possible. I was sure that I had found someone I would be able to spend the rest of my life with, someone who would always be there for me, regardless of whether or not I was still riding the crest of the wave.

Neil agreed to be best man. After the wedding at Chelsea Register Office, we held a lunch at Mark's Club in Mayfair (the proprietor was Mark Birley, who also owned Annabel's). Peter Morton then hired us the private room at Annabel's for the party to move on to for dinner. Dominic came down from Harrow to join us.

The private room at Annabel's is a long, baronial dining room done out in Mark Birley's inimitable country-house style, simultaneously grand and comfortable, like all the best aristocratic homes. Petra's family seemed a little suspicious of their new relation and one of her brothers made a speech in which he said, not very charmingly, that he hoped I wasn't marrying her for her money. All my chums like Mikey and Nagels and a few other villains seemed to find this hysterically funny, which obviously surprised my new brother-in-law who imagined he was delivering a serious warning. In my speech I said how happy I was and relieved to have found the right person at last.

At the dinner I sat next to my new mother-in-law, a very beautiful woman in her own right. Several friends made the mistake of assuming that she was the bride.

During the reception, Morton told me that he had arranged a very special present for me. I didn't discover what it was until later, when he insisted on driving past Upper Grosvenor Street on the way home. Petra and I were off on honeymoon the next day to the South of France.

Morton had always been in the habit of calling me Albert, because that was my middle name. As we approached the salon I saw that, on the wall facing one side of the American Embassy, he had had a giant message painted saying, 'Congratulations Bert of Mayfair'. It must have taken several sign-painters and a great deal of scaffolding to achieve. I had to get a team of workmen the next day to wash off the emulsion, before Petra and I could catch our flight.

As a surprise wedding present Petra bought me a gold Mercedes sports car. The whole thing was like a fairy tale. She had been to school with Nabila Khashoggi, favourite daughter of Adnan Khashoggi, who was at the time rumoured to be the richest man in the world, having made his fortune from arms dealing in the Middle

East. Nabila was also Dodi's cousin. Khashoggi had a yacht called *Nabila* which he lent us for the honeymoon. It was being moored down in the South of France.

When I actually saw the yacht I couldn't help laughing. It was the most ostentatious gin palace imaginable. Everywhere we looked there were chandeliers and kitsch gilt fittings. Anything that couldn't be made from gold was plated in it. There were immaculately uniformed staff in every room with gleaming white teeth to match their gleaming white outfits, anticipating our every whim.

We slept the first night on board and the next morning, as we breakfasted on deck in the sunshine, a beautiful converted schooner slid into the harbour.

'Now that,' I said to Petra, 'is what I call a yacht.'

As this fabulous boat moored next to ours I realised that the people on board were the Agnellis, the Italian family that own Fiat and a great deal else. In fact it turned out to be Gianni Agnelli himself and a lady who wasn't his wife but who was also a client of mine. They recognised me and invited us over. The moment we were on board I couldn't stop myself from enthusing about the boat with its beautiful wood finish and polished brasswork. It was the complete opposite of the *Nabila*.

'Do you know who she once belonged to?' Gianni asked me proudly. 'Errol Flynn.'

Throughout the days of our honeymoon we stayed on the schooner with the Agnellis, swimming, water-skiing and sunbathing, only returning to the *Nabila* to sleep.

Once we got back to England, Petra made it clear that she also wanted to be involved in the business. I was very happy for this to happen in principle, but in practice it wasn't easy. How could I hope to explain to her the idiosyncratic methods I had used to build and run the business over the previous twenty-five years? How could I explain the roller-coaster way in which money poured in and out of the till and the frequent visits from bailiffs and other creditors? When Petra held a meeting she wanted everyone to have yellow legal pads and take notes. I began to realise that perhaps she was not the pussycat I had imagined her to be.

However, she was as enthusiastic about building the House of Leonard into an international concern as I was, and she had access to the money we needed to do it. We talked endlessly about our plans, and whenever I raised any objection to something on the grounds that we couldn't afford it, she would sweep my protestations to one side and insist that we should have nothing but the best. I guess in some ways she wanted to change everything in order to wipe out any memory of Ricci's taste, even though Ricci had been gone a long while.

I was surprised to find that I was getting bills from clothes shops like Versace and St Laurent, which I knew Petra didn't frequent, signed by Mrs P. Lewis. When I went to the shops to enquire I discovered that Ricci, whose real name was Patricia, was still signing for things as Mrs P. Lewis. I decided to change my name by deed poll and for a few years I became Leonard A. Leonard.

There were several ways in which I had been planning to move the business forward. I had opened salons at two Inter-Continental hotels in London, the huge new flagship which they had erected at Hyde Park Corner, and the Britannia, just down the road from the salon in Grosvenor Square. There were plans underway for the Mayfair Hotel, and the Inter-Continental Group wanted me to open salons in their hotels in America, starting with the Berkeley in New York and moving on to the other major cities later.

It seemed like an obvious way to expand the business and to exploit the name of the House of Leonard which was so well known and respected amongst the international jet set. Many of my best clients already lived in New York and would be happy to patronise any salon I opened there.

Sheik Maktoum and Sheik Rashid had also asked me to open a salon in their Jebel Ali Hotel in Dubai. The United Arab Emirates' capital city was fast becoming the main trading port in the Middle East, attracting a very international crowd, all of whom knew the House of Leonard. Neville Shulman had managed to arrange a very good deal for me with them.

I had seen how successful Vidal Sassoon had been with his international operation, and many of the stylists whom I had trained had also set up their own salons and were coming up fast behind me. It made sense that I should be expanding too.

By the time I married Petra I was full of confidence and ambition and was going ahead with the New York and the Dubai projects at once, training staff and doing the publicity and fashion shows. I also planned to use the Dubai salon as the launch pad for an expanded range of Leonard products.

I had always had my own stuff in the salon, but I had never really tried to reach the general public with it. Vidal had done brilliantly with his products for the mass market, and we wanted to create something more up-market and exclusive. I had commissioned perfumiers to create a cologne and designers to work on the packaging and labelling.

Petra started to take over the beauty side of the London salons, which I think was a source of some bitterness amongst the more experienced staff, who wondered what this little slip of a girl knew about their industry.

It was an exciting time for both of us. Every month we were flying back and forth across the Atlantic or out to Dubai. For three years I was spending at least one week a month in New York, and Inter-Continental were nagging me to open up in all their other hotels across the States. It was a tempting prospect, particularly financially, but all my friends were back in London and I missed them whenever I was away. I missed the long leisurely lunches and dinners, the many hours we spent gossiping in hotel bars and pubs around the West End. Departure lounges, however luxurious, at airports full of people I didn't know, were a poor substitute.

There were endless meetings with designers and manufacturers and the products slowly began to take shape. We were madly optimistic about the future, but it was also very exhausting and Petra and I were often apart, flying to different locations to fulfil our obligations.

All of New York society turned out for the opening of the salon at the Berkeley, most of whom were already clients of the London salon. Pat Kluge, the wife of billionaire John Kluge, was there and asked me if I would arrange to have her husband's grey hairs dyed. I did as she asked and was surprised when she rang up a few days later to complain.

'You didn't do John's body hairs,' she protested. 'His chest is still grey. You only did his head.'

'I only do heads, Pat,' I said. 'If you want the rest done you'll have to do it yourself.'

'It's all right for you,' she grumbled. 'You don't have to sleep with him.'

Donald and Ivana Trump were New York's golden couple at the time and both arrived for the opening party. Neither Ivana nor I made any reference to our liaison many years before. She looked wonderful and had really worked on her Yugoslavian accent. I was impressed. They invited Petra and me aboard their yacht which was moored in New York harbour and I was shocked to discover that it was the old *Nabila*, which Donald had bought off Khashoggi, who was going through a bad patch. The yacht seemed to have undergone as radical a facelift as Ivana. While still one of the most over-the-top boats that ever put to sea, she was a little less gaudy than when Petra and I honeymooned on her.

Travelling is always wearying, even when you are getting upgraded to first class, which we often were because we had a contract to do the hair of many of the Pan-Am 'meet and greet' staff. I found that drinking helped me to get through the ordeal of constant travel. What else is there to do when you are trapped in planes and airports for hours on end? First-class passengers on Pan-Am flights could have their own brands of drinks stocked on board. I used to ask for bottles of my favourite French white wine called Baron de L. The air crew thought that it must be imported from my own vineyard. I didn't bother to disillusion them.

Petra and I also found time for some fun as well. We went on holiday to India with Bryan and Greta Morrison. I remember cutting Bryan's hair at sunrise in front of the Taj Mahal. I doubt if we had been to bed that night. In the cities there were hairdressers riding around on bicycles, looking for business. If you wanted a haircut you could flag them down and have it cut at the side of the road.

'If things don't go too well you could always do that round Mayfair,' Bryan joked. 'I'll stake you to a tricycle.'

Bryan had been a friend for some time. Another of life's rough diamonds, he had made his fortune from publishing the music of groups like the Bee Gees, Pink Floyd and Wham!, but his great love was polo. He had had trouble being accepted in such an establishment game and so went off and founded the Royal Berkshire Polo Club in a field near Windsor, hiring Major Ronald Ferguson (Fergie's dad), as his manager. He now entertains people like Prince Charles and the polo set on his own home territory. Bryan has made it big time.

Seldom seen without a cigar clamped between his teeth, he was always a force to be reckoned with. His wife Greta, a beautiful Sixties model, was a regular at the salon. I saw in the paper recently that Bryan is planning to broadcast live rock concerts across the Internet. If Bryan is involved, the chances are that it will turn out to be a big money-spinner.

To impress Petra on the Indian holiday I hired the private island at the Lake Palace Hotel in Udaipur and arranged for twenty-two dancers and musicians to serenade her. Petra was always taking pictures of us with our friends and lovingly compiling albums to chart our romantic life together. We used to refer to one another as 'Kuschy Bear', which sounds a bit tacky but felt very nice and cosy.

How lucky could I get? How many men would dream of meeting a beautiful young heiress who was nicer and more generous to them than anyone has ever been before? It sounds like an impossible fantasy, but it had come true for me.

Petra was also very keen for us to start a family. She adored children and dogs. She bought me a German Shepherd as a surprise. It was a lovely idea but eventually we had to get rid of it. It was just too big a dog to live in a flat. It had so much energy it was practically climbing the walls, not to mention leaving dirty footprints and balls of hair on all the white carpets. We bought the flat below ours on the Embankment and set about converting it into a nursery wing. We also bought the one above, both as a guest wing and for Dominic who was growing up and needed some privacy. We linked them with internal staircases. We were spending money like it was going out of style. I had always been extravagant by nature, but Petra put me in the shade. She wanted nothing but the best for the whole operation. The salons in New York and Dubai glistened with money and the apartment became one of the most glamorous in London.

My long-suffering accountant, Neville Shulman, was becoming more and more angry with me. He could see that our spending was out of control and that there was no way the business could ever be profitable. He had several meetings with us, warning that we had to cut back. We were just spending Petra's capital and it had to run out some day. I refused to listen. It was too exciting to have an unlimited amount to spend and Petra was either too much in love to understand or in too deep to admit to the truth. Neville couldn't change our ways and eventually stopped trying to advise us.

In our minds, we imagined we would get both the salons going and then cut down on the travel a bit. We would launch the products in Dubai, because there they seemed to love to buy anything that had a Mayfair cachet, and then, supported by a big advertising campaign, release them on to the European and American markets.

Our plans were only in their initial stages when Petra announced she was pregnant. We were both taken by surprise and then we gradually realised that this was probably not the best time to try to start a family, not when we were under so much pressure.

Looking back now, I think I probably misjudged how much Petra wanted to have that baby when I talked her into going for a termination. To my mind it was a simple postponement of the happy event. We would get the business launched, then try again. But I hadn't thought it through. If I didn't feel like having a child then, why would I feel like it in five or ten years' time?

Petra reluctantly agreed with me, at least on the surface, but I think deep down she allowed me to talk her into doing something that went against her nature. At the time, however, she seemed to be content with the decision.

Perhaps I should have made more of an effort to find out how she really felt. Perhaps I wasn't sufficiently sensitive to her needs. Women are such complicated creatures, and I had never had the time to get into the habit of caring properly for the ones who came into my life. I always thought it was enough to keep them in luxury and introduce them to the most interesting and exciting people in the world. But I realise now that they need more than that for happiness.

The business seemed to be running away with our lives. The faster things went, the more I drank to try and keep myself going. I never seemed to get the worse for drink, perhaps because I was still throwing up, although I did start to stumble and fall more often. I put it down to tiredness and jet lag and any number of other possible causes. The more business commitments we took on, the more socialising we seemed to do and the spiral increased.

In order to look after our growing empire we had to divide our energies. I left Petra in Dubai to oversee developments at the Jebel Ali and returned to London to make sure everything was running smoothly in the salons there, in Upper Grosvenor Street, the Inter-Continental and Britannia Hotels.

I have always been a great user of the telephone. I love being able to pick up a receiver and talk to anyone who has crossed my mind. In fact, I was so keen on the phone that Petra bought me a gold-plated one.

Late one evening in London I put a call through to her hotel room in Dubai. There was no reply. I tried the salon and a couple of friends to see if they knew where she might be. It was puzzling because in a Middle Eastern city there really isn't much for a woman on her own to do in the evening. If she wasn't in her room and she wasn't in the coffee shop, where was she? I even asked the manager, who was someone I knew quite well, to check her room. But it was empty.

By the end of the night I knew that she was with another man. I was devastated. I had not imagined for a single second that such a thing could ever happen. She had always been so good and kind, so caring and protective of me. I had felt so totally safe in her love and suddenly it had all vanished.

CHAPTER FOURTEEN

Petra came back to England and agreed to meet me at Brown's Hotel in Mayfair, which is usually such a pleasant, romantic and old-fashioned place to meet for afternoon tea. But this time I arrived with a heavy heart.

She told me who the man was. It was a local Dubai businessman of sorts, called Abdul, someone I would never have imagined for a second could be a rival in love. He was a bald, totally ordinary-looking man. I was mortally offended and unable to understand what could possibly have gone so terribly wrong. I felt confused and sick with unhappiness. She told me that she liked the life in Dubai and wanted to stay there. She was going to open a nursery school. All the plans I had thought we were making together crumbled to dust.

'I'm married, Leonard,' she said.

'I know we're married, Petra,' I snapped.

'No,' she said, 'I'm married to Abdul.'

'How can you be?' I scoffed. 'You're still married to me.'

'I have become a Muslim,' she explained. 'I have married him under Muslim law.'

'But you've always been an atheist!' I protested. She just shrugged and averted her eyes.

I hardly recognised the sweet girl who just a few weeks before had been so generous and supportive. She seemed to want to ruin everything I loved. Back at the apartment she destroyed the photograph albums full of our memories which she had so lovingly created. She also destroyed some of my personal treasures, like the unique sketches which Warhol and Bacon had done for me. She claimed that she had spent a very substantial amount of her inheritance on the business, so she should therefore keep all the Leonard hair-care products, which were by then sitting in a warehouse waiting to be distributed to shops and supermarkets.

I crumpled beneath the fury of her onslaught and gave her

whatever she asked for, just as I had with Ricci. More than anything, I wanted the ordeal to be over and for the pain to stop. I didn't put up any sort of a fight, I simply didn't have the spirit left for it. I had been riding so high that the fall was all the more catastrophic.

After Petra had gone back to Dubai, a large tax demand arrived which, as her husband, was my prime responsibility. I had to find the money for it. However hard I worked, it looked increasingly as if it would be impossible to get a grip on the mounting debts. My urge to work was also seeping away. I was no longer young or keen enough to stay up all night creating new styles or training new people. I felt tired and disillusioned and could see no way forward. Without Petra's cash I didn't know how to keep the empire going. Money was now haemorrhaging even faster than before on both sides of the Atlantic, and I couldn't summon the energy to work any harder.

I was grateful for my friends who rallied round me, all of them as shocked as I was that a partnership which had seemed to be going so well should have ended so abruptly and unexpectedly. None of them was sure what to say to me in my confusion and grief. To begin with a lot of them assumed that I must have been messing around. Bryan Morrison threatened to 'knock my block off' if it turned out to be my fault. It was soon obvious to them that I had no idea what I had done wrong.

Many friends had started to refer to me as 'Uncle Len', and they seemed to be taking care of me rather as one might an elderly uncle who has somehow lost his way in life. Fewer and fewer people referred to me as 'Mr Leonard' any more. It was as if I had forfeited the right to everyone's respect. They all seemed to hold me in considerable affection, but that affection seemed to be tinged with pity and disappointment, as if I had somehow let the team down, failed to fulfil the promise of my early stardom.

Petra, true to her word, returned to Dubai, opened a nursery school and very quickly became pregnant. I have since lost track of her and my friends know better than to tell me if they do come across her anywhere.

I threw Petra's Russian wedding ring, along with mine, into the Thames. Years before, in a rather more traditionally romantic setting, on the Rialto Bridge in Venice, I had marked the disintegration of my marriage to Ricci by chucking my wedding ring and, for some reason, my Cartier watch into the Grand Canal. Futile gestures, both of them.

My confidence in women had been completely smashed. I wasn't sure that it would ever be repaired. I just wanted to spend time with the guys who had stuck by me, taking refuge in bars and restaurants. I enjoyed the comfort of familiar anecdotes, accrued and embellished over thirty years and remembered through a fog of cocktails. It became hard sometimes to remember how much of my meteoric rise could have been real and how much might have been a sort of waking dream.

If it was all real then why couldn't I get myself back up to the old speed? As far as the outside world was concerned, the House of Leonard continued to be one of the great salons of London. I was still a legend as long as I was around, but increasingly I preferred to be somewhere else.

The house in Gloucestershire had been disposed of a few years before I married Petra. Now I had to get rid of Chelsea Embankment, which sold to the theatre director Trevor Nunn. I ended up renting a very nice flat in Cadogan Square. The capital raised on the sale was quickly soaked up by tax bills and other debts. Before long, I was finding it hard to meet the rent on the new flat each month. When the landlords told me I had to get out, I had nowhere to go and had to put all my furniture into storage. I then moved into a slightly more modest, but still very comfortable flat in Roland Gardens, South Kensington. Despite knowing that money was no longer available in infinite quantities, I still couldn't get out of the habit of spending. When you are used to ordering things from the best shops in large quantities, it is hard to change overnight. I once heard an ex-cabinet minister being interviewed just after his party had lost an election and overnight he found himself an ordinary MP again. He was saying how hard it was to adjust to not being able to ask people to do everything for you, not having limousines waiting for you at every door, to having to work out how to use the photocopier yourself. I can completely understand how he felt.

My way of coping with the changing circumstances was to tell myself that they didn't exist. After all, the salons were still there, the customers were still coming in, my name was as famous as ever. If I just kept going things would come right in the end. They had to. I wasn't beaten yet.

There was a young girl working as a greeter at Harry's Bar who had always been kind to me. Her name was Anna Roberts. She was beautiful, tall and leggy and very English in a Home Counties way. I had first met her while I was still married to Petra. When the marriage broke up I began to see Anna in a different light. I was aware that she fancied me and we started to become good friends in the long hours I spent over lunch and dinner in the restaurant. While I was still living at the Embankment flat I began to court her in the old-fashioned way, the only way I knew how, with armfuls of flowers and gifts. I nick-named her Bambi. On her birthday I hired a vintage Rolls-Royce, filled it with bottles of champagne and took her and a group of her friends out to dinner.

We started to have an affair. In a pattern that was by now familiar to me, her mother was horrified. I should have stayed aloof from family squabbles, I know, but I was behaving irritably with people who gave me a hard time. Why couldn't somebody actually be pleased that their daughter was involved with me? I was a nice man. I was generous. I was famous and successful. What was so terrible about me?

Anna's mother gave me a very hard time. In the end, during one heated telephone conversation, I had to remind her not to be cheeky to her elders. Anna told me she had never heard her mother stuck for words before.

Anna and her mother decided that I was drinking too much for my own good and one day, while I was at work, they poured every bottle of alcohol they could find in the flat down the drain. I was furious and immediately restocked the bar. I felt that I was perfectly capable of controlling my own habits. Anyway, I needed to have drinks there to offer to guests.

Anna and I went on a holiday to Kenya together, and took Dominic skiing in Switzerland. On the Kenya trip we went with Billy Keating, my American friend from the old days, and Angela Nevill, whose parents were best friends of the Queen. They had been together longer than most married couples, working together in the art world, and eventually got married. They used to represent Alan Bond, a larger-than-life Australian businessman, who used to be a multi-millionare until he too fell on hard times. I believe they bought a Van Gogh for him, costing tens of millions.

I loved Billy, who was very camp and a terrible fantasist. He used to tell everyone that he was from an old planter family in Savannah, Georgia, and that their family home was used to film *Gone With The Wind*. I once pointed out to him that everyone knew the film was made on a studio back-lot. Billy just laughed and waved my complaint aside. From then on I always referred to him as 'the vamp from Savannah'. Sadly, Billy, who was always fond of his drink, eventually died of liver failure. I miss him a lot.

When the millionaire entrepreneur Peter de Savary asked me if I would open a Leonard salon in his new St James's Club in Antigua, I agreed readily. It would be a chance to travel somewhere glamorous and to remind my clientele that I was still cutting the crème de la crème.

There were a lot of old friends at the club's opening, including Liza Minnelli. She always liked the spiky look for her hair which had become her trademark. I thought a softer style suited her better. I would leave it to dry naturally and keep the height down. No matter what had happened to me personally, I still knew how to cut hair and I still had an address book to die for.

In the Caribbean it was chaos everywhere. Tubs of my conditioning cream vanished from the salon and turned up in the kitchens, being used as mayonnaise. Colonel Michael Parker, the royal firework supremo, had been hired to put on a display from de Savary's yacht for the opening of the club. He stored all the explosives under his bed and lay on top of them, smoking happily as a crowd of us partied around him until late into the night.

Peter de Savary, whom everyone had nicknamed Peter UnSavoury, was finding it very hard to adapt to the Caribbean way of doing things. He wanted everything to be run as smoothly and immaculately as his other St James's Clubs in London and Los Angeles, but, no matter how much he ranted and shouted at them, the West Indian staff were not intending to change their laid-back ways for him. The atmosphere became quite unpleasant and in the end Anna and I were glad to escape to Florida for a few days with the actor Michael York and his wife Pat, who had also been guests at the opening.

I wanted the relationship with Anna to work, but I suspect I was difficult to live with at the time. The worry, the drink and the hurt all mixed up inside me to make a disturbed potion. As usual, I tried to make up for my moods by deluging her with gifts. I bought a Persian kitten when she told me she liked cats. Anna called it Monty. I called it Pushkin. Because Anna was out at work at Harry's Bar most of the day, it used to travel around in the car with me quite a bit. I took it to restaurants where it quickly developed a taste for lobster soup and skate wings.

One day when Anna was at home and I was at work I received an hysterical phone call. The cat had crawled into the washing machine with my cashmere jumpers and Anna had started the programme without realising. She had heard a clunking noise and had opened the outer door, to be confronted with a wide-eyed kitten pressing its nose against the glass as the cold water poured in on top of it.

To be honest I was more concerned that my cashmere jumpers had gone into the machine than the blessed cat. I suggested that she immediately call the fire brigade rather than bother me at work. She did as I advised and the cat survived, but my jumpers were ruined. A few days later the cat got stuck in the basement area which Anna couldn't get to. The fire brigade came to the rescue once more. This time they were less pleasant about it and warned her that if they were called again she would be receiving a large bill.

I was beginning to get bad headaches. My head throbbed worse than any toothache or hangover I had ever suffered. I put the problem down to stress and swallowed large amounts of painkillers to keep myself going. The pains were making me irritable with the people I loved.

When you run a business like a hairdresser's you cannot afford to go sick for any length of time. People's hair will keep growing and if you aren't available to cut it they will soon find someone else. The chances are they will not come back unless your replacement makes a serious mistake. So I kept going when I should have been taking time off to pull myself together.

Anna and I did have some wonderful times. As well as Kenya and Antigua we went to La Colombe d'Or Hotel in St Paul-de-Vence in the South of France. It was a beautiful place full of original Impressionist paintings, but I was taken ill with a potassium deficiency, which is a bit like having dangerously low blood pressure. I ended up in hospital, with Anna having to ferry supplies in to me. She said it was like being involved in some tribute to the Sixties and Seventies since the other guests at the hotel who helped her to look after me included Liza Minnelli, Jan and Johnny Gold from Tramp, Erroll Brown from Hot Chocolate and Mary Quant. They were all busily bringing in my favourite dishes from the hotel, plus champagne and wine. Anna was also liaising with my doctor in England, Tony Greenburgh, who has consulting rooms in Belgravia and has been a great source of help to me over the years.

I have to admit I don't mind being in hospital too much, if it is a comfortable one. All the responsibilities of life are removed from a hospital patient, if only temporarily, and one becomes the centre of attention. You get lots of fussing, good food and flowers and visits from chums. A bit like being in a hotel really.

But I sensed an air of exasperation seeping into Anna's normally patient manner. After coming out of hospital, I had another little scrape scrambling on board a boat late at night, and had to be taken off to casualty to have some stitches put in. Anna didn't know anything about it until I got back in the early hours of the morning and woke her up.

'Where have you been?' she asked, a little irritably I thought.

'I was taken into hospital,' I replied.

'No you weren't, Leonard,' she said, turning over as if to go back to sleep. 'We got you out of hospital yesterday.'

'No, I've been back, really,' I protested, and showed her the dramatic blue butterfly stitches in my knee. She seemed rather less sympathetic than I might have expected.

The relationship disintegrated soon after that, and we both have different ideas on what actually went wrong. To save face all round I told the gossip columns that I had moved out of the flat because I was allergic to the cat. The nice thing, however, was that we managed to stay good friends and Anna is one of the people I can always ring whenever I feel in need of a chat.

For a few months I moved into the Britannia Hotel in Grosvenor Square where I had one of my salons. The relationship with the Inter-Continental Group was still going well. The salon at the Inter-Continental on Hyde Park Corner, which was attached to the gym and pool, all of which was branded as 'Leonard', was always busy and attracted a lot of names. Thanks to my good friend Patrick Board, another salon was being built in the basement of his hotel, the Mayfair.

At the Britannia I had rather narrow premises which I turned into a men's salon. Dick Burnett, an architect who had helped me with a revamp at Upper Grosvenor Street and with the gym in South Audley Street, designed it to look a bit like a club car from the Orient Express. He has remained a faithful and dear friend throughout all my troubles.

Part of the deal with the hotels was that I could have accommodation whenever I needed it, so the Britannia gave me a suite. It was on the top floor and must once have been servants' quarters. It had subsequently been knocked into one big, long room. They allowed me to move in my own furniture and pictures.

I loved living in a hotel. There was none of the bother of finding people to clean and make the beds; everything was done for me. But, best of all, there was room service. No need to worry about stocking up the larder. All I had to do was pick up the phone to order and trolleys filled to bursting would be brought up in the lifts. I took full advantage of that.

I had a friend called Charlie Jenkins, a big man who ran a successful animation studio which made *Yellow Submarine* for the Beatles. He was as keen on eating and drinking as I was, and so the two of us would get stuck in and just keep the orders coming. Nagels turned up one evening to eat with us and the trolleys were coming in so fast they started to collide and one tipped over, spreading all its contents on the floor. Nagels was laughing so much he had to leave, although he had trouble getting into the lift with all the waiters, but Charlie and I kept on eating. It was good food, and we didn't intend to waste a scrap of it.

The other advantage of hotel life was the bars. All my friends knew that, at certain times of the day, I could be found drinking at the Inter-Continental or the Britannia. I just loved the relaxed, social atmosphere of these places. I would be working away in one of the salons, with customers dotted all over the place in various states of washing and cutting, and I would find the call of a convivial drink just too strong to resist. I would usually only plan to go for a quick one to give me energy, but once I got chatting to chums I would find it harder and harder to get back to work.

Five-star hotels are such interesting places to hang around in. The Inter-Continental was particularly attractive to the many wealthy Arabs who were then arriving in London with a lot of oil money to spend. The sheiks would book whole floors rather than just suites, and would carry on their lives as if they were still in their own countries. They would bring their own chefs and fleets of servants. I went up to the suite of one sheik to cut his hair and found that he had two beautiful falcons sitting patiently on perches with hoods over their heads. When I had finished my work he said he needed to exercise his birds and he opened the windows to allow them to fly out over Hyde Park and scare the pigeons. I heard later that an American woman had complained vociferously at having to share a lift with these birds. God knows how they managed to get them into the country past our customs.

On another occasion an Arab princess came down to the salon and I found she had lice in her hair. I happened to mention it to one of the managers and they immediately evacuated the entire floor and had it fumigated.

Wherever the Arabs went to stay the high-class hookers would follow in droves. There was a branch of Cartier next to the salon in the hotel and we used to watch the girls being escorted there to be given fabulous pieces of jewellery. They would come back a few days later and cash them in. I got to know a lot of the girls in the bar, and one in particular used to come in to have her hair done in exchange for services rendered.

When the Inter-Continental opened on Hyde Park Corner they hired a brilliant chef called Peter Kromberg. He had previously worked in Bangkok and at the Portman Hotel in Oxford Street. We got on well. He kept the Cristal champagne flowing whenever I was around and I encouraged him to use the gym and pool at the hotel which was part of the Leonard set-up.

Peter is still at the hotel and I pop in regularly when I am in the West End. He always ensures that I have a glass of champagne to cheer me on my way. Each time I mention to him how much Rene likes the cream cakes that they bake for the guests and he takes care that I don't leave without a bagful to take home to her. A number of people have been very kind to me in recent years and have not yet forgotten all the good times.

As I fought to keep working, the headaches were steadily growing worse. I was working out in the gym at the Inter-Continental one day when I blacked out. I have little or no memory of what happened next until I woke up in Westminster Hospital. They told me I had a brain tumour which would need to be operated on immediately.

I asked to be moved to the Wellington, a brand-new private hospital in St John's Wood. I wanted to be comfortable and also to be in a place where friends could come and visit me whenever they felt like it.

Once I had been moved, all the chums like Mikey, Anna and my son Dominic started to arrive and the room was soon filled with champagne and flowers. Mara and Lorenzo from San Lorenzo sent in my favourite cheese, Dolcelatte. Johnny Gold delivered mineral water from Tramp. Michael Birri biked over pasta from Harry's Bar. The nurses would bring refreshments from the hospital bar and I managed to keep my mind off whatever might be growing inside my skull in a whirl of entertaining from my bed.

Immediately he heard I was unwell, Neville Shulman rushed over and brought me all kinds of fruit. He was horrified to see all the champagne in my room, but I assured him it was only for my guests, and said I wasn't drinking anything. Naturally he was unconvinced and I was touched to see how worried he was about me.

Dodi dropped in to cheer me up, bringing a cap from his yacht to cover my sadly shaved head. Marie Helvin came and Estée Lauder arrived with a pot of her collagen cream which she said would help with the scars. I rather think it did help, actually.

Jack Nicholson turned up twice. The first time was in the middle of the night with Stanley Kubrick, but the security staff wouldn't let them in, refusing to believe that they were who they said they were. When he came back the next day Jack took great pleasure in teasing the staff. The nurses were positively drooling over him as he flirted at full steam with them. Other visitors came and went as he sat in the corner of the room, drinking tea as if he was entertaining the local vicar.

Ricci came in too and got talking to Anna. I dare say they were comparing notes about how impossible I was to live with. I was told that afterwards Ricci was quoted in the papers saying that I would never work again. In fact I think a few friends thought that I would only leave the hospital in a box.

The tumour turned out to be benign but somewhere along the line, during all the revelries at the Wellington, I had a fall and broke a bone in my shoulder. In my memory it happened on the way to surgery, when the porters dropped me off my trolley. Some of my friends uncharitably suggest that it was more likely that I had had a few too many vodkas from the bar and simply fell over. I considered taking legal action because the injury left me badly scarred and with limited mobility so that I was unable to work for a long time, but it's all a bit of a minefield when you haven't got any money to feed the lawyers.

The operation on my head, however, was a success, although it left something of a dent in the right-hand side of my forehead. I was eventually allowed to go home to try to piece my life together, but an unfortunate side effect was that I started having epileptic fits, sometimes as many as five a day. I didn't thrash around and froth at the mouth or anything dramatic like that, I would just have absences, or petits mals, which would mean that I would usually fall over and bang my head on something. I had these attacks everywhere: in supermarkets and in the streets, in offices and hotel lobbies. Once I collapsed on top of poor old Rene while we were out shopping in Marks and Spencer in Putney, pinning her to the floor. She had a great deal of difficulty getting out from under my new, less than slim-line figure and had to be rescued by passers-by as they waited for me to come round. I even had one in the canteen of the *Daily Express* on Boxing Day when I went to visit Richard Compton Miller. At the beginning, alarmed friends would call ambulances each time. I soon learned that if they just let me be, and provided I hadn't hurt myself badly in the fall, I would recover naturally.

It is embarrassing never to know if you are suddenly going to black out and wake up to find yourself covered in blood and surrounded by concerned people, but I was determined to keep going and not to allow it to defeat me. The doctors had me taking over twenty pills a day to try to stabilise the condition. I sometimes wondered if the pills weren't aggravating the situation, making me feel lethargic and grow fat.

While I had been in hospital I had overheard two Japanese patients talking. They were telling someone that their company had just bought the Inter-Continental Hotel chain and that they intended to get rid of the hairdressing salons and other retail operations. I knew that my leases were nearing the end and it seemed I was not going to be able to renew them as had been planned.

I also knew that there were debts piling up at Upper Grosvenor Street. The rents were colossal and I had never expected to be unable to work for several months. There were also personal debts to be cleared up from my marriage to Petra, including tax bills and lawyers' fees.

It was as if I was in a bad dream, watching my life slip away from my control. Everything I had built up and was most proud of was vanishing – my marriage, my business, my homes, my lifestyle. I had no idea what to do to stop the rot. My rise had been so effortless and unplanned; now it was all disappearing through my fingers like sand.

Most of all I wanted to continue cutting hair. As long as I could keep cutting, I told myself, I would be all right again. Before he heard I was unwell, Stanley Kubrick was asking around as to how to contact me. He was planning to make *Eyes Wide Shut* with Tom Cruise and Nicole Kidman. When he heard that I was ill he told Barbara Daly that the sort of magic I possessed in my fingers never went away. I prayed that he was right.

The bailiffs moved into Upper Grosvenor Street once more, and this time there was no way of avoiding the truth. They were going to take everything, and my landlords, the Freshwater Group, also wanted the building back. The salon which had once been the Claridge's of hairdressing was stripped bare as if the locusts had been through.

Several friends invited me to use their salons to cut clients and friends who wanted to keep coming to me, and I still went to people's hotels and homes to cut their hair. Stephen Way was particularly generous, letting me use his Bond Street salon, which is close to where it all began at Vidal's first premises all those years ago. Stephen is one of the success stories from the early Sixties, having started out with Nagels and me. He is now married to TV and radio personality, Gloria Hunniford, and has a lot of influence in the hairdressing industry.

Frank Sinatra called me up soon after I came out of hospital and I went to see him. While I was cutting his hair I admitted that I was having a problem with epileptic fits.

I noticed that he was staring at me intently in the mirror as if weighing up whether to say something or not. 'You'll learn to live with it, Len,' he said eventually. 'You'll learn to cope. I have.'

A hairdresser called Jacques Alexander, who owned a small salon in Thackeray Street, behind Kensington High Street, offered to set me up in business again. I went to work there for a while. He then opened another salon in Avery Row, a tiny side street off Grosvenor Street, and called it Leonardjacques. A number of my old clients started to come back to me. One of them was Major Ronald Ferguson's wife, Susan. I was alarmed to discover that the next-door premises contained a flat where the Major was alleged to be visiting a young lady.

Jacques was very generous in his assistance, but the partnership didn't work out. I just wasn't comfortable working in such cramped surroundings and time-keeping had never been my strong point. As long as I was the big name in the biggest salon in London, with dozens of back-up staff, I could get away with being a little vague. If I missed appointments at Leonardjacques there was no one to cover up for me and the customers were no longer as patient.

I seemed to be going in and out of hospital at a regular rate during the following years. I would have a fall, hurt myself and be whisked off by ambulance. When Nagels, with whom I had lost touch for a while, heard that I was unwell, he came to visit me in Roehampton Hospital. I could see that he was shocked by the change in me. I knew that I had put on a lot of weight and that, since my hair had grown back after the operation, I looked a bit like a mad professor.

'Hello, Nagels,' I said. 'What's brought you here?'

'I've come for a haircut,' he half joked, obviously unsure what to say.

'I haven't got my scissors,' I said.

'But you always have your scissors, Len,' he protested and for a horrible moment it occurred to me that I might never be able to cut hair again. What he said was true. I had never been without my scissors since I was fifteen years old. They were my whole reason for being as they flew through people's hair almost as if they had a will of their own. How could I possibly have left them behind? What would I do if someone really did ask me now to cut their hair? What if no one else ever did ask?

Many of my friends were very kind during this period. At one stage Bryan Morrison invited me up to his splendid Georgian country house near Windsor, along with a group of my old mates, including Clive Arrowsmith, Billy Keating and Angela Nevill, Mikey Stevenson and Anna Roberts. He sat us all down and started to talk. It felt a bit like being summoned to see some Mafia don who had decided it was time to take control of the situation. Bryan pointedly handed out glasses of champagne to everyone but me.

'Uncle Len is under a bit of stress and needs help getting back on his feet,' he growled through his cigar. Everyone muttered their agreement. I stared at my hands and kept quiet. 'And I'm going to help him. I'll set him up in a salon again. I'm willing to do that. But I've warned him that if he so much as touches a drop of drink then the deal's off.'

I heard his words and I really appreciated the way in which my friends were rallying to my cause, but I couldn't think what to say. I was aware that I did need help, and I was grateful to Bryan for being willing to take on the responsibility. There was no question that he had the ability to refinance me and get me going again, but would I be able to work for someone else after all these years of being my own boss? I don't know if I ever believed that I would be able to keep to my side of the bargain.

I convinced myself that drink wasn't my problem. I was rarely the worse for wear, and although I was very partial to a glass or three, I knew how to control it. I wasn't sure what the fuss was all about but I was willing to go along with Bryan if it meant I could get back to the top.

A few days later I slipped up, sneaking a couple of drinks while no one was looking, and had a bit of a fall on Bryan's baronial stone staircase, banging my poor old head once again. Bryan washed his hands of me.

'When I saw him lying on the steps with his brains spilled out,' he told friends later, 'I thought he was dead. It was terrible. I was playing squash the next day and it quite put me off my game.'

I tried booking into a drying-out clinic called Clouds once, but it didn't work for me. I knew I was going to have to do it by myself. For so many years I was able to eat and drink whatever I liked. Now I had to be more careful.

For all their kindness, I had become something of an embarrassment to many of my friends. I could see that. It was time to withdraw a little and recompose myself. I needed to get my life back together again and find a base from which to start rebuilding. All the grand flats had gone the same way as the business. The furniture which had been put into storage had disappeared too because I hadn't been able to keep up the payments. I had little more than the clothes I stood up in and they were getting to be pretty frayed around the edges, a far cry from my glorious wardrobes full of Turnbull and Asser shirts and St Laurent suits. If I wasn't careful, I was going to be on the street.

You certainly find out your true friends when you are really down. The best undoubtedly were Neville Shulman and Richard Compton Miller. I could ring them any time for a chat, and they both took me out for lunches and dinners. It was Neville's idea to set up a trust fund for me, to provide some financial support.

My sister Rene, now a widow, suggested I go back to stay with her for a while. She and her son Colin still live in the house where I spent most of my childhood. Nothing had changed when I came home. It was no longer a council house because they had bought it during the Thatcher years, but they had done nothing to it. Even the paintwork was as I remembered it from my youth. Rene was still talking about me as if I was ten years old, remembering the teachers who used to come knocking on the door to find out why I wasn't in school and the neighbours who despaired as to what would happen to me in life. It was as if none of the stuff in between had ever happened.

I had fallen to earth with a bang. I couldn't understand how my life could have changed so dramatically. Although some friends would still take my calls, they were always having to hurry away to work, or were about to leave on business trips to the sort of exotic locations I had once thought nothing of travelling to for a few days. My world had suddenly shrunk to an endless stream of petty worries about how to get through each day and successive health scares.

I had grown used to the frequent stays in hospital. In some ways they were something of a relief from the struggle of coping with daily living. As the doctors battled to reduce my medication from twenty-five tablets a day to a more manageable five, the fits began to become less frequent.

I applied for a council flat of my own, somewhere within walking distance of Rene. Wandsworth Council came up with one which I accepted, but I still couldn't quite face moving out of Rene's place completely, even though I knew I was driving her mad. I wanted to do up the new flat a bit and make it nice, somewhere I could invite friends for a meal. The doctors said I wasn't to have an oven in case of accidents and I would have to survive with a microwave.

The hospital authorities installed a panic button which would summon medical help if I needed it. They also paid for Adolf, a West Indian cleaner, to come in once a week to sort me out.

Dick Burnett, the architect friend who had helped me so much over the years with the design of the salons, came to help me plan what to do with the flat, but I didn't have any money to buy the sort of things that I wanted, however modest. When I can lure friends to visit me in Roehampton we head for restaurants like Blades in the Lower Richmond Road, where I am now as comfortable as I once was in San Lorenzo. It's the people who make places great, not the food nor the surroundings, and there are nice people everywhere, thank God.

For a while I used the new flat mainly as a place to sit during the day and make phone calls. The phone is my lifeline. If I can chat each day to some of my old chums, if only for a few minutes, I feel as if I am still in touch. Although many people proved to be fair weather friends, only staying around for as long as the champagne and caviar were flowing, it is touching how many others have remained faithful and supportive.

The most important thing to me was to get my health back. Without that I was as helpless as a beetle on its back.

One of my former stylists, Karen Dunford, decided to throw a 'Leonard Revisited' party at her flat for some of the people who had trained under me, and she kindly invited me along. I was staggered by the response she got. About seventy people arrived, some of them flying in from places as far afield as Paris, America, Canada and South Africa. I have never heard so many squeals of delight as old friends who hadn't seen one another for years were reunited. The flat was not big and before long you could hardly move for the crush of bodies.

Karen sat me down in a corner near the food like some old dowager, and people kept coming up to say hello and tell me what they were up to. I could see in their faces that they were surprised by how much I had changed. My weight had risen enormously due to my medication and there was still a dramatic dent in the right-hand side of my forehead.

I remember someone remarking once that the other male staff in the salon always seemed to be trying to look exactly like me in the old days, imitating my hair, my clothes and my mannerisms. They must have looked at me at that party and wondered where their glamorous role model had disappeared to.

So many of my protégés are successful and have managed to make their dreams a reality. I had so many dreams and many of them came true, but I never managed to set them on solid foundations, so that, when my health went badly wrong, there was nothing left to hold things together.

The party went on until four in the morning and then I was driven home to my flat.

CHAPTER FIFTEEN

My plight must have been weighing heavily on the minds of some of my true friends. 'Uncle Len', it seemed, needed to be sorted out a bit. As Bryan's approach hadn't worked, they were going to have to think of something else.

Richard Compton Miller wrote a long article about my problems in the *Daily Express*'s health section. A little while later he was interviewing Daniel Galvin about the fact that he was running in the London Marathon. Richard mentioned me in the conversation and said that he thought the hairdressing industry should do something about getting me back on my feet.

Daniel agreed with him and, at Richard's suggestion, wrote a letter to the *Daily Express* saying that he couldn't believe that someone who had been as big a name in the industry as I had, could be forgotten so quickly. The letter was published and Richard and Daniel, after talking to Neville Shulman, decided it would be a good idea to set up a 'Leonard Trust' as Neville suggested, both to help me financially and to create an annual prize in my name.

Daniel started contacting ex-colleagues and other people who had worked for me. John Frieda became involved and was soon the driving force behind the Trust, letting them use his office off Hyde Park Corner and his wonderful secretary, Claire Jackson. It was thrilling to have some of the greatest names in hairdressing on the Trust, including Vidal Sassoon, Daniel Galvin, John Frieda, Nicky Clarke and Michael Rasser, plus my two loyal supporters, Richard and Neville. They approached Geoffrey Bonn at the Hairdressers' Benevolent Fund, who agreed to support and administrate the Trust.

Many old clients and friends like Gillian Lynne the choreographer, Peter Morton and Paul McCartney were incredibly generous in making pledges to get the Trust started.

The next thing I knew I was the guest of honour at the annual Hairdressers' Benevolent Ball at the Dorchester. I was very touched, not just by the speeches from people like Lulu (who said that had I not been too busy to cut her hair one day she would never have met John, who then became her husband), but by the sheer fact that so many people still remembered me. They had even put together a video of the highlights of my life.

John, Richard and *Vogue*'s Kathy Phillips started talking about the many wonderful fashion and beauty pictures that came out of the period when I worked with Barbara Daly, Barry Lategan, Clive Arrowsmith and the other photographers. These pictures were now considered by collectors to be works of art, symbols of an important period in fashion history. They decided to get limited editions made of some of the best work I did for *Vogue* with photographers like Barry, Clive, Lichfield, Donovan and Bailey, get them signed and then sell them. There were pictures of Twiggy, Marie Helvin, Natalie Wood, Jerry Hall, Penelope Tree, Brigitte Bardot and other less famous faces. The exhibition was to be held at Christie's, organised by Meredith Etherington-Smith who had just master-minded the sale of Princess Diana's dresses in New York. Tickets to the event cost £75 each and *Vogue* very generously waived their copyright to the pictures.

Even Vidal flew in from America for the event. Nearly all the pictures sold at prices from £350 each. Patricia Roberts, the model, bought the picture of herself with the lit sparkler stuck in her hair. After the party Willy Bauer, another loyal friend, gave a dinner for me at the Westbury Hotel. It was an excuse for more wonderful speeches from John, Vidal, Daniel, Nicky and other members of the Leonard Trust. Even Rene joined in the celebrating. I was very moved by the time and trouble they all went to on my behalf.

The pictures sold well and a great deal of money was raised. Now my little flat is almost finished and furnished in a style which I am comfortable with. I have a wardrobe of decent clothes which fit my new shape, many of them made by Edward Sexton, Tommy Nutter's ex-partner who has been a good friend to me, and I have a bit of spare cash for socialising.

Doormen, waiters and barmen still recognise me in all the hotels and restaurants of the West End and are as kind to me as they always were. A couple of times a week I go into Stephen Way's salon to cut clients' hair; on other days I go to their homes or hotels.

Although my marriages both ended in tears, I still have my son

Dominic, who has grown up to be a happy and successful young man, working in the computer business and travelling all over the world, but always staying in touch on the phone. I feel proud that I was able to give him a good education.

Apart from my trusty scissors virtually everything else has gone now – the girlfriends, the business, the homes, the clothes, the furniture, the scrapbooks, the works of art and books. I have my memories still, of course, although they too become increasingly muddled and faded with the years.

Life is very different now. I fell down a hole outside Harrods the other day. Things like that keep happening but I'm not going to let it get me down. The people from the store were very nice.

'Can we call our in-store medic for you?' they asked.

'No, it's all right,' I said, gazing up at their concerned faces and the sky above them. 'Just call me an ambulance.'

Back once more at the Chelsea and Westminster Hospital the doctor asked what happened and I explained.

'Pity you didn't fall down inside the shop,' he chuckled, 'then you could have sued them for a fortune.'

Which just goes to illustrate, I suppose, how important it is to be in the right place at the right time.

The Sixties have become a piece of history now. I saw a photographic exhibition at the Victoria and Albert the other day, full of fashion pictures for which I remember doing the hair. Zandra Rhodes is in the process of opening a textile and fashion museum in Bermondsey, covering the Fifties to the present day. Every month new books come out as my contemporaries commit their stories to paper. Everyone's memories seem to be different.

Being at the top for all those years was like trying to stay on a bucking bronco at a rodeo, and I think I managed to hang on a good deal longer than many.